OUT
AND RUNNING

OUT
AND RUNNING
GAY AND LESBIAN CANDIDATES,
ELECTIONS, AND POLICY REPRESENTATION

Donald P. Haider-Markel

Georgetown University Press
Washington, D.C.

Georgetown University Press, Washington, D.C. www.press.georgetown.edu

Library of Congress Cataloging-in-Publication Data

Haider-Markel, Donald P.
    Out and running : gay and lesbian candidates, elections, and policy representation / Donald P. Haider-Markel.
        p.   cm. (American governance and public policy series)
    Includes bibliographical references and index.
    ISBN 978-1-58901-699-6 (pbk. : alk. paper)
    1. Gays—Political activity—United States.   2. Gay politicians—United States.
3. Political campaigns—United States.   4. Elections—United States.   I. Title.
HQ76.3.U5H34   2010
324.9730086'64—dc22

                                                            2010007034

♾This book is printed on acid-free paper meeting the requirements of the American National Standard for Permanence in Paper for Printed Library Materials.

15   14   13   12   11   10   9   8   7   6   5   4   3   2
First printing

Printed in the United States of America

CONTENTS

ILLUSTRATIONS

Figures

Tables

PREFACE

IN 1977 HARVEY MILK was elected to the San Francisco Board of Supervisors. Although he was not the first lesbian, gay, bisexual, or transgender person elected to a government office in the country, he was the first LGBT person elected in San Francisco. (Throughout this book I use the term "LGBT" to be inclusive of lesbian, gay, bisexual, and transgender individuals. However, the vast majority of LGBT candidates and elected officials are gay or lesbian, and my conclusions most directly apply to gay and lesbian candidates and officeholders.) His election and 1978 assassination brought to an end a decade-long struggle for LGBT people in San Francisco, and began a new period of activism for many LGBT people around the country.

Milk began his career in electoral politics in 1973, when he first ran for a seat on the San Francisco Board of Supervisors. He had no money to run but was convinced he could gain support from the LGBT community and liberals. Although gay issues provided him with some inspiration to run, he was also motivated by the issues of government regulations on small business and the lack of funding for public schools. In that first election he came in tenth, with 17,000 votes, out of thirty-two candidates. Following his defeat, he cut his hair and vowed to never again smoke marijuana or go to a gay bathhouse, saying, "You have to play the game, you know" (as quoted by Randy Shilts in *The Mayor of Castro Street: The Life And Times of Harvey Milk*). In 1975 Milk made his second run for the Board of Supervisors. He tried to point out to LGBT groups that all their support for moderate candidates had failed to result in a single gay appointment or the passage of a gay civil rights law. He argued, "Let them come to us. The time of being political groupies has ended; the time to become strong has begun."

Milk was defeated again but he had not lost his political ambitions. Instead he rode a wave of LGBT openness that was beginning to sweep the country, in part, following the event of two state legislators coming out and publicly declaring their homosexuality. San Francisco mayor George Moscone appointed Milk to the city's Board of Permit Appeals, making Milk the country's first openly gay appointed official. However, Milk was soon fired from the position when he decided to run for the 16th District seat in the California Assembly. At the time many LGBT leaders endorsed Milk's opponent and vehemently attacked Milk, arguing that he would be shunned in the state legislature. Even so, Milk argued in his stump speech that "a gay official is needed not only for our protection, but to set an example for younger gays that says the system works; . . . we've got to give them hope." In the end Milk lost by 3,600 votes out of 33,000. He took the defeat hard but vowed to fight on.

Before running for the third time for the Board of Supervisors in 1977, Milk helped form a new group called the San Francisco Gay Democratic Club to provide an alternative to the more moderate Alice B. Toklas Club, which some argued had gotten too cozy with the Democratic machine without asking for much in return. The new group was especially focused on ensuring that gay interests were represented in local government by openly gay appointed and elected officials, rather than sympathetic heterosexuals.

On election night Milk was finally victorious, winning two to one over his closest opponents. Nevertheless, part of his celebration included taping three messages titled "In Case," one of which included the ominous phrase, "if a bullet should enter my brain, let that bullet destroy every closet door." Milk's prophetic tapes provide the basis for the modern movement—gays and lesbians may become targets if they are open about their sexual orientation, but the movement can only succeed if its members are visible.

In many ways Milk's rise to political power mirrors that of the American LGBT movement for equity. The movement did not become visible until after World War II. By the 2000s, the movement's structure, tactics, and goals had evolved to the point where it is now a familiar fixture in local, state, and national politics. This now "mature" movement has increasingly focused on electing openly LGBT candidates to public office as a central objective in achieving its goals.

Political philosophers, scholars, and activists have long recognized that a central concern for groups in a democracy is the political representation of their interests within government institutions. Perhaps the most obvious and immediate strategy for groups seeking to achieve political representation is to elect officials who identify with the group. Such a strategy, called descriptive representation, has been used again and again by a number of minority groups and women in American politics. LGBT Americans are increasingly following this pattern but they may face some of the same electoral barriers faced by heterosexual women, African Americans, and Hispanics, among others. Although experimental studies with college students have found some evidence that openly LGBT candidates are less likely to receive electoral support, and surveys of LGBT elected officials have demonstrated that they believe their sexual orientation influences their electoral prospects under certain conditions, no systematic attempt has been made to determine if a candidate's sexual orientation influences electoral results in real-world elections.

Furthermore, there is little empirical research that evaluates whether the increased descriptive representation of LGBT Americans has in fact translated into increased substantive representation, or the infusion of LGBT preferences into the policy process. Studies at the local level suggest that higher levels of LGBT descriptive representation do in fact increase the likelihood that local governments will adopt LGBT-friendly policies, and case studies of national-level LGBT officials reveal that LGBT officials are able to influence the policy process. However, only limited anecdotal evidence from research suggests that LGBT officials increase the political representation of LGBT interests in the state policymaking process.

This book addresses the issues of whether a candidate's sexual orientation influences electoral support and election outcomes in state legislative elections, and whether increased description representation for the LGBT community increases the representation of the community's interests in the state policy process. To address these issues I employ both qualitative and quantitative analyses across selected state elections from 1992 to 2006, and the legislative consideration and adoption of a variety of gay-related policy proposals from 1990 to 2007.

The seven chapters that follow are also linked by broader questions about representative democracy, legislative coalition building, the role of interest groups, and the policy process in the states. In addition, I explore the relatively new notion that increased descriptive representation may incur political costs—a backlash—against the gains, perceived or otherwise, of the traditionally marginalized group.

Chapter 1 provides an overview of LGBT politics and related policy during the last thirty years. The purpose of the chapter is to provide general knowledge of the movement and its policy goals as well the development and historical success of LGBT candidates for offices at all levels of government. This chapter also provides a theoretical overview of political representation in the context of democratic theory. It focuses on why and how groups seek descriptive representation in elected office and what happens when they reach office. This discussion is couched in the existing literature on women's and minority groups' attempts and success with achieving substantive political representation.

Chapter 2 focuses on providing a qualitative description of LGBT candidates' experiences in running for state legislative seats. I introduce the focus on LGBT candidates by first exploring the context of public opinion toward LGBT candidates by empirically examining individual-level survey data about LGBT candidates from both national and state-level surveys. This analysis provides a basis for explaining the characteristics associated with opposition to LGBT candidates. Next, I provide a descriptive historical account of LGBT candidates for state offices. This section demonstrates how the number of LGBT candidates and LGBT state legislators has grown dramatically in the past twenty years. The remainder of the chapter focuses on surveys and interviews of LGBT candidates who ran for state legislative office between 1998 and 2006, exploring the candidate and his or her campaign(s), the candidate's interpretation of campaign events, the role of sexual orientation in campaigns, the interpretations of candidate staff, and the broader context as gleaned from local media reports. The information in this chapter is used to guide the quantitative analysis in chapter 3.

Chapter 3 empirically examines the role of a candidate's sexual orientation vis-à-vis electoral support for LGBT candidates as well as the success of those candidates. First, I examine the level of voter support for state legislative candidates from 1992 to 2006 across ten states, chosen to represent all regions of the country. On the basis of public opinion polls and extensive research, a central hypothesis posits that nonheterosexual candidates will receive a lower percentage of the vote than heterosexual candidates and that LGBT candidates will be less likely to be elected to a state legislative seat, controlling for a variety of factors. However, based on the findings from chapter 2, I also consider the possibility that LGBT candidates are strategic in terms of where and when they run for state legislative seats. From this perspective I speculate that most potential LGBT candidates avoid running in districts at points in time where their sexual orientation would inhibit being elected. In fact, many candidates have been groomed as "quality" candidates who are unlikely to face significant opposition because of their sexual orientation. The results of my analysis do indeed suggest that sexual orientation does not have a negative influence on electoral support, and in some cases may enhance electoral chances.

Chapter 4 explores the history of LGBT politics in several states, with a focus on the impact of LGBT legislators. The states examined—California, Massachusetts, Minnesota, Oregon, Virginia, and Washington—together represent all regions of the country and also all have seen at least one LGBT legislator elected to one chamber in the state legislature. I explore developments in each state to better explain the process by which LGBT legislators do or do not represent the interests of the LGBT community in the policy process. This analysis is guided by previous research on female, black, and Hispanic legislators. The findings from this chapter suggest that LGBT legislators are advocates for the LGBT community but vary in their efforts, in part depending on the context in which they operate. I find that LGBT legislators are strategic in their pursuit of advancing equality goals for the LGBT community, but the case studies demonstrate that increased descriptive representation does translate, in varying degrees, to substantive representation.

On the basis of the findings of chapter 4, chapter 5 systematically examines the influence of LGBT legislators in state legislatures. Specifically, I examine the influence of openly LGBT state legislators on the amount and types of LGBT-related legislation introduced and passed throughout the fifty states from 1992 to 2007. I find that even controlling for other factors, such as state and legislature characteristics, higher LGBT representation in state legislatures does lead to greater substantive representation in terms of LGBT-related bills introduced and adopted. I also find that a greater number of LGBT legislators is associated with a higher probability of adopting antidiscrimination laws based on sexual orientation, a primary goal of the LGBT movement.

Chapter 6 explores the potential negative consequences of increased representation for marginalized groups. Although both democratic theory and empirical evidence suggest that groups can achieve positive substantive policy representation, some scholars have suggested that there may be a backlash, or negative reaction, as a politically marginal group achieves social, economic, or political gains. For example, many have argued that the women's movement, while accomplishing many significant goals in the 1970s, created a backlash of antiwoman, or at least antifeminist, sentiment in the 1980s. Similar arguments have been made concerning the white response to the black civil rights movement, increased black political participation, and the election of black officials. I examine whether or not increased LGBT representation has led to an increase in anti-LGBT-related legislation being introduced and adopted in state legislatures. To examine this question, I conduct a quantitative analysis, which does suggest that there is a backlash element to increased representation. However, an additional analysis comparing pro-LGBT legislation with anti-LGBT legislation suggests that the net effect of increased descriptive representation is positive for the LGBT community.

Chapter 7 summarizes the findings presented in the previous chapters but also explores the broader implications of these findings for theories of political representation, state legislative politics, and LGBT candidates and officeholders. Finally, I outline potential directions for the future of LGBT representation and avenues for future research.

ACKNOWLEDGMENTS

A S WITH MOST BOOK PROJECTS, this one is a long time coming. I began to collect some of the data analyzed here more than fifteen years ago in the early years of my graduate training. Nevertheless, this project would not have been possible without the support and assistance of many people and organizations. First and foremost, this project was funded in large part by a 2003 Wayne F. Placek Award from the American Psychological Foundation. A number of students assisted in data collection for the project, including Mahalley Allen, Matt Beverlin, Aaron Clark, Matthew Kaufman, Rebecca Kuhn, Jared Schreiner, James Stoutenborough, Justin Tucker, and Andrea Vieux. The staff at Georgetown University Press were great and provided consistent support, especially Don Jacobs. I also need to thank Doug Goldenberg-Hart of CQ Press for his assistance with state legislative district data.

Many mentors have been there for me throughout the years, including Marianne Wargelin-Brown, Ken Sherrill, and Ken Meier. Each of these individuals, and many others, gave me pieces of wisdom and guidance that helped me grow as a scholar. There really is something to the notion of standing on the shoulders of giants.

Finally, I thank my wife Michele and my son Jesiah for their support and patience in putting up with an academic. Without their backing, this project would not have been possible.

Political Representation and a Brief History of the American LGBT Movement

Anything that we can do, me as an individual, or us as a state, to be leaders on this issue and be role models is excellent. The message really is: everyone deserves a stake in Washington, and everyone has a stake in Washington's future.

—Washington representative Marko Liias
on his role as an LGBT legislator

What works in New York or San Francisco doesn't work in Birmingham or other southern states.

—Lesbian representative Patricia Todd on her role in a "stealth campaign" to pass bills
on hate crimes and reducing the bullying of LGBT students in Alabama

ATTEMPTS BY LESBIAN, gay, bisexual, and transgender (LGBT) people to gain political representation have evolved out of the LGBT movement's goal of achieving equality in American society and politics. This evolution is similar to that followed by other historically marginalized groups in American politics, such as women, African Americans, and Latinos. In part these developments are based on assumptions that hurdles to being elected can be overcome, and, once elected, that officials representing the group can shape policy. To gain a deeper understanding of this pattern, this chapter explores what we know about the political representation of women and minority groups in American politics. I examine what the literature has to say about attempts by marginalized groups to obtain elective office and whether these efforts translate into policy changes. In addition, I provide a brief history of the development of the LGBT movement in the United States. I explain the growing development of LGBT attempts to achieve representation in the policy process through the election of LGBT officials and how these efforts compare with the efforts of women, and of ethnic and racial minorities.

1

Political Representation: Women and Ethnic and Racial Minorities

As LGBT people seek political representation, it seems likely that they can draw lessons from other marginalized groups that have traveled similar paths. To understand the potential lessons learned, I must first address some terminology. There are two main elements to political representation. First, if an elected official clearly belongs to or identifies with a particular ethnic, racial, or religious group, it can be argued that the group has achieved "descriptive" representation (Bratton 2002; Eulau and Karps 1977; Fox 1997; Swain 1993). Second, if a group achieves descriptive representation, many infer that the elected official will pursue the policy interests of the group with which he or she identifies, thus achieving "substantive" political or policy representation (Bratton 2002; Fox 1997; Saltzstein 1989; Swain 1993; Thomas 1994). Although substantive representation also may be achieved by electing sympathetic elites (Browning, Marshall, and Tabb 1984; Haider-Markel, Joslyn, and Kniss 2000), descriptive representation is often viewed as the most reliable way to achieve substantive political or policy representation (Gerber, Morton, and Rietz 1998). The process of translating descriptive representation into political representation is also referred to as "active" representation. In contrast, descriptive representation without political representation is "passive" representation (Bratton 2002).

In addition to active and passive representation, some scholars suggest that when population subgroups have representatives in government, the members of those groups might be more likely to perceive that government agents are acting in a legitimate manner. Indeed, Pitkin (1967) argues that the descriptive representation of subgroups can lead to symbolic representation. Having members of the subgroup in official positions works "on the minds of those who are to be represented or who are to be the audience accepting the symbolization" (Pitkin 1967, 111; see also Banducci, Donovan, and Karp 2004; Bobo and Gilliam 1990). In sum, descriptive representation can also be symbolic to population subgroups, in the sense that they see people like themselves in positions of authority. This process should lead to subgroup perceptions that the actions of these government agents are justified or legitimate. For example, blacks have higher levels of political participation, higher levels of trust, and more political efficacy in cities with black mayors (Bobo and Gilliam 1990; Gay 2001; Gilliam 1996). And African American representation in congressional districts influences political participation rates for both African American and white voters, producing lower levels of participation for whites and higher levels of participation for African Americans (Gay 2001).

The Election of Women and Minorities

Of course, descriptive representation can only occur if members of a population subgroup are elected to public office. So what do LGBT candidates have to learn from female and minority candidates? For women and minorities, achieving public office has historically meant overcoming discriminatory attitudes in the minds of voters (Baxter and Lansing 1980), and LGBT candidates may face similar attitudes. Since the 1960s blatant voter discrimination against female and minority candidates has declined but such discrimination might still shape where and when candidates chose to run and of course their success (Burrell 1994; Dolan 1998; Lawless and Fox 2005; Seltzer, Newman, and Leighton 1997; Thomas and Wilcox 2005).

Although some early research pointed to an electoral disadvantage for female candidates (Ambrosius and Welch 1984; Deber 1982; Clark and Clark 1984), one of the first systematic studies of the effect of candidate gender on electoral outcomes in state legislative races (Welch et al. 1985) found that women have suffered almost no electoral penalty since 1972 (see also Burrell 1994, 1998; Darcy, Brewer, and Clay 1984; Dolan 1997, 2004; Fox 2000; Welch and Studlar 1996). Likewise, Ekstrand and Eckert's (1981) early experimental analysis on support for female candidates also found that hypothetical female candidates faced no significant disadvantage. Zipp and Plutzer's (1985) analysis suggests that neither male nor female voters are predisposed to vote for or against a qualified female candidate. And Paolino's (1995) analysis of female voter support for female candidates suggests that female candidates can increase their support among female voters without necessarily losing male voters if they connect to their candidacy to group-salient issues, such as abortion.

An analysis of survey data also suggests that most voters are not inclined to oppose female candidates for most offices (Dolan 2004; Plutzer and Zipp 1996; Welch and Sigelman 1982). Indeed, since 1937 the proportion of the population willing to vote for a female presidential candidate has increased dramatically, so that since 1997 at least 87 percent of Americans have indicated they would vote for a woman (see figure 1.1). Additionally, Matson and Fine (2006) demonstrate that female candidates actually obtain a greater proportion of the vote in low-information elections where voters know little about the candidates or their positions.

However, if female candidates do not pay a price for their gender, how do we explain the fact that female representation in elected office does not come close to the distribution of women in the population? To address this issue researchers have increasingly focused on forces other than voter predispositions. For example, it is now clear that female candidates can face hurdles that include a lack of funding, less support from party leaders, poor media coverage, and coming to public life later in life (Dolan 2004; Fox and Lawless 2004; Oxley and Fox 2004; Sanbonmatsu 2002b, 2006; Thomas and Wilcox 2005).

Lawless and Fox (2005) argue that women are disadvantaged in obtaining elected office in large part because women are not encouraged to run and are more likely to believe that they are not qualified to run for office (see also Fox and Lawless 2004, 2005; Fox and Oxley 2003; Kahn 1996; Sanbonmatsu 2006). Female candidates also tend to worry more about fund-raising than do males, and are more likely to devote more time to fund-raising and rely on more sources of funds. Given that few candidates enjoy this task, female concern about fund-raising helps to explain why women are less likely to run for office (Jenkins 2007; Thomas and Wilcox 2005).

But the perceptions of potential female candidates do not appear to mesh with reality. For example, Hogan's (2007) analysis of candidates' spending in state legislative races across twenty states finds that female candidates spend at least as much as male candidates, which suggests that female candidates do not necessarily face financial barriers in running for office.

Figure 1.1   Would Vote for a Woman or a Black Candidate If the Party Nominated Them for President, 1937–2007

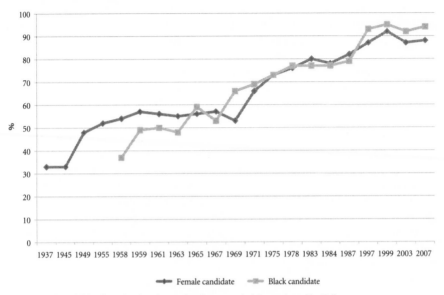

Source: Data compiled by the author based on national surveys of adults conducted by Gallup.

Even without financial barriers, female incumbents may face additional challenges. Palmer and Simon's (2005) analysis suggests that female incumbents generate greater numbers of challengers, both male and female, and across parties. Thus having a female incumbent is likely to increase the number of female candidates for that seat in the future, but perhaps not female officeholders. Indeed, Schwindt-Bayer's (2005) analysis of thirty-three national legislatures suggests because most incumbents are male, incumbency advantage tends to hinder the election of women. Across countries and over time as incumbency advantage increases, descriptive female representation decreases. And when term limits are introduced, female representation increases, also indicating that female incumbents might face more difficulty holding their seats relative to men.

And although voters do not tend to hold predispositions against voting for women, voters do hold gender stereotypes that can disadvantage women (Alexander and Andersen 1993; Dolan 2004; Flammang 1997; Fox 1997; Huddy and Terkildsen 1993a, 1993b; Kahn 1996; Niven 1998; Sanbonmatsu 2002a; Shapiro and Mahajan 1986; Witt, Paget, and Matthews 1994). However, women can take advantage of these stereotypes by campaigning on issues on which voters tend to think women are stronger and also by appealing to female voters (Brians 2005; Herrnson, Lay, and Stokes 2003; Sanbonmatsu 2006). This pattern is true for both state legislative candidates and congressional candidates.[1] But for some offices that involve issues where voters stereotype women as weak on issues such as national defense, voter stereotypes lead to a lack of support for female candidates (Lawless 2004), and female candidates are less likely to run for and be elected to these offices (Fox and Oxley 2003; Lublin and Brewer 2003; Oxley and Fox 2004). Thus, if the political climate tends to favor "men's" issues, women can face an electoral disadvantage (Lawless 2004). Likewise, if voters employ stereotypes when evaluating candidates, and tend to punish those candidates who do not fit the stereotype, this pattern may have real implications for LGBT candidates.

Whether gender stereotypes can help or hinder a female candidate might also depend on the candidate's party affiliation. McDermott's (1997) analysis of voting in low-information elections suggests that voters use gender as a cue for ideology, stereotyping women and being more liberal. This results in female Democratic candidates receiving more support from liberal voters but less support from conservative voters. For female Republican candidates, the stereotype does not hold, and thus does not provide an automatic advantage or disadvantage with ideological voters. In a similar analysis, McDermott (1998) also demonstrates that voters stereotype female candidates as being more honest. If this attribute is important to the voter, he or she is more likely to vote for the female candidate.

Racial and Ethnic Minorities and Elections

Traditionally, there has been more of an electoral disadvantage for racial and ethnic minorities than for women (Barker, Jones, and Tate 1999; Dawson 1994; Reeves 1997; Sigelman and Welch 1984). As noted in figure 1.1, in 2007 about 94 percent of Americans indicated that they would vote for a well-qualified black for president, although 10 percent of these respondents would still have reservations. By comparison, 88 percent of Americans would vote for a female president, but 11 percent of these respondents would have some reservations. About 87 percent would vote for a Hispanic presidential candidate (Newport and Carroll 2007). Thus, to a small degree, voters might be more likely to vote for a black male candidate for president than for a white female or Latino. But even though Americans generally indicate that they would be willing to vote for black candidates, in reality some whites tend to believe that white candidates would be more qualified and effective in office than a similarly matched black candidate (Philpot and Walton 2007; Williams 1989).[2]

Minority candidates may also be hindered in their campaign efforts by a lack of financial or political party support. In one report on minority candidates in all state legislative races, Sanchez (2005) found that in forty-two of the fifty states, nonminority candidates are able to raise more campaign money than their minority counterparts. However, labor unions tended to provide more money to the minority candidates who won in most states, versus white candidates who won. And minority incumbent legislators receive about the same level of party support as do white legislators.

In examinations of hypothetical elections involving black candidates, researchers have found that white voters make decisions about candidates based on the candidate's race, with black candidates receiving less support than similarly positioned white candidates (Baker and Kleppner 1986; Becker and Heaton 1967; Kinder and Sears 1981; Moskowitz and Stroh 1994; Reeves 1997; Sears, Citrin, and Kosterman

1987; Sigelman and Sigelman 1982; Sigelman et al. 1995; Terkildsen 1993; Williams 1989), but many of these studies do not consistently find a voter bias against black candidates.

Meanwhile, recent studies of real-world elections, using a variety of statistical techniques, have also drawn inconsistent conclusions on the importance of a candidate's race in elections (Bullock 2000; Bullock and Dunn 1999; Gay 1999; Voss and Lublin 2001). For example, Bullock's (2000) analysis of Georgia election returns using ecological inference concludes that black Democrats received about the same proportion of the vote as white Democrats, which suggests that race was not a factor. However, Bullock and Dunn (1999) and Gay (1999) both conclude that in congressional elections white voter support for black candidates is about 10 percentage points lower than white support for white candidates, which suggests racial animosity toward black candidates. Washington (2006) also finds that white voters, regardless of party affiliation, are less likely to vote for black candidates. And Knuckey and Orey's (2000) analysis of white voters in a statewide election clearly shows that those with high scores on symbolic racism scores were far more likely to vote for a white candidate over a black candidate.

The role of the news media in elections that involve minority candidates is less understood. In their analysis of media coverage of congressional candidates, Terkildsen and Damore (1999) found that the news media tend to focus on the race of black candidates, especially in competitive races. However, black candidates tend to downplay race except in contests where at least two candidates are black. Whether the media's focus on black candidates does anything more than label a candidate who is black as a "black candidate" is unclear, but the racial labeling of candidates clearly provides cues for voters (McDermott 1998).

To explore racial cue taking, McDermott (1998) examines voting in low-information elections. She argues that voters use race as an informational cue about a candidate's positions. Her analysis suggests that voters stereotype black candidates as more liberal and more concerned with minority rights than are white candidates. On the basis of these attributions, voters cast their ballots for or against black candidates depending on how important ideology and issue positions are to them. In a similar study, Matson and Fine (2006) find that candidates with Hispanic surnames receive a lower proportion of the vote in low-information elections where voters know little about the candidates or their positions.

However, the role of race in elections is not always so direct and is often difficult to measure. An analysis by Citrin, Green, and Sears (1990, 91) of the 1982 California gubernatorial race found that racial attitudes did shape voting decisions in that "resentment over the extent of the government's attentiveness to the demands of blacks had a consistent influence on voting decisions." In this case, voters with "antiblack feelings" were less likely to vote for the black candidate. But Citrin, Green, and Sears were unable to conclude that the candidates' race shaped voting decisions in the race. Their analysis suggests that voters with "antiblack feelings" were simply more likely to vote for the white Republican candidate, and these voters would not have been likely to vote for the Democratic candidate, even if he had been white. That said, racial attitudes did contribute to the loss of the black Democratic candidate, but voters were not strictly being racist. In addition, Highton's (2004) analysis of exit poll data clearly demonstrates that although voters may have discriminated against black candidates in the past, he could find no evidence that Democratic or Republican voters discriminated against black candidates in the 1996 and 1998 U.S. House elections.

The particular context and the quality of the candidate appear to play a substantial role in any election but these factors have particular importance for minority candidates. For example, Philpot and Walton (2007) find that black female candidates receive the most support from black female voters and considerably less support from white, male voters. However, black, female candidates who have considerable political experience were able to attract more white voters. Meanwhile, Stein, Ulbig, and Post (2005) suggest that racial voting by blacks and whites is more likely to occur with nonincumbent blacks. When a candidate is a black incumbent, approval ratings drive vote choice more than racial identification. Hajnal's (2007) analysis of support for black challengers and incumbents reaches similar conclusions, finding that the racial attitudes of whites matter less in voting considerations for a black incumbent, but racial attitudes do shape white voting preferences when the black candidate is not an incumbent. But this pattern largely occurs with white Democrats; white Republicans' racial attitudes influence their support of both black incumbents and nonincumbents.

Interestingly, the presence of black candidates on the ballot actually increases turnout among both black and white voters. Numerically, the increase in white voter turnout is higher, which appears to penalize black candidates (Washington 2006). Likewise, higher levels of black political incorporation on city councils increases black turnout in elections and decreases black voter roll-off (Vanderleeuw and Liu 2002).[3] Studies by Harris and Zipp (1999) and Herron and Sekhon (2005) also suggest that the presence of black candidates reduces black voter roll-off and invalid ballots but increases this behavior among white voters.

The racial context of elections may also play a significant role in determining whether or not both whites and blacks will vote for a black candidate. On the one hand, white support might decrease as the black population in a jurisdiction increases; this is a "black threat" or racial threat hypothesis. On the other hand, white support for black candidates may increase as black residents become the majority in a jurisdiction. Carsey's (1995) analysis of local elections in New York suggests that white voters are more likely to support black candidates as the black population increases. Liu and Vanderleeuw's (2001) analysis suggests that there is limited support for a linear "black threat" hypothesis. Instead, as the black population generally increases, white voting for black candidates tends to increase as well. Liu and Vanderleeuw suggest that white voters may be acting strategically by voting for the candidate who is likely to win or black candidates may run less racialized campaigns as the black population increases.

In contrast to women, the representation of blacks and Hispanics in local and state elections appears to, in part, be determined by the proportion of the population that is black or Hispanic. For example, black and Hispanic representation increases significantly if the group holds a majority within the district (Welch 1990). For women, the proportion of women in the district appears to matter little but more professional women in a district can increase the likelihood of female representation. Given this pattern, the proportion of LGBTs in a district could influence LGBT representation, but because LGBTs typically constitute less than 3 percent of the population, the size of the LGBT population would likely only influence LGBT representation in urban areas with district versus at-large elections.

The Role of Electoral Institutions

Electoral structures many hamper female and ethnic and racial minority representation. In studies of local elections, researchers have found that at-large city council election procedures decreased black and Hispanic representation, even though the effects for Hispanics were significant but not as severe (Fraga 1988; Jones-Correa 2001). In local school board elections, at-large districts have significantly hindered Latino representation but single-member districts (SMDs) help to enhance Latino representation (Fraga, Meier, and England 1986; Leal, Martinez-Ebers, and Meier 2004). The negative influence of at-large elections on representation of minorities has declined over time but it still hinders the election of blacks and Hispanics. In addition, at-large elections appear to provide less of a hurdle to Hispanic representation than black representation but the hurdle is more likely to exist in southern states rather than western states, such as California and in cities where the Hispanic population is not heavily segregated (Welch 1990).

Meanwhile, in state legislative races, minority candidates tend to perform better in SMDs than multimember districts (MMDs) (Grofman and Handley 1991; Grofman, Migalski, and Noviello 1986; Moncrief and Thompson 1992). For women the story is slightly different. A number of studies have suggested that women fare better in MMDs (Arceneaux 2001; Carroll 1994; Clark et al. 1984; Darcy, Welch, and Clark 1985, 1994; Clark 1994; Hogan 2001; King 2002; Matland and Brown 1992; Rule 1990; Vandenbosch 1996) but some researchers suggest that this advantage is fairly small (Welch and Studlar 1990).[4] Indeed, more women tend to run and win in MMDs than in SMDs (Darcy, Welch, and Clark 1985, 1994; Sanbonmatsu 2006), and this is true for minority women as well (Darcy, Hadley, and Kirksey 1993; Rule 1992).

Researchers have posited a variety of reasons that female candidates might be more likely to run and be successful in MMDs. Party leaders may encourage women to run in MMDs, women may choose to run in MMDs, and voters may have fewer qualms about electing women in a district where there is more than one representative (Carroll 1994; Darcy, Welch, and Clark 1985; King 2002). It seems likely that some combination of factors comes into play but if MMDs truly benefit female candidates, this benefit may also occur for lesbian candidates, and perhaps for all LGBT candidates.

In summary, although racial and ethnic minorities and female candidates have historically faced barriers to gaining voter support, much of the overt opposition has disappeared. The hurdles currently are more nuanced and tend to come from structural elements, potential candidate misperceptions, and some level of covert and overt discrimination by voters. As such, we should expect that LGBT candidates, as a sexual minority, will face some of the same hurdles as candidates. This issue is explored more deeply in chapters 2 and 3.

In the Office: Substantive (Active) Representation

Moving from hurdles to descriptive representation to substantive or active representation, it is illustrative to review the literature concerning minority and female officeholders. A considerable body of research has accumulated on substantive representation of group interests in the policy process. In general, much of the research on female and ethnic and racial descriptive representation suggests that increased descriptive representation leads to increased substantive representation in the policy process. In other words, as groups such as African Americans have achieved greater levels of greater levels of political incorporation, policy benefits to the black community have followed. However, a body of research finds little linkage between descriptive and substantive representation, and many have suggested that measurement issues abound in this literature. Here I briefly explore the findings in this literature and outline how these findings can help us to understand patterns of substantive representation for the LGBT community.

One point of clarification: One should not assume that descriptive representation equals substantive representation simply because the elected representatives who identify with a particular group are introducing and championing proposals that benefit this group—there may be additional dynamics at play. Indeed, simply having representatives of a group in a policymaking body may influence other decision makers' attitudes about the group and subsequent support for policy proposals related to the group (Barrett 1995, 1997; Bratton 2001, 2002; Browning, Marshall, and Tabb 1984; Hawkesworth 2003; Rayside 1998; Wahlke 1971; Yoder 1991). In a role model capacity, a group's elected representatives may likewise influence public perceptions of the group, and public and legislator preferences concerning policies related to the group (Barrett 1995, 1997; Hawkesworth 2003; Pitkin 1967; Smith and Haider-Markel 2002). Thus, descriptive representation may increase substantive representation not only through the policy entrepreneurship activities of the official representing the group but also because that official's mere presence may influence the behavior of other policymakers.

Ethnic and Racial Minorities in Office

In the urban and local politics literature a fair number of studies have uncovered a link between black representation and increased policy benefits to the black community, including employment and appointment opportunities as well as favorable police department policies (Browning, Marshall, and Tabb 1984; Campbell and Feagin 1977; Cole 1976; Eisinger 1982; Keech 1968; Levine 1974; Mladenka 1989; Saltzstein 1989). Likewise, research on Hispanic officials in local government has uncovered similar patterns of increased descriptive representation that lead to greater substantive representation (Browning, Marshall, and Tabb 1984; Mladenka

1989). For example, Meier and his colleagues (2001) find that increased Latino representation on school boards leads to greater numbers of Latino administrators and teachers.[5] Likewise, Meier and his colleagues (2005) find that the type of election for school boards, whether at-large or ward, shapes the degree to which descriptive representation is translated into substantive representation. In this case, greater substantive representation occurs when elections are by wards.

At the state and national levels much of the research on racial and ethnic minorities finds a connection between descriptive and substantive representation (Tate 2003). A number of studies suggest that bill sponsorship by African American legislators is significantly different from that of white legislators (Bratton 2005; Bratton and Haynie 1999; Haynie 2000; Swers 2002; Tate 2003). Grose's (2005) analysis of roll call voting found that black legislators increase substantive representation of the black community, even when effectively controlling for black population within the constituency. Likewise, studies of roll call voting in Congress tend to demonstrate that black legislators voting patterns mesh with black interests (Menifield and Jones 2001).

However, Santos and Huerta's (2001) analysis of Latino representatives in Congress suggests that although Latinos' level of legislative activity is similar to that of non-Latino legislators, Latino legislators do not actively pursue policies that would benefit the Latino community to any greater degree than their non-Latino colleagues. Santos and Huerta conclude that Latino representation in Congress has not led to an increase in substantive representation of Latino interests. Menifield (2001) finds a similar pattern at the state level—even in states with significant numbers of Latino legislators, there is little cohesion among these legislators and they do not actively pursue representation of the Latino community. Takeda (2001) also finds that descriptive representation of Asian Americans in Congress has little connection to substantive representation. More important is the representation of Asian Americans within a legislator's constituency.

A detailed analysis of African American state legislators suggests that black legislators differ from their white counterparts. King-Meadows and Schaller (2001, 181) argue that black caucuses in state legislatures are more internally cohesive than "their white counterparts who represent districts with significant African American constituencies." The strong cohesiveness of black caucuses in state legislatures increases the likelihood of substantive representation but does not guarantee substantive representation. In addition, Bratton's (2001) analysis of bill cosponsorship in several states suggests that African American legislators differ in the kinds of bills that they sponsor, and in some states, African American legislators can have more success in achieving bill passage depending who else sponsors the bill. African American legislators were most successful when they collaborated with white counterparts.

Studies of committee assignments suggest that African American legislators are more likely to serve on committees that deal with social welfare and education issues, as well as defined black issues. From their positions on these committees, black legislators are in a position to influence the political agenda on important issues to the black community, according to Haynie (2000). Likewise, on broader measures of political incorporation within legislatures, Haynie found that African American political incorporation grew considerably in the 1980s and 1990s. Interestingly, Haynie's analysis suggests that simple the descriptive representation of African Americans mattered as much or more as political incorporation.

Bratton's (2006) analysis of Latino legislators in several states finds that bill sponsorship by Latinos does differ from non-Latinos, even when accounting for constituency characteristics. In only a few states, such as Arizona, bills sponsored by Latinos were more likely to pass, and in some states, such as California, Latino legislators were more likely to see their bills fail. The committee membership patterns of Latinos did not significantly differ from those of non-Latinos. In addition, Preuhs's (2007) analysis of social welfare spending suggests that even though increases in the Latino population are associated with declines in welfare spending generosity, increases in Latino representation in the state legislature are associated with increases in welfare spending generosity.

More recent research has explored the ability of African Americans to reach positions of power within legislatures, with the presumption being that from these positions African American representatives can more easily pursue substantive representation. Orey, Overby, and Larimer (2007) examined the degree to which African American legislators hold committee chair positions. Their analysis suggests that African American legislators are not significantly underrepresented as committee chairs, relative to their presence in a legislature. And on some types of committees, such as health care and social services, African American legislators hold a disproportionate number of chairpersonships. Because these types of committees have traditionally been of greater interest to the black community, Orey, Overby, and Larimer infer that the chairpersons of these committees have had a disproportionate opportunity to influence policy in these areas. However, the number of black chairpersons has not risen as rapidly as the representation of black legislators, and African American chairpersonships are dependent on having majority-Democratic legislative chambers.

Women in Elective Office

Studies of women in state legislatures almost consistently suggest that increased female descriptive representation leads to greater substantive representation. In one early study Thomas (1991, 974) found that female legislators were more likely "to introduce and successfully steer legislation through the political process that addresses issues of women, children, and the family." Interestingly, this pattern was partly determined by context—"women appear to be more likely to introduce and pass distinctive legislation in situations in which they may find support—in this case, circumstances of increased numbers, or support from the creation of women's legislative caucuses." In other words, as the number of female legislators increases, and/or their mobilization increases within the legislature, there is a positive effect, in that individual women in those legislatures are more likely to pursue women's issues. Female legislators also tend to be more liberal in their voting records and more supportive of women's rights, generous social welfare policies, family leave

12

CHAPTER ONE

policies, environmental protection, and gun control (Boles and Scheurer 2007; Carroll 2001; Dodson and Carroll 1991; Epstein, Niemi, and Powell 2005; Reingold 2000; Swers 1998, 2001, 2002; Thomas 1989, 1991, 1994; Thomas and Welch 1991). Interestingly, female legislators also tend to be more supportive of public funding for the arts than their male counterparts, but this difference is largely between Republican women and men (Boles and Scheurer 2007.

On the basis of a survey of female state legislators, Thomas and Welch (1991) found that over time the activities of female legislators have become more similar to those of men but women are still more likely to pursue, with a higher priority, legislation that is viewed as benefiting women's interests. Women are also more likely to serve on committees that have jurisdiction over traditional women's issues, such as health, and are less likely to serve on committees that address issues such as taxes and the economy. Likewise, Schwindt-Bayer (2006) found that female legislators in Latin America were more likely to sponsor and pursue legislation that benefited women. And Dolan and Ford (1997) provided evidence that female legislators in the American states were more likely than men to serve on committees dealing with family policy, education, and social welfare and health issues. More recently, Kittilson's (2008) analysis of female legislators in nineteen parliamentary democracies suggests that descriptive representation significantly increases the likelihood of adopting family leave policies, and the scope of these policies.

Likewise, researchers have fairly consistently shown that female legislators are more likely than men to sponsor legislation that addresses the interests of women and children, education, social welfare, and health care (Berkman and O'Connor 1993; Bratton 2006; Bratton and Haynie 1999; Burrell 1997; Crowley 2004; Dodson and Carroll 1991; Menifield and Gray 2001; Saint-Germain 1989; Swers 2002; Thomas 1991, 1994; Tolbert and Steuernagel 2001). Female legislators could be more successful than men with the legislation they sponsor, depending on a variety of contextual variables (Bratton and Haynie 1999; Kathlene 1994; Saint-Germain 1989; Thomas 1994). Likewise, Menifield and Gray (2001) find that female legislator success with sponsored bills is conditioned by male legislator cosponsorship—bills introduced by female legislators are unlikely to pass without male cosponsorship. Bratton's (2001) analysis of bill cosponsorship in several states suggests that female legislators are more likely to sponsor legislation relating to women but their success in getting bills passed was also conditioned by their ability to build coalitions with their male counterparts.

However, understanding the substantive representation of women is often complicated by being able to cleanly identify policies that represent the interests of women (Swers 2002). In one case, Bratton and Ray (2002) examine the influence of female descriptive representation on municipal programs for day care. Their findings suggest that increased female representation makes the adoption of day care coverage more likely but it is clear that these polices benefit both men and women who are parents, not just women.

Finally, Bratton and Ray's (2002) important analysis also suggests that the relationship between descriptive and substantive representation may be nonlinear (see also Bratton 2005; Menifield and Gray 2001). They find that increases in descriptive representation matter most when innovative policies are first being considered and when women have achieved more than 30 percent representation in local legislatures. And Kathlene's (1994) analysis of female state legislators' behavior on committees suggests that as female representation on committees increases, male legislators become more aggressive in their language and women tend to respond by speaking less often. The presence of female committee chairs did shape committee dynamics differently than when male chairs were present but it did not decrease the verbal aggressiveness of male legislators.

Symbolic Representation

In much the same way that increased minority representation in elected office might shape the behavior and views of other elected officials, so too might the presence of minority and female officials shape the behavior and attitudes of constituents (Gay 2001, 2002). Although this book does not deeply explore this concept, the logic of this phenomenon is worth noting simply because the evidence for symbolic representation suggests that minority representatives may influence political outcomes even without engaging in active efforts to do so.

For example, Barreto's (2007) analysis of mayoral elections found that the presence of Latino candidates increased mobilization among Latinos and Barreto, Segura, and Woods (2004) found that Latino citizens are more likely to vote when they are represented by Latinos. Pantoja and Segura's (2003) analysis suggests that Latino legislators decrease alienation among their Latino constituents. Box-Steffensmeier and colleagues (2003) found that voters are more likely to support incumbents that share their race and or gender. Marschall and Ruhil (2007) find that African American attitudes about local government are more positive in localities where the proportion of elected black officials is higher (see also MacDonald and Stokes 2006; Marschall and Shah 2007; Tate 2001, 2003).[6] Likewise, Schwindt-Bayer and Mishler's (2005) analysis of descriptive representation in thirty-one democracies reveals that greater female representation in legislatures leads to increases in perceptions of government legitimacy. Atkeson (2003) and Wolbrecht and Campbell (2007) also report that increased female representation is associated with increases in female political participation, especially among young women.

Interestingly, Hajnal's (2007) analysis of black political incorporation also suggests that in localities where African Americans have served, the attitudes of white Democrats become more positive toward African Americans and policies that are believed to benefit the black community. However, the attitudes of white Republicans are not changed by the presence of black mayors. A similar analysis of female incorporation in local government legislatures concludes that increased female representation enhances trust in government among female constituents but is associated with declines in trust among men (Ulbig 2007). In a cross-national analysis, Banducci, Donovan, and Karp (2004) find that increasing descriptive representation in legislature tends to increase minority group political participation, political knowledge, and positive evaluations of government.

Nevertheless, not all research on symbolic representation concludes that the increased descriptive representation of women and minorities shapes constituent attitudes and behavior. Lawless (2004) finds that, controlling for female representatives' party affiliation and female citizens' party affiliation, women represented by women in Congress do not have attitudes that differ significantly from women who are not represented by a woman. Likewise, Dolan (2006) finds little evidence that female congressional candidates influence female voter mobilization or attitudes. Gay (2001) finds that the presence of black congressional incumbents decreases electoral participation by white voters and only occasionally increases voting by African Americans. And although constituents are more likely to contact a member of Congress who shares their race, the race of an individual's representative does not appear to shape the individual's attitudes about Congress as an institution.

Although the evidence for symbolic representation in terms of LGBT candidates and officeholders is only anecdotal, and given the evidence from the cases of ethnic and racial minorities, it does seem possible that the LGBT community is symbolically affected by the presence of LGBT candidates and officials. Indeed, at a minimum, we will see that many LGBT candidates were motivated to run for office because of the presence of such figures as the late Harvey Milk on the San Francisco Board of Supervisors and Barney Frank of Massachusetts in the U.S. House of Representatives.

Representation, Tokens, and Critical Mass

A more complex theoretical element for substantive representation has to do with critical mass, or the notion that increased descriptive representation only leads to significant substantive representation when descriptive representation passes some threshold, such as achieving a majority. For most majority groups, and perhaps even for women, reaching a majority in government positions or within a legislative chamber seems unlikely. However, there may be thresholds at lower levels, such as 30 or even 15 percent descriptive representation, where significant substantive representation can be achieved (Dahlerup 1988; Kanter 1977). At a minimum, analyses such as those presented by Schwindt-Bayer and Mishler (2005) clearly demonstrate that substantive representation tends to increase in a nonlinear pattern as descriptive representation increases. This does not preclude the notion of a critical mass or a tipping point; it simply suggests that researchers should account for a nonlinear process when examining representation.

Crowley's (2004) analysis of the likelihood of states' adoption of child support policies suggests that it increases as the percentage of female legislators increases. Interestingly, the effect of female token legislators (e.g., less than 15 percent of the legislature) was greater on policy adoption than women in those legislatures over token status. But the greatest effect on policy was just as female representation reached the threshold of 15 percent. In addition, this pattern was not a result of the ability of female legislators to form coalitions for the purpose of achieving policy goals. Likewise Menifield and Gray (2001) argue that female legislators in chambers with a large coalition of female legislators are no more successful in securing bill passage than female legislators in chambers with just a few female legislators.

Beckwith and Cowell-Meyers (2007) suggest that critical mass, or sheer numbers, oversimplifies the situation. Instead they hypothesize that the extent of descriptive representation is only part of the story. One must also account for the ideological positions of women in power, the ideology of the party in government, the strength of the opposition forces in government, the strength of the opposition forces and the represented group's forces in civil society, and public opinion. For example, even if large numbers of women are elected to a legislature, if those women are seated in a right-leaning legislature or face a non-female-friendly public, they are unlikely to achieve significant substantive representation. Indeed, Schwindt-Bayer and Mishler (2005) argue that a key component of political representation is formal representation, or the institutional elements, such as rules and electoral systems, which may enhance or decrease substantive representation. Likewise, Heath, Schwindt-Bayer, and Taylor-Robinson (2005) suggest that the mechanisms for committee assignments can decrease the ability of female legislators to actively represent women's interests (see also Schwindt-Bayer 2006).

Bratton (2005) questions the need for a critical mass of female representation above 15 percent. Her analysis of state legislatures finds that although increased substantive representation is indeed associated with increased descriptive representation, female legislators in legislatures that have not achieved a critical mass (i.e., 15 percent female representation) are still more likely than men to introduce and champion legislation on women's issues and are at least as successful as men in pursuing a legislative agenda. And as female representation surpasses a critical mass, the gender differences in sponsored legislation actually tend to decrease. Thus, not only may a critical mass be unnecessary, descriptive representation above certain levels may actually decrease active representation by female legislators.

Likewise, not everyone agrees that minorities and women can best achieve policy goals through descriptive representation. Weldon (2002) provides some evidence that women's policy goals are more likely to be achieved when there is a strong women's movement in civil society and when government agencies exist that focus on women's issues. In contrast, female representation in legislatures has no significant influence on policy adoption.

In the case of LGBT legislators, critical mass theory poses a significant problem for substantive representation. If LGBT people are somewhere between 3 and 10 percent of the general population, it seems very unlikely that LGBT legislators would ever constitute the 15 percent of a legislature that some argue is the critical mass for substantive representation. However, if we take Beckwith and Cowell-Meyers's (2007) contextual factors into account, LGBT legislators may indeed be able to achieve substantive representation even without sheer numbers.

Negative Consequences of Descriptive Representation?

Although both democratic theory and empirical evidence suggest that groups can achieve positive substantive policy representation through descriptive representation, some scholars have suggested that there may be a backlash, or negative reaction, as a politically marginal group achieves social, economic, or political gains (Blalock 1967; Bratton 2002; Cammisa and Reingold 2004; Crowley 2004; Studlar and McAllister 2002; Yoder 1991). For example, many have argued that the women's movement, while accomplishing many significant goals in the 1970s, created a backlash of antiwoman, or at least antifeminist, sentiment in the 1980s (Banaszac 1996; Faludi 1991; Haas-Wilson 1993; Thomas 1994, 1997; Yoder 1991).

In fact, several researchers have found systematic evidence of a backlash or at least the marginalization of legislators from underrepresented groups. In the case of legislatures where there are very few African American representatives, black legislators tend to find themselves and their proposals marginalized by the white majority (Barrett 1995, 1997; Button and Hedge 1996; Carroll and Strimling 1983; Githens and Prestage 1977; Hedge, Button, and Spear 1996). Haynie's (2000) analysis suggests that black representatives were viewed as less effective than their white counterparts. Female legislators have faced some of the same patterns of social isolation in legislatures (Carroll and Strimling 1983; Githens and Prestage 1977). In addition, an analysis of female incorporation in local government legislatures concludes that increased female representation enhances trust in government among female constituents but is associated with declines in trust among men (Ulbig 2007), which might be considered a backlash by male constituents.

Bratton (2002) found that an increase in the number of female state legislators is associated with a legislative backlash—an increase in antiwoman legislation. Crowley (2004) found evidence of a decline in the impact of female legislators once female representation reaches 15 percent, which she interpreted as a potential backlash (see also Thomas 1997; Yoder 1991). Heath, Schwindt-Bayer, and Taylor-Robinson (2005) found that female legislators in Latin America are marginalized after being elected by being denied access to key legislative committees. Kathlene's (1994) analysis of state legislative committee hearings suggests that male legislators tend to become more verbally aggressive when there are more female legislators on a committee. Kathlene argues that this behavior is evidence of a backlash against female representation within a masculine institution.

Preuhs's (2005) analysis of states' adoption of English-only laws suggests that although greater numbers of Latinos in legislative leadership positions decreases the likelihood that a state will adopt an English-only law, the presence of the citizen initiative process leads to a policy backlash—and the combination of the initiative and higher levels of Latino incorporation into legislative leadership positions makes the likelihood of adoption more likely. And according to Bratton and Haynie's (1999) analysis, state legislation sponsored by African Americans was significantly less likely to pass in half the states they examined. Likewise, Bratton's (2006) analysis of Latino state legislators found that in some states, such as California, Latino legislators were more likely to see their bills fail.

However, Bratton and Ray's (2002) analysis of female representation in Norway did not find evidence that increased representation leads to a policy backlash. And an analysis of the success of female legislators on bills they have sponsored shows that women are at least as successful as men in having their bills passed (Saint-Germain 1989; Thomas 1994).

A Brief History of the LGBT Movement in America

In comparison with other minority groups, LGBT people have only recently appeared on the U.S. political scene. Indeed, not until 1969 did LGBT equality became part of the American political agenda. A riot by transvestites and gay men outside the Stonewall Inn, a gay bar in New York City raided by the police in June 1969, created the impetus for a full-fledged movement over LGBT rights, which continues today. This section outlines the origins of the movement and provides a historical overview of how the movement has manifested itself in American politics. In addition, I explain the growing development of LGBT attempts to achieve representation in the policy process through the election of LGBT officials and how these efforts compare with the efforts of heterosexual women, and of ethnic and racial minorities.

Early History and Stonewall

Before 1969 the debate over gay and lesbian rights in the United States was frequently confined to discussions of the deviant status—or treatment as such—of homosexuals in American society. However, interest groups focused on protecting the civil rights and liberties of homosexuals existed as early as 1924. In the 1950s a number of relatively secretive homosexual groups formed on both the East and West coasts and created what came to be known as the homophile movement. These early groups typically provided a safe space for members to talk with other homosexuals, but some began initial efforts to protect the free speech rights of homosexuals and overturn government laws and regulations that specifically discriminated against homosexuals. For example, efforts were made to overturn federal laws that banned the employment of homosexuals and the immigration rights of gays and lesbians (D'Emilio 1983).

During the 1950s, one early gay group called the Veterans Benevolent Association worked with African American groups in an effort to end the military's arbitrary use of undesirable discharges. Also in the 1950s gay groups were successful in securing their right to send material with homosexual content in the U.S. mail. Following demands made by members of Congress, the U.S. postmaster ruled in 1954 that a gay magazine (*One*) could not be sent through the U.S. mail. Gay groups challenged the decision, and the Supreme Court overruled the postmaster in 1958. Further, in states and localities, early homophile groups made efforts to overturn laws that banned same-sex relations between consenting adults and to prevent the police from harassing homosexuals in bars and bathhouses. However, the successes were limited to larger cities on the coasts and in those states that were conducting overall revisions of their criminal codes in the 1960s (D'Emilio 1983).

Following the Stonewall Inn riot in 1969, gays and lesbians began to develop a broader notion of gay and lesbian rights that included both personal and societal liberation. They argued that not only should homosexuals not hate themselves but neither should society. Gay liberationists argued that homosexuals must publicly declare their homosexuality in order to stop self-hatred. This process came to be known as "coming out" or "coming out of the closet." Liberation activists set out to transform traditional notions of sex and gender by educating homosexuals and the larger public, and by changing government policies to ensure that the civil rights and liberties of homosexuals were not violated (Rimmerman 2008).

But coming out to friends, family, and coworkers was not enough for some activists. The liberationists also believed that gays and lesbians must take to the streets and the halls of government to make their existence known. Throughout the 1970s liberationists engaged in protest politics by marching in the streets, staging media events, and dogging elected officials about their stance on gay civil rights.

Other gay and lesbian activists, called assimilationists by liberationists, focused their attention on more mainstream forms of political participation, such as political party activism, forming interest groups, litigation, and lobbying elected officials. Gay activists formed many new interest groups at the local, state, and national levels, and some of these groups, such as the National Gay (now Gay and Lesbian) Task Force and the Lambda Legal Defense Fund, still operate today. Within the Democratic Party, gay activists increased their political muscle, forming caucuses and drafting platform planks that supported lesbian and gay civil rights. But not all gay interest groups could be called purely assimilationist or liberationist. For example, some hybrid groups, such as the Gay Activists Alliance in New York City, combined protest politics with mainstream lobbying and political campaign participation. During the early 1970s, the alliance directly lobbied politicians and conducted "zaps" (organized protests) outside the homes and offices of politicians during the group's initial attempt to pass a New York City ordinance banning discrimination against homosexuals (Smith and Haider-Markel 2002).

Although the stigma attached to homosexuality remained largely unchanged throughout the 1970s, the gay movement began to build a list of impressive victories in government policy, private employment practices, and the media's depiction of homosexuality. Elected officials began to be open about their sexual orientation, and open gays and lesbians were being elected for the first time. In cities such as San Francisco and New York, gays and lesbians were being appointed to official government positions (Smith and Haider-Markel 2002).

Local governments on the coasts and in the heartland also began to adopt policies that prohibited discrimination based on sexual orientation in public employment, housing, and even private employment. State courts increasingly overturned archaic laws regarding sexual relations between adults, cross-dressing, and the civil liberties of homosexuals. State legislatures also began to repeal laws banning homosexual relations, and state legislators began introducing legislation to ban sexual orientation discrimination. By the late 1970s, even the U.S. Congress began to hold hearings on issues related to homosexuals, and the first bills banning discrimination on the basis of sexual orientation were introduced. Furthermore, a federal policy barring gays from employment in the Foreign Service was lifted in 1977, the same year that gay and lesbian activists were invited to the White House for the first time. The Internal Revenue Service canceled a policy that had forced homosexual educational and charity groups to publicly state that homosexuality is a "sickness, disturbance, or diseased pathology" before being given tax-exempt status (Haider-Markel 2001a).

However, the successes of the gay movement also brought a political backlash. Believing that their religious values were under attack, conservative Christians began to exert their political muscle. By the late 1970s, gays and conservative religious groups were facing off in local and state battles, with both sides believing that their rights were under attack. In Florida, Anita Bryant led a successful 1977 ballot initiative campaign to overturn a Dade County policy that banned discrimination because of sexual orientation. National attention to the battle meant that other ballot contests soon followed in Eugene, Oregon; Saint Paul; Seattle; and Wichita; gay rights forces lost in all these contests except Seattle; and in California, a 1978 ballot initiative that would have prevented homosexuals from teaching in the public schools failed but only because even some conservatives, such as Ronald Reagan, viewed the measure as draconian (Vaid 1995).

The 1980s

As the 1970s came to a close, the movement for gay and lesbian rights had made considerable strides. But the rise of a conservative religious right, the public shift to conservative values, and the outbreak of a terrible new disease offered complex challenges to the young social movement.

In 1981 religious conservatives were celebrating the presidential inauguration of their chosen candidate, Ronald Reagan. At the same time, the free-wheeling counterculture of gay liberationists was forced to confront what some called the excesses of the movement as the first cases of what was first called "gay cancer" or Gay-Related Immune Deficiency began to appear in young, gay men throughout the country. The disease, acquired immunodeficiency syndrome (AIDS), disproportionately affected gay men and intravenous drug users, two social groups that were already seriously stigmatized.

AIDS came to redefine both homosexuality and the gay movement. Religious conservatives saw it as a sign from God concerning the evils of homosexuality and used the opportunity to roll back the policy victories of the gay movement and to block increased legal protections based on sexual orientation. In states across the country, fears about the spread of AIDS led to legislative efforts to criminalize and regulate the behaviors of persons with AIDS. In California, religious conservatives placed a number of measures before voters to stop the spread of the disease, including one that would have allowed people with AIDS to be quarantined. The ballot measures all failed as gays and lesbians mobilized against them but in many states gays were increasingly losing political battles (Haider-Markel 1999a).

At the national level Democrats in Congress championed funding for AIDS research, education, and health care by 1985, even as President Reagan refused to publicly use the word AIDS. Interestingly, congressional action on AIDS appears to have been partly motivated by increasing numbers of public figures who declared that they had AIDS, were gay, or both. In fact, the first openly gay member of Congress was Representative Gerry Studds (D-MA), who revealed that he was gay in July 1983. Although Studds served until 1996, the second member of Congress to come out was Representative Barney Frank (D-MA), who revealed his sexual orientation in May 1987. And even though Frank's public declaration followed a personal scandal involving sex, he has consistently been reelected, gained prominence in both the House of Representatives and the Democratic Party, and he serves as a national role model for LGBT Americans (Rayside 1998).

By 1987 a few conservative members of Congress, including Senator Jesse Helms (R-NC), began to successfully attach amendments to AIDS funding bills that explicitly banned the use of federal funds to "promote homosexuality." Religious conservatives gained more fodder against the gay movement in the late 1980s, when controversy erupted over museum exhibitions of the homoerotic photography of Robert Mapplethorpe, which was partially funded by taxpayers through the National Endowment for the Arts. At the behest of conservative religious groups, for several years conservative members of Congress subsequently tried to end or limit the endowment's funding, but they only succeeded in slightly cutting its budget. Progay Democrats in Congress had joined forces with moderate Republicans and largely fended off the attacks by religious conservatives. Nevertheless, all proposed legislation seeking to protect gays from discrimination or hate crimes died in Congress during the late 1980s. These battles helped to reinforce and expand the increasingly partisan spilt on gay issues in Congress, with Democrats tending to be more supportive and Republicans tending to be less supportive (Haider-Markel 2001a).

Litigation successes for the LGBT movement were also few during the 1980s, with state courts consistently deciding child custody cases against homosexuals, allowing sodomy laws to stand, and upholding the rights of individuals and groups to discriminate on the basis of religious beliefs concerning homosexuality. The most important court decision of this period was the 1986 Supreme Court decision in *Bowers v. Hardwick*. Gay litigation groups had brought the case to challenge Georgia's law banning homosexual sodomy under the constitutional right to privacy of sex acts in one's own home. The Supreme Court rejected the claim of a right to privacy by a man who had been convicted of illegal homosexual sodomy under the Georgia law, thereby ensuring that similar laws would remain on the books throughout the country. The case still stands as the most significant legal defeat for the gay rights movement (Anderson 2005).

AIDS and the Republican presidents of the 1980s also appear to have provided a greater incentive for gays and lesbians to join forces and create more interest groups at the national, state, and local levels, including the Human Rights Campaign, the Gay and Lesbian Alliance Against Defamation, Right to Privacy in Oregon, the Lobby for Individual Freedom and Equality in California, the Municipal Elections Committee of Los Angeles, and the Los Angeles Gay and Lesbian Center (Smith and Haider-Markel 2002). The number of gay groups grew steadily throughout the 1980s, with some focusing exclusively on AIDS issues (Haider-Markel 1999a). Further, by the late 1980s some of the new groups reintroduced radical protest tactics in their calls for AIDS funding and ending the cultural stigma attached to gays and lesbians. Such groups included the AIDS Coalition to Unleash Power (known as ACT UP) and, later, Treatment Action Guerrillas, Queer Nation, and the Lesbian Avengers. The attention-grabbing actions of these groups brought media attention to the movement and helped to mobilize a new generation of activists. But by the mid-1990s, most local chapters of these groups had disappeared (Vaid 1995).

New gay groups also formed at the state and local levels during the 1980s, and many of these groups were increasingly successful at securing new legal protections for gays and lesbians. In 1982 Wisconsin became the first state to pass a law banning discrimination in public employment based on sexual "preference," but other states, such as Oregon, Maine, New York, and California, had begun to see gay rights legislation introduced on an almost annual basis. Several governors signed executive orders protecting state employees from sexual orientation discrimination, including in New York, Washington, Oregon, and Ohio. The number of local ordinances banning sexual orientation discrimination grew to 100 by the end of the decade, even though religious conservatives had increasingly mobilized to defeat these measures (Haider-Markel 2000). When religious groups failed in their efforts to block these policies, they increasingly turned to the ballot box, ousted elected officials who supported these polices, and, where available, placed proposals on the ballot to repeal these policies. Indeed, more than 20 of these measures were voted on during the 1980s, with religious conservatives successfully repealing gay rights laws most of the time, including a state measure in Oregon, several local measures in California, and a city ordinance in Houston (Haider-Markel 2000).

From 1990 to the Present

When the 1990s began, the gay movement appeared to be riding a favorable wave of public tolerance and policy success. In 1990 a Democratic Congress and Republican president enacted both a hate crimes policy that included sexual orientation and the Americans with Disabilities Act, which, among other things, protects persons with HIV/AIDS from discrimination. In 1992 gay groups helped to elect gay-friendly candidates to Congress, and contributions of more than $3.2 million to the Democratic Party helped to ensure the election of a gay-friendly president, Bill Clinton. Further, gay rights legislation was increasingly passing in the states, with Connecticut, Hawaii, Massachusetts, Minnesota, and New Jersey all providing legal protections by 1993 (Haider-Markel 2000; Vaid 1995). Local governments continued to codify gay rights, and more also began to adopt domestic partner policies for government employees, which allowed for the committed partners of gays and lesbians to obtain a variety of benefits, such as health insurance, usually reserved for the spouses of married employees (Haider-Markel, Joslyn, and Kniss 2000). And within the movement, the concerns of bisexuals and transgender individuals were beginning to be addressed by groups such as the National Gay and Lesbian Task Force. Further, states and localities increasingly adopted policies that not only banned discrimination on the basis of sexual orientation but also on the basis of gender identity (Vaid 1995).

However, even as gay activists celebrated these victories, religious conservatives redoubled their efforts to protect traditional values. These groups increasingly attempted to repeal or prevent the passage of gay rights laws by using the ballot initiative process. Their campaigns were successful nearly all the time, but the key successes were in Cincinnati and Colorado. In 1992 a majority of Colorado voters supported Amendment 2, a referendum that sought to repeal existing local gay rights laws and ban localities and the state from passing any new gay rights laws. The vote was a significant victory for conservative religious groups but the Colorado Supreme Court soon overturned the election results, and in 1996 the U.S. Supreme Court upheld the earlier decision in *Romer v. Evans*, ruling that Amendment 2 was unconstitutional because it prevented homosexuals from using the political process to achieve policy goals. In the Cincinnati case, voters were asked in 1993 to repeal a 1992 gay rights law passed by the City Council (Anderson 2005). Voters overwhelmingly passed the measure by mobilizing church members and the black community and arguing that traditional religious values were under fire. Gay groups challenged the election outcome in court but the City Council repealed the ordinance in 1995, largely making the challenges moot. The lesson for the gay movement in nearly all these ballot contests was that codified legal recognition of their civil rights would lose in a popular vote (Vaid 1995).

Religious conservatives also won a major victory against gay rights in 1993 when they soundly defeated President Clinton's effort to allow homosexuals to serve openly in the U.S. military. Candidate Clinton had promised his gay supporters that he would overturn the ban but once in office President Clinton attempted to convince Congress to repeal the ban rather than doing it himself through an executive order. Religious conservatives overwhelmed members of Congress by voicing their support for the ban (Rayside 1998). Gay groups were outgunned and arrived at a compromise policy called "Don't Ask, Don't Tell," which many have argued is worse than the original policy.[7]

The 1994 congressional elections brought more conservatives to Washington, many of whom had drawn their support from religious activists in the Republican Party. This shift in power meant that legislation supporting gay rights made little headway in Congress during the remainder of the 1990s, and gay groups had to spend most of their time defending themselves against anti–gay rights legislation. However, new opportunities were created for gay people who worked within the Republican Party as a federation of local gay Republican groups established a national office in Washington in 1993. This new group, the Log Cabin Republicans, formed a political action committee that raises tens of thousands of dollars per election cycle for Republican candidates, and which by 1996 had six staff members and an annual budget of $700,000 (Smith and Haider-Markel 2002).

Throughout the 1990s, gays also faced an increasingly conservative Supreme Court. In *Dale v. Boy Scouts of America* (2000), the Court ruled that the Boy Scouts of America could ban homosexuals from joining its local troops in order to maintain its moral objectives (Anderson 2005). However, President Clinton continued to support the gay movement, issuing official recognitions of Gay Pride Month each June, signing an executive order in 1998 that banned discrimination against civilian federal employees on the basis of sexual orientation, and appointing 150 gays and lesbians to federal positions throughout his two terms in office (Smith and Haider-Markel 2002).

Same-sex marriage also became a significant gay rights issue in the 1990s. Although gays had tried to legally marry in the 1970s and 1980s, their efforts had always failed. Then in 1993 a Hawaii Supreme Court ruling in *Baehr v. Lewin* (later *Baehr v. Miike*) argued that the state could not prevent same-sex marriage because such a policy violated the Hawaii Constitution's ban on gender discrimination. Religious conservatives around the country were outraged by the case and argued that homosexuals would travel to Hawaii, get married, and return to their home states to try to force recognition of their marriages. In late 1994 and early 1995 a number of national conservative groups formalized a national campaign to introduce legislation banning same-sex marriage in all fifty states and in the U.S. Congress. The organized effort manifested itself mainly through a coalition of groups called the National Campaign to Protect Marriage, which included groups such as the American Family Association, the Christian Coalition, Concerned Women of America, and Focus on the Family. These groups were the force behind state legislative attempts to ban same-sex marriage (Haider-Markel 2000, 2001b).

Related national legislation on same-sex marriage, deemed the Defense of Marriage Act (DOMA), passed overwhelmingly in 1996. Although DOMA allowed states to do as they pleased on the issue, the legislation banned any federal recognition of same-sex marriages and allowed states to refuse to recognize same-sex marriages performed elsewhere. State governments followed a similar path. By March 1998 all but two states had considered legislation banning the recognition of same-sex marriages, and twenty-eight had adopted such policies. By 2002 at least thirty-three states had passed similar policies, even though the threat from Hawaii marriages never materialized. Furthermore, at the end of 1999 the Vermont Supreme Court ruled that the state must provide the benefits of marriage to same-sex couples either by allowing same-sex couples to marry or by recognizing the relationship in some other manner. This ruling led to the state's passage of the nation's first same-sex civil union law in 2000, which gives same-sex couples the right to form state-sanctioned civil unions and take advantage of nearly all the benefits, rights, and responsibilities that are available to heterosexual married couples (Mucciaroni 2008).

Even facing a largely hostile U.S. Congress as the 1990s progressed, gay rights advocates achieved new victories in state and local public policy, political representation, and shifts in national public opinion. By the end of the 1990s more than two hundred local governments had adopted some form of legal protections for gays and lesbians and more than eighty provided some type of domestic partner benefits. In addition a number of states and localities, including Minnesota and Boulder, Colorado, adopted policies banning discrimination based on gender identity (Haider-Markel 2000).

By 2009 more than 270 localities and twenty states had laws banning discrimination on the basis of sexual orientation. In addition, all but seventeen states had adopted some form of hate crimes law that explicitly or implicitly included sexual orientation. And in terms of relationship recognition, Massachusetts (2004) allowed for full marriage rights for same-sex partners; Vermont (2000), Connecticut (2005), New Jersey (2006), and New Hampshire (2007) provided civil unions; California (2005) and Oregon (2007) allowed domestic partnerships; and Hawaii, Maine, and

Washington provided for a limited recognition of domestic partnerships. Figure 1.2 shows the pattern of local antidiscrimination laws over time. Further, direct democracy challenges to these policies began to decrease in the 1990s, and those that did reach the ballot were increasingly voted down. But religious conservatives in Maine successfully repealed statewide gay rights laws twice in the late 1990s, even as local governments in the state passed local antidiscrimination ordinances.

The 1990s also witnessed a tremendous increase in the number and scope of gay and lesbian officials in government positions. The first openly gay person to run for public office was Jose Sarria, who ran for the San Francisco Board of Supervisors in 1961. He lost his race but his effort inspired other gays and lesbians to run for public office. Throughout the 1970s and 1980s most of these candidates also lost their races, and by 1987 the movement could only claim 20 openly gay or lesbian elected officials in the country, with most of these positions being in local government. But by 1990 there had been a total of 50 openly gay officials, and in 1991 there were 52 openly gay elected officials in office. By April of 1998 this number had jumped to 146 and spanned twenty-seven states and the District of Columbia. In 2002 the number had risen above 200, but this was still a small fraction of the more than 500,000 elective offices in the United States. Still, the 2002 figures included 3 openly gay members of Congress, 47 state legislators, and a scattering of other state-level positions; the rest were local officials, including mayors and local legislative officials. Interestingly, the city of Wilton Manors, Florida, even had a gay majority on its City Council (Smith and Haider-Markel 2002). According to the Gay and Lesbian Victory Fund, by 2009 the total number of LGBT officials had swelled to more than 450.

Figure 1.2   Local Government Bans on Sexual Orientation Discrimination, 1972–2007

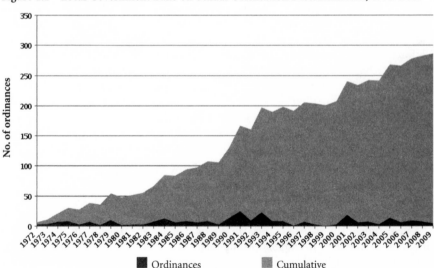

Note: The data were compiled by the author from Smith and Haider-Markel (2002) and historical data from the National Gay and Lesbian Task Force.

Furthermore, in the 1990s open lesbians increasingly began to seek elective office at the state and national levels. Lesbians secured state legislative seats in California, Maine, Montana, New Mexico, New York, and Oregon. Indeed, some called 1998 the "year of the lesbian" as four lesbians ran for seats in the U.S. House and another ten ran for state legislative seats. The only lesbian House candidate to win her race was Representative Tammy Baldwin (D-WI), who made history by being the first lesbian elected to Congress, as well as the first nonincumbent gay person elected to Congress. In the 2000 elections only two lesbians ran for Congress, in addition to the first transgender candidate, but more than twenty lesbians ran for state legislative seats.

Some reporters also declared the 1998 election year the "year that gay politicians came of age" (Brelis 1998). Massachusetts alone had a record ten openly LGBT candidates running for state or national offices. And these candidates were no longer simply defined as "gay" candidates; instead, they were being judged on the basis of their positions on particular issues (Brelis 1998). Susan Tracy, an out lesbian candidate for the 8th District U.S. House seat in Massachusetts, discovered this when she failed to receive the endorsements of the state's main LGBT group and main LGBT newspapers. Similar problems faced other LGBT candidates in the state as LGBT groups endorsed "gay-friendly" incumbents over openly LGBT challengers (Brelis 1998). This does not mean that a candidate's sexual orientation is not ever an issue. In fact, as chapter 2 demonstrates, for some voters it may always be an issue, even in very liberal areas.

Like racial and ethnic minorities and heterosexual women before them, successful gay candidates were increasingly discovering that they must speak to a broader constituency. Without the support of heterosexuals, gay candidates cannot expect to be victorious in diverse districts (see Fox 1997; Frank 1994; Haider-Markel 2000). For example, after a Rhode Island race where the openly gay incumbent representative Michael Pisaturo (D-Cranston) was accused of making gay and lesbian issues his only concern by his losing opponent, Pisaturo said that his victory was evidence that "gay baiting doesn't work anymore and a candidate's sexual orientation is much less important to voters than policy positions and advocacy on the issues of the district." Nonetheless, Pisaturo went on to say "I could not have run solely on lesbian and gay issues and expected to win" (Boyce 1998).

Opponents of gay civil rights continued their attempts to marginalize LGBT candidates and portray them as representing a special interest group. The president of the anti-LGBT political action committee Campaign for Working Families argued that gay candidates were running for office to increase their efforts at "promoting homosexuality as an acceptable alternative lifestyle" (Polman 1998). During Wisconsin representative Tammy Baldwin's historic 1998 campaign, her sexual orientation was an issue during the primary but not during the general election. Ron Greer, a Republican candidate for the congressional seat, raised Baldwin's sexual orientation during the primary as a way to mobilize religious conservatives in the district. Greer lost the primary, and Baldwin's opponent in the general election was far more moderate. In the relatively liberal Madison district, Baldwin's openness mattered less than her party affiliation and positions on the issues (Smith and Haider-Markel 2002).

In addition to elected positions, gays and lesbians were increasingly being appointed to various government positions. At the national level, Jimmy Carter was the first president to appoint an openly gay person to a national office but appointments did not take off until President Clinton took office in 1993. Clinton thanked the gay movement for its support by appointing 150 open gays and lesbians to positions in the executive branch. Although only five of these appointments required Senate confirmation, at least two were confirmed even over loud objections from religious conservatives. Presidential candidate George W. Bush had indicated to religious conservatives in the Republican Party that he would not appoint openly homosexual individuals during the 2000 campaign (Smith and Haider-Markel 2002), but according to the *Washington Blade* by 2007 he had appointed ten openly gay people to his administration.

Perhaps the most interesting change for the LGBT movement over the past thirty years has been the increased tolerance toward LGBT people and the increased support for LGBT rights. Although many Americans still opposed the hiring of homosexuals for positions that involve children, such as education, Americans increasingly supported protecting gays and lesbians from discrimination. Figure 1.3 shows this trend over time. In the 1970s only small majorities were willing to support gay civil rights and liberties in the areas of allowing homosexuals to speak in public, allowing books on homosexuality in the public library, allowing homosexuals to teach in colleges or serve openly in the military, or supporting the equal rights

Figure 1.3   Support for Gay Civil Rights, 1977–2009

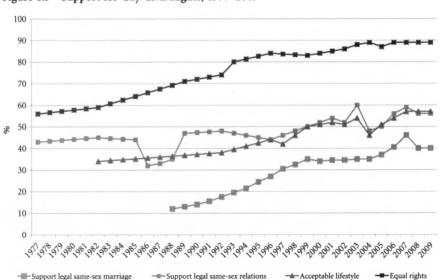

Source: Data compiled by the author based on national surveys of adults conducted by Gallup.

of gays and lesbians. By the late 2000s support in all these areas increased, with the greatest support for a vague notion of equal rights or for policies that would protect gays and lesbians from job discrimination. And as Lax and Phillips (2009) point out, in most states large majorities favor antidiscrimination policies for gays and lesbians as well as legal protections against hate crimes. For example, in Massachusetts an estimated 70 percent of the public support antidiscrimination laws in employment and 81 percent support hate crimes laws that include LGBT people. Meanwhile in Mississippi, an estimated 55 percent of the public support antidiscrimination laws and 64 percent support hate crimes laws that include LGBT people. Although majorities favor these policies in both states, one might clearly surmise that an LGBT candidate would likely find a more favorable electoral environment in Massachusetts.

However, even as Americans have increasingly become more supportive of gay and lesbian rights, the arguments made by opponents appear to fit with American attitudes toward homosexuals as a group and toward the "rightness" of same-sex sexual relations. Although Americans have become more tolerant of homosexuals as a group and have become less averse to the notion of same-sex sexual relations, most Americans still appear to believe that homosexuality is objectionable behavior and that homosexuals as a group should not be supported. Figure 1.4 demonstrates this point by plotting average American attitudes about homosexuals with a feeling thermometer. Survey respondents are asked to state their feelings toward a group using a scale from 0 to 100, where a score of 50 to 100 indicates favorable or warm feelings and 0 to 50 suggests an unfavorable or cold feeling. For many years the American National Election Study has used feeling thermometer questions to access feelings or affect toward groups, such as homosexuals and environmentalists.

Although affect toward gays and lesbians has "warmed" over time, the mean scores suggest that most Americans still have an unfavorable or cool affect toward gays and lesbians. Indeed, from 1984 to 1996 gays and lesbians scored lower than any other group except illegal immigrants (Yang 1999). By 2008 gays and lesbians had moved to a mean score of 49 on the thermometer but they still had lower affect scores than most other groups, including 16 points lower than for Jews and Hispanics and 19 points lower than for African Americans.[8] In addition, about 65 percent of respondents rated gays at or below the midpoint of 50, and the standard deviation was also almost twice as large as for most racial, ethnic, and religious minorities. By 2008 the only other groups with comparable levels of affect coolness were Muslims, atheists, and illegal aliens. So, although the increase in warm affect continues to trend upward, it is clear that LGBT people are less than popular.

Of particular importance is that respondents' affect toward homosexuals varies by individual characteristics; people who live in urban areas, people who have higher levels of education, people who identify as liberal and who belong to the Democratic Party, and heterosexual women have a higher affect toward homosexuals (Haeberle 1996; Haider-Markel and Joslyn 2008; Wilcox and Wolpert 2000; Yang 1999). Using the relatively low affect as a baseline, we can expect that the initial public response to LGBT candidates will not be very positive. However, certain

Figure 1.4   Public Feelings (Affect) toward Gay Men and Lesbians, 1984–2008 (mean score on 0 to 100 feeling thermometer)

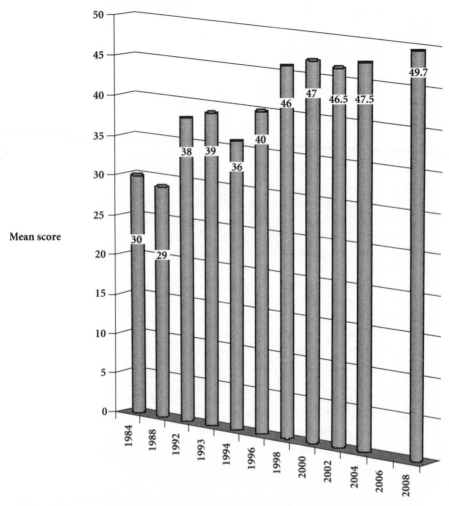

Source: The data were compiled by the author from the American National Election Study.
Note: Respondents were asked to state their feelings toward a group using a scale from 0 to 100, where a score of 50 to 100 indicates favorable or warm feelings and a score from 0 to 50 suggests an unfavorable or cold feeling with the following question: "how would you rate the following groups . . . gay men and lesbians, that is, homosexuals?"

groups in the population, such as liberals and the educated, should be more positive, and we should expect that LGBT candidates will face less negative attitudes over time.

Furthermore, Americans tend to oppose allowing homosexuals to teach elementary school children and allowing homosexual couples to legally marry. A Gallup poll from 1977 found that 65 percent of respondents opposed the hiring of a homosexual as an elementary school teacher. By 2001 opposition had decreased to 40 percent, but the level of opposition still suggests a rejection of gay civil rights in employment under some circumstances. Gallup polls from 2006 to 2008 also suggest that majorities also oppose same-sex marriage and civil unions for homosexuals, akin to the civil union policy adopted in Vermont. However, Gallup and Pew Center polls from 2008 and 2009 suggest that when given a choice between no recognition, recognition of same-sex civil unions, and recognition of same-sex marriage, a majority of Americans support either civil unions or same-sex marriage. Men tend to be slightly more opposed than women, and Republicans, conservatives, and frequent churchgoers are also more opposed to civil unions. This pattern is consistent with other national polls on gay rights and clearly reflects the religious, partisan, and ideological divide on the issue (Haider-Markel and Joslyn 2008).

In June 2003, the Supreme Court reached a landmark decision concerning the rights of gays and lesbians. In *Lawrence v. Texas*, the Court ruled six to three that Texas's antisodomy law was unconstitutional. The ruling reversed the Court's own ruling of 1986 allowing for the constitutionality of a similar Georgia law. The ruling was hailed by many in the LGBT community as vindicating their rights to full and equal citizenship. Conservatives, including dissenting justice Antonio Scalia, said that the Court was going along with the "so-called homosexual agenda," and many feared that the ruling would eventually call into question laws against homosexual marriage (Stoutenborough, Haider-Markel, and Allen 2006).

Indeed, most national polls taken in July and August showed a reversal in the upward favorable public opinion toward homosexuals and LGBT equality (Stoutenborough, Haider-Markel, and Allen 2006). Gallup national polls of adults—which asked "Do you think homosexual relations between consenting adults should or should not be legal?"—found that support for "legal" dropped from a record high of 60 percent in May 2003 to 48 percent in July 2003. In addition, the proportion of adults who believed that homosexuality should be considered an acceptable alternative lifestyle dropped from 54 percent to 46 percent in the same period, and the proportion of the public supporting civil unions for homosexual couples dropped from 49 percent to 40 percent. Likewise, support for a constitutional ban on same-sex marriage increased to 52 percent (Stoutenborough, Haider-Markel, and Allen 2006).

The public opinion backlash against the Supreme Court's June 2003 decision may have been compounded by a November decision by the Massachusetts Supreme Judicial Court in *Goodridge et al. v. Department of Public Health*, which allowed for legal same-sex marriage. Nevertheless, by 2005 the short-term decline in support as a result of the *Lawrence* and *Goodridge* decisions began to reverse itself, and 2007 polls suggest that public support for gay civil rights has returned to its previous levels (see figure 1.3).

Following the decisions in *Lawrence* and *Goodridge*, politicians in many states and the national government promised to promote legislation and constitutional amendments that would define civil marriage as solely between a man and a woman. Before 2004, there had been six statewide initiative votes on banning same-sex marriage: Alaska (1998), California (2000), Hawaii (1998), Nevada (2000, 2002), and Nebraska (2000). In each case the measures were introduced as part of a national response to the 1993 Hawaii same-sex marriage ruling. But the 2003 *Goodridge* decision generated a backlash that was focused on amending state constitutions to ban same-sex marriage. And the 2004 election season brought the issue of same-sex marriage to the forefront of the national political agenda. In early 2004 officials in California, Oregon, New Mexico, and New York began to issue marriage licenses to same-sex couples, which created a national uproar (Mucciaroni 2008).

Between August and November 2004 thirteen states voted on referendums that amended their constitutions to ban the recognition of same-sex marriage and, in some cases, civil unions between same-sex couples. Some of these measures, such as those in Michigan and Ohio, banned virtually any recognition of same-sex relationships. Missouri voted on its measure during an August primary and adopted the change in a vote of 71 to 29 percent. Louisiana considered its measure in September, whereas the remaining states all held their elections to coincide with the general election in November. In addition, Kansas adopted a constitutional amendment similar to those in Michigan and Ohio during an April 2005 primary election in a vote of 70 percent to 30 percent. Texas followed suit in 2005, and nine other states voted on constitutional bans in 2006. Nearly all the twenty-four bans considered between 2004 and 2006 passed by lopsided margins, but Arizona became the only state to vote to reject a ban (Lofton and Haider-Markel 2007). Arizona did adopt a constitutional ban in 2008, along with California and Florida, even as Connecticut, Iowa, Maine, New Hampshire, and Vermont were legalizing same-sex marriage in 2008 and 2009. The issue of the legal recognition of same-sex couples presently dominates the debate over LGBT equality.

Summary and Conclusions

My review of the history of the LGBT movement, the existing literature on the election of women and minorities, and the literature on women and minority legislators engaging in substantive representation in state legislatures allows us to draw four important implications for understanding LGBT representation. First, the LGBT community has moved from a broad form of social movement politics to a more institutionalized movement that seeks representation in the policy process. This shift increasingly encourages more LGBT people to run for public office at all levels of government. At the same time public opposition to gay civil rights and homosexuality has generally declined, providing a more amenable electoral environment for LGBT candidates. In this environment more LGBT candidates have achieved state-level offices.

Second, although women and ethnic and racial minorities faced discrimination from voters in the 1960s and 1970s, much of this opposition appears to have declined. In addition, because underrepresented groups are more likely to identify as Democrats than as Republicans, some existing opposition to these candidates is likely to be partisan rather than racially or gender based. However, voters still clearly hold stereotypes about candidates based on race and gender, and these stereotypes may limit electoral support. Candidates appear to be able to limit and even take advantage of these stereotypes in some circumstances.

In the 1980s and early 1990s LGBT candidates were facing the same pattern of opposition from the electorate as had other minorities, but as we will see in later chapters opposition has been eroding, following a trajectory similar to that of other minority groups. The trends in public attitudes concerning LGBT people support the notion of declining opposition. Nevertheless, the literature suggests that a candidate's strategy and the electoral context will likely enhance or limit opposition to LGBT candidates.

Third, although many studies suggest that the descriptive representation of previously underrepresented groups leads to increased substantive representation, a number of studies also indicate that substantive representation is limited, perhaps by critical mass elements, a backlash phenomenon, or other processes. At a minimum, we cannot assume that we can easily discern a causal connection between LGBT descriptive representation and substantive representation. In addition, we must consider the possibility that increased descriptive representation in state legislatures may result in a policy backlash against the LGBT community.

Fourth and finally, whether or not we find evidence of discrimination against LGBT candidates that inhibits their electoral viability or substantive representation, we must be cognizant that there are other methods for achieving policy representation and that descriptive representation may have positive outcomes for the LGBT community besides substantive representation, such as increased political participation or confidence in government.

Notes

1. However, Dolan's (2005) analysis of congressional candidate websites in 2000 and 2002 suggests that neither male nor female candidates focus on issues that enhance gender stereotypes.

2. Of course the 2008 election year demonstrated that women can seriously contend for a major party presidential and vice-presidential nomination and that an African American can be elected to the presidency. In fact, Senator John McCain's age may have been a bigger barrier to his presidential candidacy than was Barack Obama's race.

3. "Roll-off" refers to casting a ballot where the individual selects candidates near the top of the ballot but declines to select candidates that appear further down on the ballot. The practice is especially common when a presidential contest is on the ballot.

4. Cross-national research suggests that proportional MMD structure increases female representation to an even greater degree (Vengroff, Nyiri, and Fugiero 2003).

5. The analysis in Meier et al. (2001) also suggests that the increase in Latino teachers resulting from greater Latino representation on school boards is associated with improvements in Latino student educational performance.

6. In contrast, the analysis of perceptions of judicial fairness by Overby et al. (2005) suggests that the election of blacks to judicial offices does not increase black perceptions that the judicial system is fair.

7. No serious effort was made to overturn the compromise policy until 2010, when President Barack Obama asked the Joint Chiefs of Staff to study the issue and the White House began working with Democratic leaders in Congress to draft a bill that would allow gays and lesbians to serve openly in the military.

8. Among younger respondents answering the feeling thermometer questions, gays and lesbians have rated considerably better in all polls since 1996, which suggests that the positive affect will likely increase in the future.

See How They Run: Voter Preferences and Candidates' Experiences with the Role of Sexual Orientation in State Elections

What I think it signifies for the state is that this is a fairly tolerant state and that voters are making decisions on people's character, and not their sexual orientation.

—Washington gay senator Ed Murray in response to a question on the large number of LGBT legislators in the state

LIKE OTHER GROUPS, the LGBT community can try to achieve political representation by electing openly LGBT candidates to public office, ensuring that LGBT people are appointed to official positions, or by influencing the behavior of sympathetic heterosexual and closeted homosexual officials. However, as with any other career, LGBT persons seeking public office are often hesitant to be open or public about their sexual orientation. For LGBT public officials, being out means publicly stating one's sexual or gender orientation. But being out for officials may also mean discrimination, a lack of public support, or even the threat of physical violence. Even so, overall opposition to LGBT people, LGBT equality, and LGBT public officials appears to be declining by significant margins.

This chapter examines the role that a candidate's sexual orientation plays in an election by focusing largely on public support for LGBT candidates in state-level elections. My analysis proceeds in two parts. First, I provide an overview of public attitudes about LGBT candidates and explore the individual-level characteristics associated with opposition to LGBT candidates for state office. Second, I shift to the perspective of LGBT candidates for state legislative office. I analyze the survey and interview responses about LGBT candidates who ran for state legislative seats between 2003 and 2004. Finally, I summarize the results of my analysis and draw conclusions about the role of a candidate's sexual orientation.

An Overview of LGBT Candidates and Public Opinion

To assess the importance of a candidate's sexual orientation, we need to start with the basic facts. Although more than 730 LGBT officials held public offices in 2009, from local sheriff to the U.S. Congress, this is still a tiny fraction of all officeholders in the country. Yet, following the 2008 elections, only three states had no LGBT elected official at any level and only twenty states had no LGBT state legislators. LGBT elected officials have certainly increased, from less than 20 for all the years before 1991, to 78 in 2009 (of 7,382 seats), but there are clearly very few. Even if the low estimates of LGBT people in the population are correct (about 3 percent), the LGBT community would have to increase the number of LGBT officials in all offices by more than 500 percent simply to approach matching descriptive representation in offices with representation in the population.

However, this is not to say that the low numbers of LGBT officials simply reflect a lack of public support for LGBT candidates. Indeed, women, African Americans, and Hispanics are not represented in elected offices to the same degree that they are represented in the population anywhere in the country. As chapter 1 suggests, the lack of representation for LGBT people, women, and ethnic and racial minorities likely reflects the limited pool of candidates from these communities as much as it reflects any aversion in the population toward these groups.

With that said, it is quite clear that as a group, LGBT Americans are not viewed in a positive manner by many people. As chapter 1 makes clear, although affect toward gays and lesbians has "warmed" over time, the mean scores suggest that most Americans have an unfavorable or cool affect. Indeed, from 1984 to 1996 gays and lesbians scored lower than any other group except illegal immigrants, and in 2008 they scored lower than all but three groups (see figure 1.4 in chapter 1). And although supermajorities now support antidiscrimination and hate crimes laws for LGBT people, 15 to 30 percent of adults still oppose these laws, which simply suggests that a portion of the public is unlikely to find an LGBT candidate acceptable.

Nearly all previous research on the impact of a candidate's sexual orientation on voter evaluations, candidate success, or the candidate's electoral margins has been conducted through experiments in which voters (usually college students) evaluated fictional candidates (see Golebiowska 2001; Golebiowska and Thomsen 1999; Herrick and Thomas 1999). One exception is Golebiowska's (2002) study of LGBT candidates and elected officials. She conducted a survey of these individuals and asked them to assess the impact that sexual orientation had in their election contests. Her findings were consistent with experimental research (including Golebiowska 2001; Golebiowska and Thomsen 1999; and Herrick and Thomas 1999), which suggests that LGBT candidates receive lower evaluations than their heterosexual counterparts and that LGBT candidates are less likely to receive (fictional) votes. This pattern is especially true for gay male candidates who fit a gay male stereotype (Golebiowska 2001).

Herrick and Thomas (1999) used an experimental research design that involves creating hypothetical elections where respondents are asked more directly to state their voting preferences and their perceptions of candidates. Controlling for a variety of other factors, including gender and ideology, they find that a candidate's sexual orientation does have a slight influence on voting preference and on perceptions of a candidate's electoral viability (ability to win the election). Interestingly, lesbians are not viewed any more negatively than gay men, a finding that is consistent with the literature on women in politics that suggests voters only sometimes vote based on a candidate's gender (Fox 1997; Jewell and Morehouse 2001).

In addition, unpublished experimental research suggests that although lesbian and gay candidates might face stereotyping, not all stereotyping is negative and does not appear to decrease electoral support. Tadlock and Gordon (2003) conclude that their research on college students suggests that candidates who are labeled as openly lesbian or gay in hypothetical news accounts are stereotyped by observers. However, candidates labeled gay and lesbian are not less likely to be supported than their heterosexual counterparts in a hypothetical election and even appear to be preferred over heterosexual candidates with the same qualities.

In a very real sense, voting for a candidate is similar to hiring someone for a job. Therefore, we can first look to evidence of opposition to LGBT candidates by examining opposition to LGBT individuals in various professions. If we examine support for homosexuals across a variety of professions over time, we begin to see how a negative affect toward gays and lesbians might translate into support or opposition to LGBT political candidates. Table 2.1 displays the percentage of American adults who responded affirmatively to this question: "Do you think homosexuals should be hired for the each of the following occupations?" Since 1977 this question has been asked in a variety of Gallup and *Newsweek* polls. Besides a drop in support since 2003, across most professions listed, support has increased considerably since 1977. However, support for homosexual teachers and clergy is still fairly low. And about 10 percent of the population opposes homosexuals even being salespersons, which suggests that there is a percentage of the population that opposes homosexuals being employed in virtually any profession. The only political office listed is membership in the president's Cabinet. Since 1999 at least 70 percent of adults have indicated that homosexuals should be able to serve in this position, and the most recent polls indicate that roughly one-quarter of the population remains opposed to homosexuals serving as political appointees in national office. This finding indicates that though a strong majority of adults would not oppose LGBT candidates or appointed officials, a significant portion of the population is opposed to gays and lesbians serving in high-profile national offices.

However, we also have polling data on stated support for LGBT candidates for various offices in the abstract. Of course these data are imperfect—attitudes and state behavior may not coincide with actual behavior—but they do offer some guidance for observing changes over time and identifying likely opponents and supporters. National Gallup poll surveys on voting for a presidential candidate if the candidate is homosexual reveal a pattern of decreased opposition over time (figure 2.1). In 1978, 1983, 1999, and 2007 Gallup asked: "Between now and the [year] political conventions, there will be discussion about the qualifications of presidential candidates—their education, age, religion, race, and so on. If your party nominated a generally well-qualified person for president who happened to be a

Table 2.1 Support for Homosexuals in Different Professions, 1977–2005

Do you think homosexuals should be hired for each of the following occupations? (% responding "should")

	Doctors	President's Cabinet	Armed Forces	High School Teachers	Elementary Teachers	Salespersons	Clergy
Change since 2003	−4	−4	−4	−5	−7	−2	−7
May 2–5, 2005	78	75	76	62	54	90	49
May 19–21, 2003	82	79	80	67	61	92	56
April 25–26, 2002	—	—	—	—	—	—	40
May 10–14, 2001	78	75	72	63	56	91	54
February 8–9, 1999	75	74	70	61	54	90	54
July 28–30, 1998	70	—	66	60	55	88	51
November 21–24, 1996	69	71	65	60	55	90	53
June 4–8, 1992	53	54	57	47	41	82	43
October 12–13, 1989	—	—	60	47	42	79	44
June 17–20, 1977	44	—	51	—	27	68	36

Source: Compiled by the author based on national survey data of adults reported by Bowman and Foster (2006) and Saad (2005).

Figure 2.   Percentage Who Would Support Their Party's Nominee for President if the
Party Nominated a Well-Qualified Person Who Happened to Be a Homosexual, 1977,
1983, 1999, and 2007

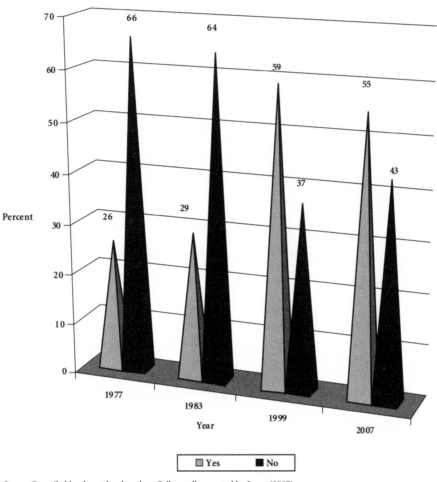

Source: Compiled by the author based on Gallup polls reported by Jones (2007).

homosexual, would you vote for that person?" In 1978, only 26 percent of respondents said yes; in 1983, 29 percent said yes; but by 1999, 59 percent said yes. The
increase in support between 1983 and 1999 was large and significant, and support
for a homosexual candidate has increased at a much faster rate than for women,
blacks, Catholics, and Jews. However, in the February 2007 survey the proportion
of adults indicating that they would support a homosexual for president declined
to 55 percent, whereas opposition increased from 37 percent in 1999 to 43 percent
in 2007 (Jones 2007).[1] Although the Gallup question is asked too infrequently to
capture clear trends, the decline in support for a homosexual candidate (and for a

homosexual cabinet member, as shown in table 2.1) may have been a result of a
negative reaction to court rulings on sodomy laws and same-sex marriage in 2003
(Stoutenborough, Haider-Markel, and Allen 2006).

There were significant ideological differences among those who would vote for a
homosexual for president and those who would not. An analysis of the 2007 Gallup
poll reveals that 81 percent of liberals would support a homosexual for president,
57 percent of moderates, and only 36 percent of conservatives. By comparison,
support for a Catholic, black, or Jewish candidate did not significantly differ across
ideological groups (Jones 2007).[2]

Likewise, the public does not perceive that Americans are ready to elect a gay or
lesbian candidate for president. Table 2.2 displays the results of a September 2006
Gallup national poll of adults, in which respondents were asked "Do you think
Americans are ready to elect a/an _____ as president, or not?" In the blank, a
variety of candidates were included—from a woman to an Asian to a gay man or
lesbian. Overall more respondents felt the country was ready to elect a woman (61
percent), but only 7 percent believed that Americans were ready to elect a gay man

Table 2.2   Perception of Public Support for a Female or Minority President (percent)

Generally speaking, do you think Americans are ready to elect a/an _____ as
president, or not?

	Yes, ready	No, not ready	No opinion
Woman	61	38	1
African American or Black	58	40	2
Jew	55	42	3
Hispanic	41	58	1
Asian	33	64	2
LDS/Mormon	29	66	5
Atheist	14	84	2
Gay or lesbian	7	91	2

Perceptions that Americans are ready to elect a president with following characteristic,
by party affiliation

	Democrat	Independent	Republican
Woman	64	65	54
Black	49	59	67
Jew	48	59	58
Hispanic	34	42	46
Asian	26	39	35
LDS/Mormon	21	29	37
Atheist	8	21	14
Gay	7	10	4

Source: Gallup national poll of adults, September 21–24, 2006.

or lesbian. Indeed, twice as many respondents believed that Americans would elect an atheist president over a gay or lesbian president. Furthermore, these perceptions differed little across partisan groups, with independents being the most likely to think the country was ready to elect a gay or lesbian president.[3]

Responses to survey questions on LGBT candidates for other offices also reveal a pattern of increased support for homosexual candidates over time. Table 2.3 displays the responses to a variety of poll questions conducted since 1991. Across each of these polls about 25 percent or more were opposed to supporting an openly homosexual candidate for elective office. In a 2000 Fox News / Opinion Dynamics poll the respondents were asked a question that refers to a candidate who had a homosexual relationship. A bare majority of registered voters indicated that they would still vote for such a candidate, but 14 and 26 percent, respectively, indicated that they would probably or definitely vote against such a candidate. By comparison, more respondents said that they would definitely vote against a candidate who had a homosexual relationship than would vote against a candidate who abused alcohol (11 percent), had an extramarital affair (13 percent), used marijuana (17 percent), or been treated for a mental illness (25 percent). However, fewer respondents would vote against a candidate who had a homosexual relationship than would vote against a candidate who lied on his résumé (34 percent), used cocaine (37 percent), or cheated on his taxes (38 percent) (Bowman and Foster 2006).

Likewise, in a March 2004 poll of national adults, the *Los Angles Times* found that 32 percent would not be willing to vote for an openly gay candidate running for an unspecified elective office. The gender of a homosexual candidate seems to matter little to Americans. A November 2003 national poll of adults conducted by Scripps suggests that 27 percent of respondents would oppose a gay congressional candidate, whereas 28 percent would oppose a lesbian congressional candidate.

In the same 2003 Scripps poll, respondents were asked a number of questions regarding the personal attributes of gay and lesbian candidates as well as how competent gay and lesbian candidates would be on specific issues. The distribution of responses to these questions is displayed in table 2.4. In terms of the honesty, morality, and strength of gay and lesbian candidates for Congress, the great majority of respondents indicate that there would be no difference compared with the typical congressional candidate. However, at least 9 percent suggested that gay and lesbian candidates would be at least somewhat less honest, 17 percent indicated that gay and lesbian candidates would be at least somewhat less moral, and 13 percent suggested that lesbian and gay candidates would be at least somewhat less strong than the typical candidate for Congress. In terms of negative attributes, such as being less strong, respondents ranked gay and lesbian candidates nearly the same, but they did attribute slightly more negative characteristics to gay male candidates.

The lower half of table 2.4 displays attitudes concerning the competency of gay and lesbian candidates on education, military, and tax issues. Across all three issues, at least 76 percent of respondents believed that gay and lesbian candidates would be at least as competent as the typical candidate for Congress. About 5 percent of respondents thought that gay and lesbian candidates would be more competent, whereas at least 8 percent thought that gay and lesbian candidates would be less

Table 2.3 Opposition to Gays and Lesbians in Political Office (percent)

Please tell me whether you would or would not do each of the following: Vote for a political candidate who is homosexual

	Yes	No
June 15–16, 1994, Yankelovich/CNN/*Time*	48	45
October 14–15, 1998, Yankelovich/CNN/*Time*	58	36

Let me mention several things you might learn about a candidate running for president. For each one, please tell me whether this should or should not disqualify them from becoming president of the United States. If someone is gay or lesbian, do you think this should or should not disqualify this person from becoming president of the United States?

	Should Disqualify	Should Not Disqualify
October 25–29, 1991, NBC/*WSJ*	47	47
February 28–March 2, 1992, NBC/*WSJ*	42	53

I'd like to ask whether certain information about a candidate for political office would cause you to vote against him, regardless of other factors. What if you found out that the candidate was a homosexual. . . . Would that alone cause you to vote against him?

	Yes	No
September 19–20, 1996, PSRA/*Newsweek*	37	58

Do you think homosexuals should or should not be hired for each of the following occupations? (major political officeholders)

	Should	Should Not
July 30–31, 1998, PSRA/*Newsweek*	68	27
Mar. 9–10, 2000 PSRA/*Newsweek*	71	24

Let's go through this list again, this time please tell me if you were considering a candidate whom you would otherwise support, and you discovered that they had had a homosexual relationship, would you still vote for them, probably vote against them, or definitely vote against them (asked of registered voters)?

	Still Vote For	Probably Vote Against	Definitely Vote Against
May 10–11, 2000, Fox News / Opinion Dynamics	53	14	26

Would you be willing or not willing to vote for a well-qualified candidate running for an elected office if that person was openly gay?

	Willing	Not Willing	Don't Know
March 27–30, 2004, *Los Angeles Times*	59	32	9

Table 2.3.   *(Continued)*.

If a candidate for Congress said publicly that she is lesbian, would that make you more likely to vote for her, more likely to vote against her, or have no effect on your vote? (Scripps Survey Research Center, Ohio University, October 20–November 4, 2003)

More likely to vote for	3
No difference	66
More likely to vote against	28
Don't know	3

If a candidate for Congress said publicly that he is gay, would that make you more likely to vote for him, more likely to vote against him, or have no effect on your vote? (Scripps Survey Research Center, Ohio University, October 20–November 4, 2003)

More likely to vote for	2
No difference	67
More likely to vote against	27
Don't know	4

Source: Compiled by the author based on Bowman and Foster (2006) and Hargrove and Stempel (2003).

competent than the typical congressional candidate. Between gay and lesbian candidates there are some small differences. Gay male candidates were seen as less competent on education and military issues than were lesbians.

Predicting Attitudes about Gay and Lesbian Congressional Candidates

To better explain who opposes gay and lesbian congressional candidates and who attributes negative characteristics to gay and lesbian candidates, we need to undertake a multivariate analysis of individual-level responses. The Scripps Survey Research Center data from 2003 (discussed above) allow for such an analysis.

Research on attitudes toward gays and lesbians as well as support for gay and lesbian civil rights can readily inform models of attitudes toward homosexual candidates. An analysis of attitudes toward gays and lesbians, gay civil rights, and same-sex marriage reveals that women and people who are educated; Democrat; liberal; young; and nonreligious, infrequent churchgoers tend to be more supportive (Brewer 2003a, 2003b; Egan and Sherrill 2005; Haider-Markel and Joslyn 2005, 2008; Herek 2002). As such, in my multivariate model predicting opposition to gay and candidates and attitudes about candidates' attributes, I included variables to account for living in the South, gender, being born-again, Protestant, church attendance, education, race, ideology, partisanship, age, and city size for place of residence.

The first dependent variables employ the last two questions from table 2.2. Respondents were asked: "If a candidate for Congress said publicly that he is gay, would that make you more likely to vote for him, more likely to vote against him, or would it have no effect on your vote?" The same question was asked with regard to a lesbian candidate for Congress. Because respondents were allowed three scaled

Table 2.4 Attitudes Concerning Gay and Lesbian Political Candidates (percent)

Think about how honest the typical candidate for Congress is. By comparison, how honest would a _____ candidate likely be?

Gay Male		*Lesbian Woman*	
Much more honest	4	Much more honest	3
Somewhat more honest	7	Somewhat more honest	5
No difference	81	No difference	82
Somewhat less honest	5	Somewhat less honest	5
Much less honest	4	Much less honest	5

What about moral? How moral would a _____ candidate be compared to the typical candidate for Congress?

Gay Male		*Lesbian Woman*	
Much more moral	2	Much more moral	3
Somewhat more moral	6	Somewhat more moral	4
No difference	73	No difference	76
Somewhat less moral	9	Somewhat less moral	9
Much less moral	10	Much less moral	8

What about strong? How strong would a _____ candidate be compared to the typical candidate for Congress?

Gay Male		*Lesbian Woman*	
Much more strong	3	Much more strong	3
Somewhat more strong	5	Somewhat more strong	4
No difference	73	No difference	80
Somewhat less strong	11	Somewhat less strong	7
Much less strong	8	Much less strong	6

Think about how competent the typical candidate for Congress is on the following issues. By comparison, how competent would a _____ candidate likely be on education?

Gay Male		*Lesbian Woman*	
Much more competent	4	Much more competent	4
Somewhat more competent	4	Somewhat more competent	2
No difference	83	No difference	86
Somewhat less competent	5	Somewhat less competent	3
Much less competent	4	Much less competent	5

What about military issues? How competent would a _____ candidate be compared to the typical candidate for Congress?

Gay Male		*Lesbian Woman*	
Much more competent	3	Much more competent	2
Somewhat more competent	2	Somewhat more competent	3
No difference	76	No difference	80
Somewhat less competent	10	Somewhat less competent	8
Much less competent	9	Much less competent	7

Table 2.4.   (Continued).

What about on taxes? How competent would a _____ candidate be compared to the typical candidate for Congress?

Gay Male		Lesbian Woman	
Much more competent	1	Much more competent	2
Somewhat more competent	3	Somewhat more competent	2
No difference	88	No difference	88
Somewhat less competent	4	Somewhat less competent	4
Much less competent	4	Much less competent	4

Source: Compiled by the author based on a Scripps Survey Research Center, Ohio University, October 20–November 4 national survey of approximately 950 adults as reported in Hargrove and Stempel (2003).

responses—from more likely to vote for, to no difference, to more likely to vote against—predicting responses requires the use of ordered logit.

The results are displayed in table 2.5. The fit statistics suggest that the models reasonably predict the likelihood of voting against a gay or lesbian congressional candidate. Voting against a gay male congressional candidate is significantly shaped by gender, religion, religiosity, education, ideology, partisanship, and age. Consistent with more general research on gay issues, respondents who are male, born-again, attend church frequently, less educated, conservative, Republican, and older are more likely to vote against a gay congressional candidate. With the exception of education, respondents with these same characteristics are more likely to oppose a lesbian candidate for Congress. Educational differences among respondents are not statistically significant predictors of voting against a lesbian candidate. However, the coefficient is in the expected negative direction, and the standard error is smaller than the coefficient. Thus for the most part there is little substantive difference between predicting voting against a gay congressional candidate versus a lesbian congressional candidate.

Table 2.5 also contains columns headed "mfx" for marginal effects. Each of these coefficients are marginal effects coefficients, which are estimated following the estimation of the original model with the value of the dependent variable set to (3) "More likely to vote against." Marginal effects coefficients allow for the direct comparison of the relative influence of each variable on the probability of voting against the candidate. Thus, because the coefficient for church attendance is twice as large as the coefficient for gender, this indicates that the relative influence of church attendance in this model is greater than that of gender (actually twice as large). In the first model we can also conclude that although ideology and partisanship are important predictors, the religion (born-again) and church attendance variables are considerably more important predictors of vote choice. We can also compare the relative role of variables across the model for a gay candidate versus a lesbian candidate. By comparing the relative size of the coefficients across the models, we can see that there is little difference in the importance of variables across the models. Thus, these models clearly indicate that religion, gender, ideology, and partisanship strongly shape the likelihood of supporting a gay or lesbian congressional candidate.

Turning to respondent attitudes regarding the attributes of gay and lesbian candidates, we can also develop a multivariate model to predict opinion. However,

Table 2.5   Predicting Opposition to Gay and Lesbian Candidates, 2003 National Polls

Independent Variable	Vote against Gay Candidate		Vote against Lesbian Candidate	
	Coefficient	Mfx	Coefficient	Mfx
South	.205		.261	
	(.186)		(.184)	
Female	−.432*	−.081	−.417*	−.079
	(.180)		(.177)	
Born-again	.637**	.123	.756**	.149
	(.199)		(.196)	
Protestant	.222		.241	
	(.189)		(.186)	
Church attendance	.880**	.165	.834**	.159
	(.193)		(.189)	
Education	−.164*	−.031	−.123	
	(.078)		(.077)	
White	−.214		−.255	
	(.254)		(.250)	
Ideology > liberal	−.396**	−.074	−.404**	−.077
	(.087)		(.085)	
Party > Democrat	−.275**	−.051	−.279**	−.053
	(.071)		(.070)	
Age	.023**	.004	.021**	.004
	(.006)		(.006)	
Place size > urban	−.085		−.068	
	(.082)		(.081)	
/cut 1	−6.120		−5.835	
/cut 2	−.709		−.578	
Log likelihood	−440.662		−456.293	
Pseudo R^2	.18		.18	
Chi square	188.02**		203.06**	
N	743		757	

Source: Scripps Survey Research Center, Ohio University, Oct. 20 to Nov. 4, 2003, national poll of adults.

Note: Coefficients are ordered logit coefficients; standard errors are in parentheses. ** $p < .01$, * $p < .05$, # $p < .10$. Marginal effects (Mfx) estimated following ordered logit model estimation with the value of the dependent variable set to "More likely to vote against" (3); marginal effects for dichotomous variables capture the discrete change from 0 to 1.

recall that the questions displayed in table 2.3 had five possible responses. Given the small percentage of responses in each category that is positive, these responses were combined with the "no difference" response and coded as 0. The responses for the negative attributes were combined and coded as 1. For example, regarding whether or not gay candidates are less honest, responses for "much more honest," "somewhat more honest," and "no difference" were all coded 0. Affirmative responses for "somewhat less honest" and "much less honest" were coded 1. Given the binary nature of each dependent variable, models were estimated using logistic regression. In each model all the variables from table 2.5 were included.

The results are reported in tables 2.6 and 2.7. Overall the models predicting attitudes toward lesbian candidates have more robust fit statistics than do the models predicting attitudes toward gay candidates. In addition, all the variables perform inconsistently, and we see much the same pattern as we saw in table 2.4; gender, religion, religiosity, education, partisanship, ideology, and age are relatively consistent predictors of opinion. However, there are some interesting variations. For example, gender and urbanism are more often significant predictors of opinions about a lesbian candidate than a gay male candidate. Additionally, the coefficient sizes indicate that religion and partisanship are somewhat more important in the models predicting attitudes toward lesbian candidates.

Opinions on State and Local Candidates

Although national polls that focus specifically on gay and lesbian candidates for state or local office find similar levels of opposition as those found in polls regarding generic offices or congressional offices, there does seem to be more acceptance of homosexual candidates for subnational offices. For example, a 1999 poll asked respondents if they would support gay candidates for local or state offices. More than 77 percent said they would (Cassels 1999). Likewise, support for LGBT candidates varies by state. A 1989 New Jersey poll by The Record found that only 23 percent of respondents in that state said that whether or not a person is gay should be considered when the person is a gay man running for political office, and 65 percent said it should not be considered.[4] A more direct 1994 poll of California adults conducted by Political Media Research found that 2 percent of respondents would be more likely to vote for a lesbian or gay candidate, 41 percent would be less likely, and 55 percent said it would have no effect on their vote (Smith and Haider-Markel 2002).

Although dated, a 1994 Harris poll conducted in New York provides an interesting perspective. Table 2.8 displays the questions and frequency of responses for this poll. Respondents were asked to assess how a candidate's characteristics and issue positions influence they way people in their communities vote. About 61 percent suggested that a gay or lesbian candidate would influence the way people in the community vote with no indication if this characteristic would make people vote for or against such a candidate. By comparison, 76 percent of respondents thought a candidate's race would influence voting in their community at least quite a lot, whereas about 63 percent felt that way about abortion. As such, respondents perceived that a candidate's sexual orientation was on par with their abortion positions but was somewhat less important for their community than was race. Interestingly, however, for these three questions the largest percentage of respondents indicating that it would make no difference at all (18 percent) was for a gay or lesbian candidate.

Table 2.6 Predicting Beliefs about the Attributes of Gay and Lesbian Candidates (Honesty, Morality, and Strength)

Independent Variable	Gay Candidate Less Honest	Lesbian Candidate Less Honest	Gay Candidate Less Moral	Lesbian Candidate Less Moral	Gay Candidate Less Strong	Lesbian Candidate Less Strong
South	.268 (.294)	.612* (.285)	.087 (.208)	.143 (.219)	.379# (.209)	.321 (.236)
Female	-.147 (.291)	-.534# (.286)	-.306 (.203)	-.551* (.214)	-.309 (.207)	-.383# (.232)
Born-again	1.199** (.349)	1.157** (.338)	.977** (.229)	.900** (.239)	.548* (.235)	.569* (.262)
Protestant	-.161 (.313)	-.037 (.305)	-.136 (.217)	-.108 (.229)	-.146 (.222)	-.122 (.249)
Church attendance	-.252 (.319)	.327 (.320)	.416# (.221)	.670** (.235)	.240 (.225)	.620* (.257)
Education	-.310* (.124)	-.451** (.126)	-.265** (.089)	-.382** (.095)	-.223* (.090)	-.325** (.100)
White	-.095 (.432)	-.860* (.396)	-.205 (.291)	-.558# (.296)	-.139 (.301)	-.168 (.342)
Ideology > liberal	-.256# (.139)	-.099 (.135)	-.276** (.098)	-.150 (.102)	-.172# (.099)	-.123 (.111)
Party > Democrat	-.100 (.111)	-.436** (.115)	-.170* (.080)	-.292** (.085)	-.168* (.082)	-.219* (.092)
Age	.035** (.009)	.033** (.009)	.017** (.006)	.016* (.007)	.021** (.006)	.024** (.007)
Place size > urban	-.118 (.133)	-.232# (.132)	-.224* (.093)	-.126 (.098)	-.090 (.094)	-.150 (.107)
Constant	-1.905# (1.043)	.380 (1.001)	.657 (.711)	1.363# (.743)	-.310 (.756)	-.269 (.815)
Log likelihood	-179.839	-179.401	-322.342	-293.279	-316.616	-259.288
Pseudo R^2	.14	.21	.14	.16	.09	.12
Chi square	59.55**	95.59**	105.97**	108.11**	59.60**	70.08**
N	728	741	744	734	737	736

Source: Scripps Survey Research Center, Ohio University, October 20–November 4, 2003, national survey of adults.

Note: Coefficients are logit coefficients; standard errors are in parentheses. ** $p < .01$, * $p < .05$, # $p < .10$.

Table 2.7 Predicting Beliefs about Gay and Lesbian Candidates' Lack of Competency on Issues

Independent Variable	Gay Candidate Less Competent on Education	Lesbian Candidate Less Competent on Education	Gay Candidate Less Competent on Military	Lesbian Candidate Less Competent on Military	Gay Candidate Less Competent on Taxes	Lesbian Candidate Less Competent on Taxes
South	.584*	.903**	.261	.263	.771*	.779*
	(.273)	(.304)	(.206)	(.222)	(.291)	(.290)
Female	−.384	−.760*	−.555*	−.788**	−.645*	−.505#
	(.276)	(.310)	(.203)	(.219)	(.296)	(.293)
Born-again	.638*	1.277**	.537*	.847**	.349	.982**
	(.313)	(.367)	(.227)	(.247)	(.330)	(.340)
Protestant	.271	.181	.112	−.201	.610#	.173
	(.293)	(.324)	(.214)	(.233)	(.315)	(.310)
Church attendance	−.076	.133	.396#	.298	.118	.368
	(.301)	(.344)	(.222)	(.240)	(.325)	(.328)
Education	−.386**	−.493**	−.206*	−.300**	−.514**	−.412**
	(.119)	(.138)	(.089)	(.096)	(.130)	(.128)
White	−.379	−.116	−.006	−.214	−.233	−.506
	(.401)	(.480)	(.298)	(.316)	(.440)	(.427)
Ideology > liberal	−.342*	−.277#	−.295**	−.175#	−.515**	−.242#
	(.134)	(.148)	(.099)	(.106)	(.149)	(.139)
Party > Democrat	−.225*	−.321**	−.116	−.229*	−.204#	−.279*
	(.108)	(.121)	(.079)	(.087)	(.113)	(.114)
Age	.030**	.034**	.012*	.017*	.028**	.033**
	(.009)	(.010)	(.006)	(.007)	(.009)	(.009)
Place size > urban	−.193	−.409**	−.090	−.261*	−.178	−.297*
	(.126)	(.142)	(.093)	(.099)	(.134)	(.135)
Constant	.052	.391	.400	1.407#	−.858	−.164
	(.964)	(1.120)	(.709)	(.762)	(1.034)	(1.035)
Log likelihood	−196.332	−156.897	−324.915	−285.769	−172.494	−173.000
Pseudo R²	.15	.25	.10	.13	.20	.20
Chi square	70.44**	107.00**	70.09**	86.30**	84.64**	88.70**
N	739	737	738	736	733	735

Source: Scripps Survey Research Center, Ohio University, October 20–November 4, 2003, national survey of adults.

Note: Coefficients are logit coefficients; standard errors are in parentheses. ** $p < .01$, * $p < .05$, # $p < .10$.

Table 2.8   New York State Poll on Gay Candidates, 1994 (percent)

How much difference do you think each of the following makes to the way people in your community vote?

	A Great Deal	Quite a Lot	Not Much	No Difference at All
The candidate is gay or lesbian	35	26	21	18
The candidate's race	45	31	15	9
The candidate's stand on abortion	28	35	25	12

Do you personally agree or disagree that if a candidate says they are gay or lesbian then you should not vote for that candidate?

Agree	12
Disagree	88

Specific questions regarding Karen Burstein, a lesbian candidate for New York attorney general.

Have you seen, read, or heard anything about voters not voting for a candidate who says they are gay or lesbian, or not? (962 respondents)

Have	38
Have not	62

Which candidates have said they are gay or lesbian? (365 respondents)

Karen Burstein	47
Don't know	53

Does the fact that Karen Burstein says she is a lesbian mean that you are more likely to vote for her for attorney general, less likely, or does it not make a difference to you on how you will vote? (174 respondents)

More likely	4
Less likely	18
No difference	78

Source: Data compiled by the author from an October 14, 1994, Louis Harris and Associates random sample survey of New York adults.

Respondents were also asked this question: "Do you personally agree or disagree that if a candidate says they are gay or lesbian then you should not vote for that candidate?" Compared with perceptions of how the community might vote, here a far smaller percentage of respondents appears to have been willing to indicate that they would vote against a candidate for being gay or lesbian (12 percent). Given the national polls discussed above, where an average of one-quarter of respondents would oppose a gay or lesbian candidate, New Yorkers are significantly less likely to reject candidates based on sexual orientation.

The poll, conducted on October 14, 1994, was fielded in the middle of an election season where the Democratic candidate for attorney general, Karen Burstein, publicly stated that she was a lesbian. Her sexual orientation became an issue in the race, and although she won her party's nomination, she lost the general election. Three specific questions were asked regarding knowledge of a gay candidate, identification of that candidate, and whether the fact that the candidate was a lesbian would influence the likelihood of voting against her (see table 2.8). Interestingly, less than 40 percent of respondents had heard anything about a gay candidate, and of those who had heard, fewer than half could identify Burstein as the lesbian candidate. Of this small (174) group of respondents, 18 percent indicated that Burstein's sexual orientation would make them less likely to vote for her.

A multivariate analysis of responses to the candidate questions in the New York poll reveals that respondents' preferences are somewhat less predictable than in national polls. Table 2.9 displays the results of models that predict perceptions of community attitudes, the likelihood of voting against a gay candidate, and voting against the lesbian attorney general candidate; each model controls for the respondent's gender, age, education, race, religion, partisanship, ideology, and rural-versus-urban context. Educated male respondents were somewhat more likely to indicate that it would matter to their community if a gay or lesbian candidate was running for office. However, religion, partisanship, and ideology apparently play little role in shaping this perception.

Individual preferences on voting for gay and lesbian candidates in New York are more predictable. Liberals, Democrats, whites, the educated, youth, and women were more likely to indicate that they would vote for a gay or lesbian candidate. Meanwhile, the results from the model predicting opposition to the lesbian candidate Burstein are similar; women, youth, the educated, and Democrats were more likely to indicate that they would vote for Burstein. Religion and ideology did not play a statistically significant role. However, this analysis was conducted only for those respondents who were aware that Burstein was a lesbian—a very small subset of the survey sample.

An additional analysis (not shown) of these data reveals that gender, race, and ideology had the strongest relative role in predicting opinions for each model. In addition, if we reestimate the model predicting voting against any gay or lesbian candidate and control for the respondent's belief about how his or her community would vote for such a candidate, the results indicate that a belief that the community would oppose such a candidate strongly increases the likelihood of the individual voting against a gay or lesbian candidate. Indeed, the relative influence of this factor is greater than gender, race, or ideology in predicting voting preference.

One final poll is especially relevant to our discussion of LGBT candidates for state office. In March 2006 Zogby America conducted a national random sample telephone survey of likely voters. For this poll the Victory Fund commissioned a series of questions related to gay and lesbian candidates for state legislative seats. The full wording of the questions and descriptive statistics are displayed in table 2.10. On the first question regarding an openly gay or lesbian candidate running

Table 2.9   Predicting Attitudes on Gay and Lesbian Candidates, New York, 1994, Harris Poll

Independent Variable	Matters to Community if Candidate Is Gay	Should Not Vote for Gay Candidate	Vote against Lesbian Attorney General Candidate
Female	−.334*	−.834**	−1.830**
	(.124)	(.232)	(.624)
Age	−.008*	.015*	.037*
	(.004)	(.007)	(.019)
Education	.092#	−.177#	−.768**
	(.057)	(.101)	(.265)
White	.189	−.680*	1.587
	(.197)	(.339)	(1.229)
Protestant	.180	−.021	.161
	(.147)	(.248)	(.715)
No religion	−.198	−.620	−.231
	(.245)	(.625)	(.999)
Party > Democrat	.004	−.340*	−.803*
	(.077)	(.138)	(.383)
Ideology > liberal	−.106	−.494**	−.732
	(.094)	(.172)	(.493)
Place size > rural	.204	.152	.282
	(.083)	(.150)	(.417)
Constant		.763	2.506
		(.779)	(1.985)
/cut 1	−.785		
/cut 2	.305		
/cut 3	1.385		
Log likelihood	−1163.098	−287.127	−50.350
Pseudo R^2	.01	.09	.34
Chi square	29.69**	57.29**	51.15**
N	870	881	161

Source: The data are from an October 14, 1994, Louis Harris and Associates random sample survey of New York adults.

Note: The coefficients in the first column are ordered logit coefficients; the coefficients in the second and third columns are logit coefficients; standard errors are in parentheses. ** $p < .01$, * $p < .05$, # $p < .10$.

for the state legislature, respondents were asked if they would vote for this candidate if the candidate was the one who most shared their views. Consistent with virtually all the polls we have discussed, just more than 26 percent of respondents indicated that they would probably or definitely vote for someone else. When the same respondents were asked a similar question, but this time regarding an incumbent state legislator who is later found out to be gay or lesbian, slightly fewer (22 percent)

Table 2.10   Attitudes on Gay and Lesbian Candidates, March 2006, Zogby Poll (percent)

1. If an openly gay or lesbian candidate were to run for state legislature in your district and they were the candidate that most shared your views on political issues would you . . . ?

Definitely vote for the gay or lesbian candidate	45.2
Probably vote for the gay or lesbian candidate	25.6
Probably vote for someone else	11.5
Definitely vote for someone else	14.9
Not sure	2.9

2. Let's say there's a candidate who ran successfully for state legislature in the last election and you supported them because he or she shares your views on most political issues. What if you later found out this candidate is gay or lesbian? Would you . . . ?

Definitely still vote for this person	51.2
Probably still vote for this person	23.2
Probably vote for someone else	10.7
Definitely vote for someone else	11.2
Or are you not sure?	3.7

3. Let me read you the opinions of two people. One person says that a gay candidate does not share our values and would focus too much on gay issues. Another says sexual orientation is not important to the job as long as the candidate has a strong record of getting things done for everyone in the community. Do you . . . ?

Strongly agree that gay candidate does not share our values	13.2
Somewhat agree that gay candidate does not share our values	8.6
Somewhat agree that sexual orientation is not important	24.7
Strongly agree that sexual orientation is not important	47.4
Neither/not sure	6.0

4. Let me read you the opinions of two people. One person says that a lesbian candidate does not share our values and would focus too much on gay issues. Another says sexual orientation is not important to the job as long as the candidate has a strong record getting things done for everyone in the community. Do you . . . ?

Strongly agree that lesbian candidate does not share our values	16.1
Somewhat agree that lesbian candidate does not share our values	8.2
Somewhat agree that sexual orientation is not important	21.0
Strongly agree that sexual orientation is not important	46.5
Neither/not sure	8.2

5. I am going to read you the description of two candidates for office. Please tell me which candidate you would be more likely to vote for—A or B?

A is gay and has openly and frankly discussed his sexual orientation in the media on multiple occasions. B is gay but retained his sexual orientation as a private matter until he was outed by the media.

Candidate A	32.9
Candidate B	38.8
Neither/no difference	19.0
Not sure	9.3

Source: Compiled by the author from a national poll of likely voters conducted by Zogby America, March 14–16, 2006, for the Victory Fund.

said that they would probably or definitely vote against this candidate. Thus, for LGBT state legislative candidates, the data suggest that the levels of opposition from voters will be similar to that faced by LGBT congressional candidates or hypothetical LGBT candidates for generic offices. At its base, about one-quarter of the general public, and also likely voters, appear ready to oppose LGBT candidates for virtually any office, but the public may be slightly more supportive of LGBT candidates who come out as incumbents.

In addition, the Zogby poll also separated the sample in half. One half of the sample was asked about a gay candidate (question 3), and the other half was asked about a lesbian candidate (question 4). More than 72 percent of respondents at least somewhat agreed that the sexual orientation of a candidate is not important. However, for a lesbian candidate somewhat fewer (less than 68 percent) felt the same way.

For the final question on candidates, likely voters were presented with two hypothetical candidates. Candidate A was gay and had consistently been public about his sexual orientation; candidate B was also gay but had never been public about his sexual orientation until he was outed by the media. Respondents were asked which candidate they preferred. Respondents who indicated both or neither were unfortunately grouped in a third category. Respondents had an almost 6-percentage-point preference for the candidate who was outed versus the candidate who was open about his sexual orientation, but 19 percent said it made no difference or preferred neither candidate. Another 9 percent were unsure. The results suggest that voters have a slight preference for gay candidates who are more private about their sexual orientation, but overall they are accepting of both openly gay candidates and those who are outed.

To disentangle attitudes about the candidates referred to in the Zogby poll, I estimated multivariate models to predict responses to each question. Based on the demographic questions asked in the poll, the models control for gender, age, size of place, race, education, ideology, partisanship, living in the South and East, being a born-again Christian, and having children under the age of eighteen. The results of this analysis are displayed in table 2.11. Overall the models predict voting preferences and attitudes fairly well. Likely voters were more likely to say that they would vote against an openly gay or lesbian state legislative candidate if they were male, older, lived in a rural area, less educated, conservative, Republican, not from the East, born-again, and had children under eighteen. For an incumbent state legislative candidate the results were slightly different; here gender was a slightly more important predictor but age and size of place were less important. In this model whites were somewhat more likely to support the candidate, those from the South were less likely to support the candidate, and having children made no significant difference.

The models that predict belief that the sexual orientation of a gay candidate is not important in half the sample versus a lesbian candidate in the other half of the sample are similar, but they differ in some interesting ways. In the model for the

Table 2.11 Predicting Attitudes about Gay and Lesbian State Legislative Candidates, March 2006, Zogby Poll

Independent Variable	Vote against Out Candidate	Vote against Outed Incumbent	Fact That Candidate Is Gay Not Important	Fact That Candidate Is Lesbian Not Important	Multinominal Logit Prefer Outed Candidate	Prefer Neither/ No Difference
Female	−.351*	−.567**	.623**	.513*	.102	−.016
	(.136)	(.140)	(.197)	(.205)	(.177)	(.210)
Age	.009#	.002	−.011	−.002	.010#	.005
	(.005)	(.005)	(.007)	(.007)	(.006)	(.007)
Place size > rural	.216*	.103	−.011	.032	−.111	.016
	(.092)	(.096)	(.138)	(.136)	(.120)	(.144)
White	−.318	−.428*	−.350	.173	.213	.557#
	(.211)	(.217)	(.323)	(.302)	(.255)	(.324)
Education	−.368**	−.416**	.149	.343**	.072	.153
	(.078)	(.080)	(.121)	(.116)	(.102)	(.123)
Ideology > conservative	.645**	.616**	−.591**	−.507**	.322**	.066
	(.079)	(.082)	(.113)	(.113)	(.095)	(.113)
Party > Republican	.159#	.170#	−.189	−.268*	.343**	.190
	(.085)	(.089)	(.125)	(.127)	(.111)	(.133)

Table 2.11 (Continued). Predicting Attitudes about Gay and Lesbian State Legislative Candidates, March 2006, Zogby Poll

Independent Variable	Vote against Out Candidate	Vote against Outed Incumbent	Fact That Candidate Is Gay Not Important	Fact That Candidate Is Lesbian Not Important	Multinominal Logit Prefer Outed Candidate	Prefer Neither/ No Difference
South	.137	.309#	-.027	.110	.118	.517*
	(.156)	(.160)	(.223)	(.237)	(.213)	(.245)
East	-.471*	-.320#	.760*	.507*	-.084	.168
	(.172)	(.181)	(.283)	(.241)	(.213)	(.258)
Born-again	.801**	.705**	-.531*	-.607*	.023	-.092
	(.154)	(.158)	(.230)	(.232)	(.214)	(.253)
Children < 18	.372*	.068	-.417	.062	-.077	-.279
	(.176)	(.183)	(.262)	(.257)	(.222)	(.269)
Vote against gay	—	—	—	—	.188*	.579**
					(.095)	(.109)
/Cut point 1	1.631	.925	-4.453	-2.494	-2.496**	-3.441**
/Cut point 2	3.161	2.387	-3.664	-1.843	(.672)	(.811)
/Cut point 3	4.040	3.202	-2.393	-.581		
Log likelihood	-979.177	-915.848	-477.096	-453.061	-259.288	
Pseudo R^2	.12	.12	.10	.09	.06	
Chi square	277.20**	245.15**	107.72**	90.07**	103.33**	
N	886	883	431	409	806	

Source: The data are from a Zogby America Omnibus national random sample telephone survey of adults conducted March 14–16, 2006.

Note: Except final two columns, coefficients are ordered logit coefficients; standard errors are in parentheses. ** $p < .01$, * $p < .05$, # $p < .10$.

gay candidate women, liberals, those living in the East, and those who are not born-again were more likely to say that the candidate's sexual orientation does not matter. For the lesbian candidate, these same characteristics predicted attitudes, but education and partisanship were also important, with the educated Democrats being more likely to say that the candidate's sexual orientation is not important. It is not clear why partisanship and education matter more when the hypothetical candidate is a lesbian, especially because the aggregate attitude toward a gay versus lesbian candidate differed little. The results may simply indicate that female candidates, regardless of their sexual orientation, face a slightly more hostile electorate than do male candidates. And attitudes toward female candidates generally are more strongly shaped by partisanship and education (Fox 1997).

Finally, recall that the last question on gay and lesbian candidates presented the respondent with two hypothetical candidates: Candidate A was gay and had consistently been public about his sexual orientation; candidate B was also gay but had never been public about his sexual orientation until he was outed by the media. Respondents who indicated both or neither were unfortunately grouped in a third category. Because a choice of one candidate or the neither category precludes choosing another candidate or category, I modeled preferences on this question using multinomial logit. Here a single equation was estimated with the choice of candidate A, the openly gay candidate, as the baseline or reference category. Thus the model predicts the likelihood of choosing candidate B or neither/no difference instead of (or relative to) candidate A. Because it was not clear which candidate would be most attractive to voters who are less supportive of gay candidates overall, I included responses to the question about voting against an openly gay state legislative candidate as an independent variable. Voters who were older, more conservative, and Republican, and those who indicated that they would vote against a gay state legislative candidate, were more likely to prefer the candidate who was outed versus the candidate who was openly gay. Likely voters who indicated neither candidate or said no difference were somewhat more likely to be from the South and white than those who supported candidate A. These voters were also more likely to have said they would vote against a gay state legislative candidate.

Overall this final set of results indicates that a strong preference for a candidate who is private about his or her sexual orientation is greatest among voters who are older, conservative, and Republican, and those who would prefer not to vote for a gay candidate at all. This also means that an openly gay or lesbian candidate, versus one who is private about their sexual orientation, is preferred by liberals, Democrats, and youth. Given that the characteristics of voters who prefer the more closeted candidate are the same as those voters who are unlikely to vote for gay and lesbian candidates in the first place, there does not appear to be an electoral advantage for a candidate who attempts to keep his or her sexual orientation private, especially if it is likely that the candidate will be outed at some point.

The Views of LGBT Candidates and Elected Officials

Now that we have a preliminary understanding of the preferences of the electorate faced by LGBT state legislative candidates, we can turn to exploring how LGBT candidates view this electorate and the role of sexual orientation in their campaigns. The analysis of individual voting preferences given above clearly demonstrates that segments of the population are unlikely to vote for gay and lesbian candidates. However, some segments of the electorate may actually be more supportive of openly gay and lesbian candidates than candidates who are less open about their sexual orientation. In other words, being openly gay or lesbian may sometimes provide an electoral advantage.

During the 1994 race for New York attorney general, Republican Dennis Vacco repeatedly insisted that his openly lesbian opponent, Karen Burstein, represented special and narrow interests. Vacco argued: "I have no problems with that sort of agenda, but I think the people of the state should know that that's her agenda" (Polman 1998). Vacco won the race but he lost four years later after being accused of pursuing a very narrow conservative political agenda. In Connecticut an openly bisexual state representative, Evelyn Mantilla, won a landslide victory in 1998 even though her challenger, the Reverend Gabriel José Carrera, tried to appeal to Latino voters by arguing that Mantilla's bisexuality and support of lesbian and gay issues ran contrary to their values (Boyce 1998). In his 1998 reelection attempt to the Oregon State House, Representative Chuck Carpenter faced a concerted effort by conservative religious groups to defeat him. Conservatives within the state Republican Party recruited an ultraconservative candidate, Bill Witt, to challenge Carpenter in the Republican primary. Witt was a founding member of the Oregon Christian Coalition and a major donor to the Oregon Citizens' Alliance, a group that has repeatedly tried to pass antigay ballot initiatives (Gay and Lesbian Victory Fund 1998).

But many other candidates see little of this antigay rhetoric during campaigns. Take an example from Rhode Island. When Representative Michael S. Pisaturo ran for office in 1994, he was public about his sexual orientation from the start. He discovered that, even in Cranston, Rhode Island, being openly gay worked in his favor. He recalled: "People would say, 'I don't agree with gay rights, but you're honest and I like that.'" He has even come to believe that being out can be an asset for politicians. Even so, he says he knows of at least six Rhode Island legislators who are secretly gay. Although being gay is only part of his political life, he has been involved in trying to restore AIDS funding, he has sponsored bills on gay civil rights and same-sex marriage, and he publicly supports LGBT organizations. Alan Spear, Minnesota's Senate president, largely agrees with Pisaturo's comments. Spear was elected to the Minnesota Senate in 1972, and he came out in 1974. During his three decades in office he has seen little of the backlash reported by some LGBT candidates. Furthermore, as noted by Annisa Parker, an out lesbian on the Houston City Council, being open may have helped her win by providing considerable free media attention to her candidacy. However, she says, "There aren't many city issues that are gay issues. City government is concerned with potholes and sewers and such, not social and sexual matters" (Freyer 1999). In sum, as we consider how being gay may hurt a candidate's electoral chances, we must also consider that there may be benefits to being openly gay as well.

To assess the role of sexual orientation in state legislative elections, I contacted all openly LGBT candidates who ran for state legislative offices in primary and/or general elections across thirty states during the 2003–4 elections. Candidates were identified through LexusNexus newspaper database searches; contact with national gay and lesbian groups, such as the Log Cabin Republicans, the Gay and Lesbian Victory Fund, Human Rights Campaign, and the National Gay and Lesbian Task Force; as well as contact with state-level gay and lesbian interest groups. Given the newspaper search and group contact, it is fairly certain that all openly LGBT candidates for state legislative office in 2003 and 2004 were identified.

Each candidate was contacted and asked to complete a questionnaire and also was asked for permission to pose follow-up questions. The candidates were promised anonymity. In the 2003–4 cycle there were ninety-five LGBT candidates running for state legislative offices. In twenty-four (25 percent) of these races, candidates were running for the upper legislative chamber, typically called the State Senate. Most candidates (seventy-three) ran as Democrats or for the Democratic nomination, but seventeen ran for the Republican nomination or on the Republican ticket, and five candidates ran on the Green Party ticket. In total, twenty-one (22 percent) of the candidates lost in the primary election, withdrew, or failed to file enough signatures to obtain a spot on the general election ballot.

The candidates were contacted by mail, with follow-up contact via e-mail and telephone. Only nine candidates had no reliable contact information (i.e., mailings returned by the U.S. postal service). Of the remaining eighty-six candidates, thirty-eight completed the survey questionnaire. Although the response rate was 44 percent, the respondents were generally representative of the population of candidates.

Follow-up e-mails, phone calls, and visits were made to some of the candidates who responded to the survey. In part the follow-up interviews were conducted for those candidates who completed the survey before Election Day, November 2004, but some respondents were questioned in greater detail about their responses to the survey. The following discussion summarizes responses to the questionnaire, but it is also informed by the unstructured follow-up interviews. Because all the questions were open-ended, here I summarize the responses rather than providing descriptive statistics (see appendix A for the list of questions that were asked).

Most respondents to the survey ran in districts that favored Democrats in voting registration numbers, past voting, or both. In fact, all the Democratic candidates ran in districts that favored their party and only Republican candidates ran in districts that were not favorable to their party. Interviews with candidates helped to confirm that this pattern was not an accident. Most openly LGBT candidates tend to run as Democrats and select districts where they believe their sexual orientation will be less of an issue. Many candidates had prior political experience in the district, through activism, a staff position, or holding lower-level offices, so they were familiar with the ideological and partisan orientations of the district. Even Republican candidates ran in districts that were socially liberal and potentially favorable only to moderate Republican candidates. Indeed, the notion that LGBT candidates select districts carefully is highlighted by the fact that several races saw openly LGBT candidates facing off in either the primary or general election.

In terms of how candidates came to decide to run for a state legislative seat, many describe a process of being recruited or encouraged by others, including sitting legislators, party activists, and party leaders. Indeed, most candidates indicated that they were recruited or encouraged to run by others. About half the candidates were encouraged to run because they had either held a lower-level office previously or established their viability in a previous race or in internal party elections. For most of the candidates the decision to run was based in part on a seat coming open through retirement, term limits, or the pursuit of a higher office by an incumbent.

The candidates were asked to assess the support of the gay and lesbian community for their candidacy and the extent to which they participated in any gay and lesbian social or political events. Many suggested that the LGBT community was very supportive and they had participated in community events during the campaign. One respondent even indicated that 50 percent of her volunteers and more than 50 percent of her contributions were from the LGBT community. Other candidates indicated that they had the support of the LGBT community but either did not attend events or the community's support was less than vocal. The remaining candidates received little support from the community. In some cases the community supported another LGBT candidate, while in others the community supported a heterosexual Democrat over the openly LGBT Republican candidate. In at least one case the candidate suggested that some lesbians preferred the heterosexual female candidate to his own candidacy.

Because LGBT candidates often *appear* to face organized opposition from conservative religious groups, candidates were asked about the appearance of such campaigns. Surprisingly, few respondents indicated that there was any active opposition by religious conservatives against them, and only about half these candidates described significant efforts by religious conservatives to defeat them. For example, one candidate described the formation of a new group whose sole purpose was to oppose her candidacy. Most opposition campaigns were led by local chapters of the Christian Coalition, the Eagle Forum, and right-to-life groups.

When asked about media coverage of their races, not surprisingly most candidates indicated that the media did not print or air more than a few reports on their race. In fact, most state legislative races receive little media coverage (Hamm and Moncrief 2008). However, a few candidates did report a considerable amount of coverage, and in most of these cases the coverage tended to focus on the fact that one or more candidates in the race were openly gay or lesbian. Virtually all the candidates reported that coverage was fair and tended to be accurate. And although sexual orientation was mentioned in media reports in virtually all the races, it was not usually the main focus of coverage. Indeed, for many candidates the only news media stories that focused heavily on sexual orientation were those in the LGBT press. In one case a candidate indicated that her sexual orientation was highlighted by the national news media but also that the attention may have helped her campaign. Overall, the candidates' responses suggest that the news media did not hype their sexual orientation and that coverage did portray openly LGBT candidates in a negative light.

The costs of campaigns for state legislative seats vary considerably depending on the state and even the district, with races in states like California with more professionalized legislatures running into the hundreds of thousands of dollars, but those in a state like Montana only costing a few thousand dollars in many districts. In addition, some states place significant limits on campaign contributions and/or may provide public funding for campaigns (Hamm and Moncrief 2008). LGBT state legislative candidates were quite mixed in response to questions regarding their ability to finance their campaigns, size of contributions, and ability to raise money from political action committees (PACs). Most respondents indicated that they had no problems raising money, and nearly all candidates received at least some money from PACs. Most candidates received small individual donations. Some candidates received bundled contributions from the Victory Fund, a national group that focuses on electing LGBT candidates. Most of the Democratic candidates received contributions from labor, environmental, and pro-choice organizations, but some also received contributions from a variety of business and development organizations. Several candidates indicated that it is either "very easy for a gay candidate to raise money in my state" or that close to half their contributions came from the LGBT community or LGBT organizations. The view that raising money is easy as an LGBT candidate was especially prevalent among incumbents, with challengers being less likely to espouse such a view. At the same time, many challengers still indicated that raising money for their campaigns was not too difficult.

LGBT candidates also suggested that group endorsements were relatively easy to obtain. Almost all the candidates received some endorsements; groups affiliated with the Democratic Party, such as environmental, pro-choice, and labor organizations, endorsed most Democrats. Often these endorsements came through local and state groups but some endorsements came through chapters of national organizations, such as the National Organization for Women, along with strictly national groups, such as Democracy for America. Openly LGBT Republican candidates had far more difficulty obtaining endorsements. These candidates likely faced this problem because they were running as long-shot challengers in Democratic districts.

Most candidates reported that their party supported their candidacy following the primary election, if one was held. Some candidates received direct support from legislative leadership or funds from legislative leadership PACs. And most candidates who ran in states that had public funding received some public funding for their campaigns. Other candidates did not receive financial support or endorsements from leaders but did receive nonmonetary support, such as help from campaign workers.

In terms of incumbency and previous political experience, some LGBT candidates were incumbents running for reelection for their current office, 38 percent had held previous office but were running for a higher office, and a small portion had never before been elected to an office. In addition, nearly all incumbents had previously served in a lower office, including state assemblies, city councils, and county positions. A few respondents who had not been elected previously had run for a local or state office in the past. The pattern and experience of these candidates is fairly consistent with that of most state legislative candidates (Hamm and Moncrief 2008). However, it does appear that the average LGBT state legislative candidate is somewhat more likely to have previously served in a public office.

Respondents were asked to list the four central issues in their campaign. Most candidates listed education, or support for public schools. About half listed environmental issues—and about the same percentage listed health care issues. Others mentioned job creation or economic issues, and a few focused on government overspending or state budget problems. Only a few listed equality or civil rights issues as being primary to their campaign. This suggests that the average LGBT candidate runs for state office campaigns on staple party issues and does not emphasize issues that are directly related to gay civil rights.

However, when asked directly if gay civil rights were important to their campaign, only a few said the issue was not important at all. In fact, about half of the LGBT candidates indicated in one way or another that the issue was very important to their campaign. For some this meant that their literature and campaign speeches discussed the issue, while for others it was because their voting record on LGBT issues was raised during the campaign. Most of the remaining candidates indicated that the issue played some role in the campaign. For these respondents the issue was often couched in the broader terms of protecting the civil rights of all citizens or in opposing measures that would ban same-sex marriage. Thus, although some candidates indicated that the issue was important, very few actively campaigned on it, and for some candidates it became important because opponents raised it or external events, such as ballot measures to ban same-sex marriage, forced it into the spotlight. One candidate even indicated that the issue had to be addressed because opponents accused him of being a single-issue candidate given his sexual orientation.

The candidates were asked to assess the campaign, spending levels, and tactics of their opponents during the primary election. About half of the LGBT candidates either had no primary or were unopposed in the primary, which is a higher rate than normal for state legislative elections (Hamm and Moncrief 2008). In other races the primary is the key race simply because the district is heavily partisan, often Democratic, in one direction. Only a few respondents described the primary race as fairly nasty in terms of attacks, and a small number of candidates even faced opponents who were also gay or lesbian. One candidate even indicated that her opponent said she "wasn't gay enough." A few indicated that their opponents tried to make an issue of their sexual orientation.

In terms of general election campaigns, only a few candidates faced no opposition but many respondents indicated that their main opponent mustered little in the way of campaigning. Thus, in most of the races all the candidates involved actively campaigned and raised a reasonable amount of money for a race. Only a few candidates described activity by their opponent to make sexual orientation an issue in the campaign. None of these candidates lost their races. As such it does appear that a candidate's sexual orientation played little role in the outcome of these elections. At a minimum, candidates running in general elections did not suggest that sexual orientation played a significant role in the electoral outcome.

The candidates were also asked to name one issue or event that had the most influence on the campaign's outcome. Many indicated that campaign resources, including money, determined the outcome. Most of the remaining candidates indicated that their incumbency, or that of their opponents, or the partisan leaning of the district determined the outcome. A few candidates mentioned key endorsements by elected officials or newspapers, or their previous political experience in the district or state as being central factors. But overall incumbency and the partisan composition of the district appeared to play the greatest role in most races, which is consistent with research on state legislative elections generally (Hogan 2007, 2008).

The respondents were also asked directly if sexual orientation played any role in the campaign. Many candidates indicated that sexual orientation played no role in the campaign but a fair number did say that sexual orientation played a small, negative role. In most of these cases sexual orientation became important because opponents raised the issue of same-sex marriage. In other cases a same-sex marriage ban was being considered by the state and the issue was brought into media coverage of the campaign; in only a few races did respondents indicate that the issue became significant in a negative manner. One respondent said: "My opponent made it a central part of her campaign—it backfired on her. I had Republicans donating to my campaign to defeat her." In another race the respondent said that the state Republican Party had funded telephone push-polls that scared voters into believing that they might elect a lesbian who could become a legislative leader in their state. One respondent also indicated that his opponent attempted to argue that LGBT candidates might have policy interests that are different from heterosexuals, making it difficult for an LGBT candidate to represent the interests of the heterosexual majority. At the same time, many incumbent legislators indicated that the issue had been significant in past campaigns but was no longer an issue. But even for incumbent legislators, the role played by sexual orientation in past elections was not a deciding factor in the election outcome. And no single respondent indicated that they had ever lost a race because of their sexual orientation.

Interestingly, several candidates suggested that being an LGBT candidate was actually an asset. One respondent said that her candidacy rallied political progressives and the LGBT community in her district, and this may have made opponents afraid to attack her sexual orientation. Two candidates said that being openly LGBT gave them a volunteer network and staff that they otherwise would not have had.

Both candidates indicated that the volunteers were important in their election victories. And one incumbent candidate indicated that although the issue had been important for her in past campaigns, at this point being an openly lesbian legislator seemed to help her maintain her seat.

The candidates were also asked how their race might have been different if it had occurred in another district or state. Nearly all the candidates who won their races suggested that their sexual orientation would have played a larger role in races outside their district. They indicated that most other districts in their state, as well as other states, would have been more difficult to run in as an LGBT candidate. Although the evidence is limited, the comments are suggestive toward a notion that LGBT candidates target the districts in which they will be willing to run. For some candidates these were clearly their home districts; for others it was simply a function of knowing the district and having a sense of how being a gay or lesbian candidate would play. This is not to suggest that all potential LGBT candidates move to new districts and establish residency to run in a "friendly" district; but some clearly do, especially in urban areas where moving a few blocks away would place you in another district. Instead, candidate comments suggest that potential LGBT candidates may simply choose not to run in districts where they believe sexual orientation may play a role. In addition, the biographies and résumés of the respondents in the sample suggest that most are well prepared for a political race before their run.

Finally, the candidates were asked to explain any lessons they had learned from being an openly LGBT candidate for state office. Many said something along the lines of "Be who you are; don't listen to political advisors about this issue; just acknowledge and move on (then it becomes a nonissue)." One candidate phrased it this way: "Don't limit yourself. I almost didn't run because I was convinced that sexual orientation would be a huge deal and that I would never win." Another group of respondents suggested that you cannot be "the gay candidate" or the "single-issue candidate." These respondents suggested that LGBT candidates had to focus on representing all their constituents and spend considerable time meeting people in person. Some candidates suggested that this face-to-face contact was very important in eliminating notions that LGBT people are different—"it makes you more 'real.'" Still others suggested that LGBT candidates have to be smarter and more qualified, with a proven track record, than the average candidate for state office. And one candidate emphasized a need to capitalize on the LGBT community to raise funds and obtain volunteer campaign workers. Indeed, at one point or another in the survey, nearly all the candidates made reference to reliance on the LGBT community and/or LGBT political organizations for volunteers and financial support.

Summary of Surveys and Interviews

The results of the surveys and interviews of LGBT state legislative candidates from the 2003–4 elections suggest a number of interesting findings. First, LGBT candidates tend to be somewhat more experienced and better prepared than the average state legislative candidate (Hamm and Moncrief 2008). They are just as likely to be self-motivated to run as they are to be recruited but either way most of them have previous experience in elected positions. And if they obtain a legislative seat, like most incumbents, they are reelected. Second, based on candidate comments and other evidence concerning where candidates run, it seems as though LGBT candidates are quite selective in choosing when and where and how to run. The average LGBT candidate runs as a Democrat in a left-leaning district. These candidates appear to be quite aware that their district is likely to be accepting of an LGBT candidate, whereas many other districts may not be. Combined with the political experience of most of these candidates, the average Democratic LGBT candidate may actually be more successful than the average Democrat running for state office. LGBT Republicans, conversely, are likely to face uphill battles as Republicans in Democratic districts or as Republicans in Republican districts where voters may not be so accepting of an openly LGBT candidate. Indeed, most of the successful Republican LGBT candidates were not public about their sexual orientation until they had served a term or more in office.

Finally, the surveys and interviews also make it clear that sexual orientation is not a deciding factor in most, if any, races. Even in the few races where LGBT candidates faced a mobilized campaign by religious conservatives or a candidate who tried to make sexual orientation a focus of the campaign, the candidates did not suggest that these efforts did or could have defeated them. In fact, some candidates indicated that they had managed to capitalize on being LGBT to win their elections by attracting contributors and volunteers. This is not to say that sexual orientation does not matter for state legislative candidates, only that given that it could be a factor, as indicated by the polling data presented above, potential LGBT candidates are strategic in choosing when, where, and how they run. These strategic maneuvers tend to downplay or eliminate the potential negative role that sexual orientation could play in a state legislative campaign.

Conclusion

In an effort to better understand the political representation of the LGBT community, this chapter has explored whether a candidate's sexual orientation influences the level of support for candidates for state offices. I examined this issue first through the context of public opinion toward gay and lesbian candidates by empirically examining individual-level opinion toward openly gay and lesbian candidates. This analysis included multivariate models for predicting attitudes, and the data employed are from several state and national polls. Second, I provided a qualitative description of gay and lesbian candidates' experiences in running for state legislative seats using surveys and interviews with gay and lesbian candidates for state legislative office in 2003 and 2004. The results of both sets of analyses reveal several important conclusions.

First, an analysis of national- and state-level surveys reveals that in most parts of the country, a core of about 25 percent of adults are unlikely to support a gay or lesbian candidate for state or national office. In addition, this opposition has changed little during the past fifteen years, even as support for gay civil rights has increased.

Second, an analysis of individual-level preferences reveals that, regardless of the office, older, Republican, conservative, religious, males with less education are more likely to oppose an openly gay or lesbian candidate. The evidence indicates that these individuals likely constitute the consistent 25 percent of the population that would not vote for a gay or lesbian candidate.

Third, potential LGBT state legislative candidates are strategic in their pursuit of office. They tend to have greater experience and resources than the average state legislative candidate, and they appear to typically run in districts where voters are less likely to oppose an openly gay candidate. Indeed, the candidates suggested that being openly LGBT can even be an electoral advantage, at least for those running as Democrats.

Finally, an analysis of candidate surveys and interviews suggests that the political strategies employed by LGBT candidates make it relatively rare for a candidate's sexual orientation to play a significant role in state legislative elections. Those candidates who have political experience extending back a decade or so indicate that sexual orientation was often a campaign issue in the past, but it has become less so. And even in past races none of those interviewed suggested that their sexual orientation was a major factor in the campaign or in the election outcome. In addition, none of the candidates surveyed or interviewed indicated that sexual orientation cost them the election. These observations support the notion that a candidate's sexual orientation may play a role in some campaigns, but potential LGBT candidates are strategic enough to ensure that they run in districts where the issue will not doom their candidacy. As more LGBT candidates run for state offices, it is likely that more LGBT candidates will run in less friendly districts, and we could see an increase in races where sexual orientation is a significant issue. Conversely, if public attitudes continue to become less negative toward LGBT people and candidates, the possibility that sexual orientation will be a factor in races should decline.

Notes

1. By comparison, in the 2007 Gallup poll support for various presidential candidates was as follows: Jewish (92 percent), atheist (45 percent), black (94 percent), Catholic (95 percent), homosexual (55 percent), a heterosexual woman (88 percent), Mormon (72 percent), and Hispanic (87 percent). Thus only an atheist would receive less support than a homosexual in 2007.

2. A 2007 survey by the Pew Research Center found that 46 percent of adults would be less likely to vote for a homosexual candidate for president, whereas 1 percent would be more likely and 51 percent said it would not matter for their vote. Comparable negative candidate characteristics in the Pew survey were candidates who had never held public office, had no college degree, did not believe in God, were Muslim, and had used drugs in the past (Pew Research Center for People and the Press 2007).

3. The perceptions of others' preferences survey questions should be interpreted with caution; the average person is simply not very good at predicting the behavior of others.

More than 40 percent of the public did not believe that America was ready to elect a black president, and yet we did in 2008.

4. In 1994 New York City's Staten Island borough president Guy Molinari said that someone who is gay or lesbian is not fit for public office. During a *New York Times* / CBS News state poll following the comment, respondents who knew about Molinari's statement were asked if the statement bothered them. More than 60 percent of respondents said the comments bothered them but 38 percent said the comments did not bother them (Smith and Haider-Markel 2002).

CHAPTER THREE

Assessing the Role of Sexual Orientation in Elections: LGBT State Legislative Candidates, 1992–2006

O N THE BASIS OF THE DISCUSSION and analysis presented in chapter 2, we can now move to a systematic analysis of how a candidate's sexual orientation influences state legislative election outcomes. Although much of the (especially early) research on female and minority candidates would suggest that LGBT candidates are likely to receive less support than their heterosexual counterparts, the conclusions in chapter 2 indicate that if LGBT candidates are strategic, their sexual orientation is not likely to significantly hinder their election opportunities. Ideally, an analysis of election outcomes would examine both primary and general elections simply because in many state legislative districts the most competitive election is the primary election. My analysis is limited to general state legislative elections from 1992 to 2006 across ten states. However, the interviews with candidates analyzed in chapter 2 suggest that for most candidates, the role of sexual orientation is similar in both primary and general elections.

Theory and Previous Research

I begin with the simple notion that a candidate's characteristics influence the level of voter support. These characteristics can include major factors, such as incumbency and party but might also include issue positions, gender, attractiveness, charisma, and sexual orientation. Simply put, voters are likely to take many factors into account when deciding which candidate to support, but in many contests, a candidate's party and incumbency are likely to be the main factors. In addition, the structural elements of a given race and district are likely to shape the outcome, including a candidate's spending and the district's socioeconomic characteristics (Hogan 2001, 2007).

Furthermore, because Lax and Phillips (2009) establish that attitudes about LGBT equality vary across states, we might also expect opposition to or support for

LGBT candidates to vary over time and across states, and no existing research has attempted to evaluate this potential variation. Thus this chapter examines three questions: What factors influence the likelihood that a LGBT candidate will run in a given state legislative district? Does a candidate's sexual orientation influence the level of voter support in state legislative elections? And does a candidate's sexual orientation influence the outcome of state legislative elections?

A Candidate's Sexual Orientation

As noted in previous chapters, most research on the impact of a candidate's sexual orientation on the candidate's evaluations, success, or electoral margins has been conducted as experimental studies in which fictional voters (usually college students) evaluated fictional candidates (see Golebiowska 2001; Golebiowska and Thomsen 1999; Herrick and Thomas 1999). One exception is Golebiowska's (2002) study of LGBT candidates and elected officials. She conducted a survey of these individuals and asked them to assess the impact sexual orientation had in their election contests. Her findings were consistent with similar, experimental research.

These studies have provided our first empirical support for accepted anecdotal evidence indicating that the sexual orientation of openly gay and lesbian candidates is a factor in their campaigns (see DeBold 1994; Rayside 1998; Smith and Haider-Markel 2002). Furthermore, the experimental research supports public opinion findings from chapter 2 that voters do consider a candidate's sexual orientation when evaluating how a candidate's positions might actually translate in to real-world voting behavior.

However, as chapter 2 makes clear, voters who are likely to vote against a candidate based on sexual orientation are not likely to have much impact on the outcome of the race. Since voters who oppose LGBT candidates are likely to be conservative Republicans, and LGBT candidates are likely to be Democrats or moderate or liberal Republicans, the candidates would be unlikely to receive their voting support regardless of their sexual orientation. Thus, though sexual orientation could play a role in electoral campaigns, its influence on electoral outcomes should be fairly minimal. In addition, the strategic behavior of LGBT candidates should be evident in terms of where and when they choose to run for state legislative office. In particular LGBT candidates should be more likely to run in districts where voter demographics indicate a more liberal populace.

Research on State Legislative Elections

The other body of literature relevant to this chapter concerns state legislative elections in particular, and state and local elections generally, and comes largely from political science. Approximately forty years of research on the outcomes of state and local elections has consistently found that the strongest influences on electoral margins and candidate victory are (1) traditional district support for the candidate's party, (2) incumbency, and (3) campaign spending (Hogan 2007, 2008; Krebs 1998; Thompson and Moncrief 1998; Carey, Niemi, and Powell 2000; Jewell and More-house 2001).

Research on state legislative elections specifically uses a number of approaches to developing dependent variables—measures of election outcomes. Each of these approaches is useful in its own right. For example, Tucker and Weber (1987) measured electoral margins by using the percentage of votes cast for the Democratic candidate as one dependent variable, and the percentage of votes received by the Republican candidate as a second dependent variable (see also Gierzynski and Breaux 1993). This allowed them to treat each candidate as a case and compare across the models for differences across party. Others, such as Gierzynski and Breaux (1991), have used similar techniques but examined the vote share for incumbents in one model and challengers in another model. Other recent studies have estimated the probability of a given incumbent candidate's election by using a binary dependent variable (win/loss) with logistic regression (Carey, Niemi, and Powell 2000; Hogan 2007, 2008). Overall, the literature makes it clear that a variety of dependent variables should be employed to examine the potential impact of contextual factors on election outcomes, especially when examining elections over time, across states, or both (Hogan 2008; Jewell 1994; Jewell and Morehouse 2001).

Individual candidates' characteristics seem only to influence vote share on the margins but researchers have found that women and minorities tend to receive slightly less support than do similar white or male candidates (Bullock 1987; Bullock and Gaddie 1987; Grofman, Migalski, and Noviello 1986; Grofman and Handley 1991; Hogan 2001; Jewell 1994; Krebs 1998), especially if they are running in multimember districts rather than in single-member districts (Jewell 1994; Gerber, Morton, and Rietz 1998). However, King's (2002) findings suggest that female candidates benefit under multimember districts rather than single-member districts. Either way, district type is potentially an important force influencing election outcomes (Carey, Niemi, and Powell 2000; Jewell and Morehouse 2001).

In addition, a considerable amount of research on public opinion and voting in direct democracies suggests that voting on LGBT-related issues is shaped by religious values (e.g., see Haider-Markel, Querze, and Lindaman 2007; Haider-Markel and Kaufman 2006; Lofton and Haider-Markel 2007). Thus it would seem reasonable to account for the religious denominational affiliations in state legislative districts, with particular attention given to Protestant fundamentalists. Likewise, the size of the LGBT population in a district could play an important role in attracting LGBT candidates and in their electoral success. As the LGBT population in a district increases, so too should the likelihood of both LGBT candidates running in the district and their electoral success.

Nevertheless, because the impact of gender and race on state and local election outcomes has been fairly small, we should expect that the impact of sexual orientation, if significant, would also only be on the margins in most races, if any. Furthermore, the impact of sexual orientation may be subdued by other candidate characteristics. For example, incumbency is a key factor in state and local races (Caldeira and Patterson 1982; Carey, Niemi, and Powell 2000; Jewell and Morehouse 2001; Hogan 2003, 2007, 2008), and it seems that LGBT incumbents are less likely to lose vote share over their sexual orientation than are LGBT challengers.

Meanwhile, LGBT challengers running against heterosexual incumbents are less likely to be victorious simply because of their challenger status.

The literature also suggests a number of other factors to consider when explaining state legislative outcomes. For example, Hogan (2003) examined the potential impact of divisive primaries on general election outcomes and suggests that divisive primaries can decrease a candidate's support in the general election. And although conventional wisdom indicates that a candidate's spending determines election outcomes, Caldeira and Patterson (1982) found that the relationship between campaign spending and vote margin is curvilinear rather than linear—meaning that its influence is greatest when spending is quite low or quite high.

Meanwhile, Jewell (1994) suggests that researchers of state elections should control for national trends, such as the shift toward Republicans in 1994, but provides little guidance as to which trends are most important to take into account. However, his argument suggests that any analysis of state legislative elections over time should account for time in the models. For LGBT candidates, we especially need to consider that fact that affect toward homosexuals and attitudes about LGBT equality began to rapidly change in the late 1990s (see chapter 1).

Incumbency is certainly an important factor in national elections (Carson, Engstrom, and Roberts 2007) but the same is true in state elections (Carey, Niemi, and Powell 2000; Hogan 2008). Indeed, Holbrook and Tidmarch (1993) found that incumbents in legislative leadership positions have higher vote margins than their counterparts (see also Carey, Niemi, and Powell 2000). Chapter 2 also made it clear that LGBT challengers face an uphill battle against incumbents. At the same time LGBT incumbents suggested that their sexual orientation was less significant in campaigns once they had achieved office. As such, the incumbency advantage should benefit LGBT incumbents in the same way that it helps heterosexual incumbents.

Additionally, researchers have demonstrated the impact of redistricting on state election outcomes, minority representation, and party control (Gerber, Morton, and Rietz 1998; Lublin and Voss 2000; Jewell and Morehouse 2001), and these studies suggest that aggregate factors in a state can play an important role in election outcomes but their effects tend to be relatively difficult to measure. Interviews with LGBT candidates in several states did indeed suggest that redistricting shaped their elections but these cases were few in number and difficult to quantify. Nevertheless, as more LGBT candidates run for office and more LGBT legislators face reelection, it is likely that they will face electorates that may be less supportive of an LGBT candidate.

However, almost none of the studies using multivariate analyses use district-level control variables that account for constituency characteristics other than support for a political party (Jewell 1994; but see Hogan 2007, 2008). And although district support for a candidate's party is likely to play an important role in explaining a candidate's vote share, other factors—such as education, income, and the racial composition of a political jurisdiction—have consistently been shown to influence election outcomes in a variety of contexts and should be taken in account (Haider-Markel and Meier 2003; Krebs 1998; Thompson and Moncrief 1998; Jewell and Morehouse 2001).

In the case of LGBT candidates the importance of an LGBT presence within a district as well as the religious orientation of the district could likely play an important role in determining whether LGBT candidates run and how they perform in elections. For example, it is clear that these factors matter in determining the outcomes of ballot measures related to LGBT citizens (Haider-Markel et al. 2007).

Research Design and Variable Measurement

The heart of the analysis for this chapter follows that of traditional studies of state and national legislative elections, with the addition of tracking candidates' sexual orientation (Jewell and Morehouse 2001; Hogan 2003). I collected data on state legislative districts and elections across ten states from 1992 to 2006. Where the data were available, the selected years cover eight election cycles, occur following the 1990 census redistricting and after the 2002 census redistricting, and offer a variety of electoral contexts. The ten states selected are Arizona, California, Georgia, Maine, New Hampshire, New York, Oregon, Vermont, Virginia, and Wisconsin.[1] These states represent each region of the country, offer a diverse set of electoral and district conditions, and have witnessed at least one openly LGBT candidate running for state legislative office since 1990 (Smith and Haider-Markel 2002). On average each state has about 150 legislative seats across two chambers.[2]

In the first set of models I examine the likelihood of an LGBT candidate running in a district with a dependent variable coded 1 if a candidate in a race is LGBT, and 0 otherwise. I estimate separate models based on party and a final model for all LGBT candidates.

In the second set of models I examine the likelihood of a candidate winning an election. I begin this portion of the analysis with a dichotomous dependent variable coded 1 if the Democratic candidate wins the election, and 0 otherwise. The second model in this series codes the dependent variable 1 if the Republican candidate wins the election, and 0 otherwise.

In the final series of models I examine voting support for candidates. The first dependent variable in this series is measured simply as the percentage of the two-party vote received by the Democratic candidate in one model, and the percentage of the two-party vote received by the Republican candidate in the second model. My multivariate analyses are conducted with ordinary-least-squares regression (for dependent variables that are in percent) and logistic regression (for dependent variables that are dichotomous). Models are estimated separately for Republicans and Democrats, as well as both together.

Independent Variables

Several independent variables are relevant for this analysis. Most important, each model will include an independent variable coded 1 if the candidate's sexual orientation is LGBT and 0 if the candidate is heterosexual. In the 1990s the number of LGBT candidates for state offices began to increase dramatically. However, it is difficult to say with complete certainty that one can create a database that includes every LGBT person who has run for a state legislative seat. I created an extremely reliable database for 1992 to 2006 by tracking LGBT candidates in LexisNexis newspaper databases; using tracking lists developed by LGBT interest groups (Gay and Lesbian Victory Fund, Human Rights Campaign, National Gay and Lesbian Task Force); keyword searches of LGBT newspapers, such as the *Washington Blade*; and through contacts with LGBT groups in thirty-five states.[3] This technique should ensure that the database includes all openly LGBT candidates who ran for state legislative office during this period, in part because I define open candidates as those who have been public about their sexual orientation through the news media or through their own campaign materials. Thus, the data used here are the most comprehensive ever collected on LGBT candidates. The final data set from 1992 to 2006 contains 201 LGBT candidates. Because the overall number of LGBT candidates tended to go up with each election cycle, I include a counter variable in each model to reflect the years from 1992 to 2006.

Each model controls for whether or not the candidate is an incumbent state legislator. Incumbency is simply a dichotomous variable coded 1 if the Democratic candidate is an incumbent in the Democratic models and 0 otherwise. The Republican models follow the same pattern.[4]

District characteristics are included in the models as rough surrogates for voter preferences. For example, in chapter 2 we found that on average individuals with higher levels of education were more likely to support an openly gay or lesbian candidate. Likewise, an analysis of public opinion polls consistently shows that those with more education are more likely to have a positive affect toward gays and lesbians and be more supportive of gay civil rights (Brewer 2002; Haider-Markel and Joslyn 2005, 2008). As such we can hypothesize that in state legislative districts with higher levels of education, it should be more likely that an LGBT candidate will run for office. I measure education as the percentage of the population twenty-five years or older who have a college education.[5]

Although income and race are not consistent predictors of attitudes toward gays and lesbians or LGBT-related policy (Brewer 2002; Haider-Markel and Joslyn 2008), as a means to capture constituency characteristics they may play a role in predicting which types of candidates run for legislative seats and how successful they are (Hogan 2001, 2007). Higher-income districts may be more attractive to LGBT candidates on their face, considering that higher-income areas reflect more cosmopolitan attitudes (Florida 2002), which should make voters in these districts appear to be more supportive of LGBT candidates. However, these areas may in fact be less supportive of LGBT candidates in elections largely because higher-income individuals are more likely to support Republicans (Brooks and Brady 1999), and LGBT candidates are more likely to run as Democrats (see chapter 2). And although African Americans and Latinos tend to be somewhat less supportive of gay civil rights policies because they hold conservative social attitudes in general (Herek 2002; Layman and Carsey 2002), they may or may not be more supportive of LGBT candidates in the aggregate, in part, because they may be less likely to vote against a Democratic candidate, which is the party of most LGBT candidates (see chapter 2). I measure income as the average household income in a district and race with variables capturing the percentage of African Americans and the percentage of Hispanics in a district.[6]

Of course, income and education are simple surrogates for voter preferences; other factors could be more important for LGBT candidates, including the religious orientation of a district and the size of the LGBT population in a district. Political jurisdictions with more conservative religious denominations have consistently been shown to be less supportive of LGBT civil rights, whereas jurisdictions with higher LGBT populations have been more supportive (Haider-Markel, Querze, and Lindaman 2007; Haider-Markel and Meier 1996). Here I measure religious orientation with a variable that captures the percentage of Protestant fundamentalists in a district.[7] Because denominational data are only available by county and not by district, I estimated the Protestant fundamentalist population by first determining the district population in each county that overlapped the district and the Protestant fundamentalist population in each of those counties, and then creating a measure of the percentage of the district population that is Protestant fundamentalist, weighted by the proportion of the district that is represented by each county's population. I expect that districts with a higher Protestant fundamentalist population will be less likely to have an LGBT state legislative candidate, and if they do, they will be less supportive of the candidate at the ballot box.

Likewise, I measured the LGBT population with a surrogate, the percentage of same-sex households within a district.[8] Same-sex household data are available by county but not by legislative district. I estimated same-sex households by first determining the district households in each county that overlapped the district and the same-sex households in each of those counties, and then I created a measure of the percentage of the district households that are same-sex households, weighted by the proportion of the district that is represented by each county's population. Although this measure is not precise, because it only captures same-sex couples living in the same household, it is the best surrogate for the LGBT population (Haider-Markel 1997). I expect that districts with a higher LGBT population will be more likely to have LGBT candidates run for legislative office and be more supportive of these candidates.

In addition there were a number of relevant variables for which only incomplete data were available. For example, some states had party registration data available for some but not all election years. Party registration is measured as the percentage of voters who are registered as Democrats, for the Democratic models, and the percentage of the voting population who are registered as Republicans, for the Republican models. I use caution in estimating models with partisanship data; the gaps in data cannot be assumed to be random, and here I assume that they may bias the results.

Also, on a limited basis, I was able to collect data on candidate gender, candidate spending, percentage living in poverty, and urbanism of the district (in percent). Although not all models making use of these variables are included, I report results that diverge from the models with more complete data.

Results and Discussion

Table 3.1 displays the results for my model estimating the likelihood that an LGBT candidate will run for a state legislative seat in a given district. The first column displays the results for Democratic candidates, the second column for Republican candidates, and the third column for all candidates.

Given the large number of cases, the models predict the presence of LGBT candidates reasonably well. The results for the time counter variable indicate that LGBT Democratic candidates have been more likely to run for state legislative seats over time, which is consistent with expectations; in nearly every election cycle since the late 1980s, more LGBT candidates have run for state legislative seats. District characteristics, such as education and income, appear to influence the likelihood of Democratic LGBT candidates running in a given district—higher education levels

Table 3.1 Influences on the Likelihood That an LGBT Candidate Will Run in a State Legislative District, 1992–2006

Independent Variable	Likelihood of LGBT Democratic Candidate	Likelihood of LGBT Republican Candidate	Overall Likelihood of LGBT Candidate
District average income	−.000*	.000	−.000#
	(.000)	(.000)	(.000)
% college educated	.014**	.016**	.015**
	(.003)	(.005)	(.003)
% African American	−.022*	−.029	−.023*
	(.019)	(.034)	(.010)
% Hispanic	.020**	.023	.020**
	(.006)	(.020)	(.006)
% Protestant fundamentalist	−.064**	.023	−.051**
	(.020)	(.039)	(.018)
Same-sex households	.110#	.006	.096
	(.062)	(.247)	(.061)
Year counter	.070**	−.014	.064*
	(.022)	(.065)	(.021)
Constant	−144.810**	19.926	−131.495**
	(43.301)	(129.568)	(41.229)
Log likelihood	−836.387	−116.671	−901.452
Pseudo R^2	.04	.03	.04
LR chi-square	66.59	7.90	67.28
Probability chi-square	.000	.341	.000
% correctly predicted	99.11	99.91	99.03
No. of cases	17,153	17,153	17,153

Note: Coefficients are logistic regression coefficients. Standard errors are in parentheses.
Significance levels: ** < .01; * < .05; # < .10.

increase the likelihood, whereas higher income levels decrease the likelihood of Democratic LGBT candidates running. Potential Democratic LGBT candidates may perceive that an educated populace will be more tolerant, whereas higher average income may betray an underlying leaning toward Republican candidates.

The racial composition of a district also plays a role, with Democratic LGBT candidates being more likely to run in districts with a higher Hispanic population but somewhat less likely to run in districts with a higher African American population. Why such a pattern appears is not entirely clear, but because African Americans have tended to be less supportive of LGBT civil rights and have a lower positive affect toward gays and lesbians (Herek 2002), it could be that LGBT candidates may be deterred from running in districts with high African American populations. Meanwhile, Latinos tend to be more socially conservative but apparently this is not a deterrent to LGBT candidates.

Interestingly, whereas Democratic LGBT candidates appear to be significantly less likely to run in districts with higher Protestant fundamentalist populations, they are only marginally more likely to run in districts with a higher LGBT population. This pattern could appear because although there is some variation across districts in terms of same-sex households, the variation is fairly small. In the case of Protestant fundamentalists, there is a considerable population concentration variation across states and districts. In addition, though there are parts of the country that have state legislative districts with high enough populations of Protestant fundamentalists to constituent a voting majority (an overall mean of 7.24 percent and a maximum of 55.3 percent), same-sex households never constitute more than a small percentage of all households in most districts (a mean of 0.57 percent and a maximum of 5.6 percent).

Turning to Republican candidates, it becomes clear that predicting where LGBT Republicans (second column) are more likely to run is more difficult, in part, because these candidates are few in number. The results of my analysis suggest that LGBT Republicans are more likely to run in districts with a more highly educated population, just as Democrats are, but other factors—such as average income, racial composition, religious orientation, and LGBT population—appear to play little or no statistically significant role. Indeed, even the time counter has no significant influence on the likelihood of an LGBT Republican running in a given district. This set of findings indicates that potential Republican LGBT candidates may simply use district education levels as a gauge for their candidacy, and ignore or downplay other district characteristics. Perhaps this is not too surprising. For a potential LGBT Republican candidate, the district characteristics that are likely to be favorable for an LGBT candidate, such as a higher LGBT population and fewer Protestant fundamentalists, are likely to be unfavorable for a Republican candidate.

The model with all candidates (third column) is similar to the model for Democratic LGBT candidates, largely because the model is driven by the higher number of LGBT Democrats in the sample. However, the results indicate that state legislative districts with a more educated population, a higher Hispanic population, and, to some degree, a higher LGBT population, are more likely to see LGBT candidates run for office. Other factors do not appear to attract LGBT candidates. In the overall model, LGBT candidates are less likely to run in districts with a higher average income, a higher African American population, and a higher Protestant fundamentalist population.

Of course, some of the district characteristics discussed suggest that some districts lean toward the Democratic Party while others lean toward Republicans. So why not simply include party registration variables? Recall that the limited availability of voter registration data means that including party registration figures leads to a significant drop in the number of districts (cases) included in the model. Nevertheless, it is illustrative to see how including party registration influences the models.

Table 3.2 displays the results for the same models from table 3.1 but includes the percentage of voters registered as Democrats in the models. The results are similar to those shown in table 3.1—LGBT candidates are more likely to run in districts with a more educated population, a lower average income, fewer African Americans, and a higher LGBT population. Interestingly, the Hispanic population appears to have little influence, whereas the Protestant fundamentalist population appears to positively increase the likelihood of an LGBT Republican candidate running in a district. Because the percentage of registered Democrats has a positive influence on the likelihood of an LGBT candidate running, especially a Democratic LGBT candidate, the influence of Protestant fundamentalists is likely confounded by its collinearity with party registration.[9]

Although they are not shown here, additional models have been estimated that include other independent variables that were available for only a subset of districts. Few of the results for these models are notable. However, the results for these models suggest that (1) LGBT candidates are no more likely to run in single-member districts versus multimember districts, (2) districts with a higher proportion of households below the poverty level are somewhat more likely to have an LGBT candidate, (3) districts with a higher proportion of the population living in urban areas are more likely to have an LGBT candidate, and (4) LGBT candidates are less likely to run in districts that have a higher proportion of their economy based in farming. This pattern is also suggestive of districts that lean Democratic and confirms the pattern that LGBT candidates are simply more likely to appear in districts that favor Democratic candidates.

Overall, this set of results indicates that the districts in which LGBT candidates seek office are different from those in which no LGBT candidates run. Consistent with the findings of chapter 2, LGBT candidates appear to be strategic in terms of where, how, and when they run for state legislative seats. Some potential candidates select residency based on the district but others may simply time their run strategically. Although many state political candidates are strategic in terms of choosing to run for office (Hamm and Moncrief 2008; Rosenthal 1998), the probable difference for LGBT candidates is that they can potentially greatly decrease their odds of being opposed by a significant proportion of voters because of their sexual orientation if they run in districts with populations that are, for example, less affluent, more educated, and less Protestant fundamentalist.

Table 3.2 Influences on the Likelihood That an LGBT Candidate Will Run in a State Legislative District; Voter Registration Included, 1992–2006

Independent Variable	Likelihood of LGBT Democratic Candidate	Likelihood of LGBT Republican Candidate	Overall Likelihood of LGBT Candidate
District average income	−.000*	−.000#	−.000**
	(.000)	(.000)	(.000)
% college educated	.081**	.155**	.094**
	(.021)	(.044)	(.019)
% African American	−.059*	−.012	−.053*
	(.019)	(.061)	(.023)
% Hispanic	−.006	−.052	−.004
	(.017)	(.074)	(.016)
% Protestant fundamentalist	.046	.348*	.094#
	(.060)	(.140)	(.053)
Same-sex households	1.323*	1.679	1.341**
	(.062)	(1.342)	(.432)
% registered Democrats	.039*	−.026	.028*
	(.016)	(.035)	(.015)
Year counter	.079	−.065	.054
	(.062)	(.136)	(.056)
Constant	−166.443	119.580	−115.065
	(123.235)	(270.595)	(111.234)
Log likelihood	−167.867	−47.790	−198.540
Pseudo R^2	.18	.22	.18
LR chi-square	72.90	27.21	88.21
Probabilty chi-square	.000	.001	.000
% correctly predicted	98.75	99.70	98.46
No. of cases	3,043	3,043	3,043

Note: Coefficients are logistic regression coefficients. Standard errors are in parentheses.
Significance levels: ** < .01; * < .05; # < .10.

Predicting Electoral Support and Election Outcomes

With the understanding that state legislative districts do not witness a random distribution of LGBT candidates, we can now examine how district and candidate characteristics influence election outcomes. If LGBT candidates are in fact more likely to run in some districts versus others, it should decrease the likelihood that a candidate's sexual orientation will have a negative influence on electoral support or election outcomes. Indeed, if LGBT candidates are very selective in choosing where, when, and how to run, they could actually perform better, on average, in elections than their heterosexual counterparts, as was suggested in chapter 2.

Table 3.3 displays the results for the models that estimate the likelihood of electoral victory for Democratic (first column) and Republican (second column) candidates. Both fit the data fairly well, and the control variables tend to perform as expected. In the model that estimates the likelihood of victory for Democratic candidates, candidates are more likely to achieve victory if they are incumbents and they are in a district with a lower average income, a higher rate of residents with a college education, fewer Protestant fundamentalists, more same-sex couples, more Hispanics, and more African Americans. Of particular importance is that LGBT candidates are more likely to achieve victory relative to their heterosexual counterparts. Although this finding is consistent with the conclusions drawn from Democratic LGBT candidates in chapter 2, it is somewhat inconsistent with the literature

Table 3.3 Influences on the Likelihood That a State Legislative Candidate Will Win the General Election, by Party, 1992–2006

Independent Variable	Democratic Candidate	Republican Candidate
LGBT candidate	.608*	−.169
	(.237)	(.746)
Incumbent candidate	3.334**	3.118**
	(.075)	(.073)
Average income	−.00001**	.00002**
	(.00000)	(.00000)
% college educated	.004#	−.015**
	(.008)	(.003)
% African American	.056**	−.043**
	(.003)	(.003)
% Hispanic	.027**	−.013**
	(.003)	(.003)
% Protestant fundamentalist	−.063**	.051**
	(.003)	(.004)
Same-sex households	.083**	.037
	(.027)	(.028)
Year counter	−.008	−.023**
	(.007)	(.008)
Constant	15.359	45.547**
	(13.884)	(15.369)
Log likelihood	−4,573.1784	−4,084.771
Pseudo R^2	.36	.33
LR chi-square	5,170.59	4,028.43
Probability chi-square	.000	.000
% correctly predicted	79.54	78.14
Number of cases	10,755	8,847

Note: Coefficients are logistic regression coefficients. Standard errors are in parentheses.
Significance levels: ** < .01; * < .05; # < .10.

on minority candidates. Recall from chapter 1 that female and minority candidates tend to perform less well in elections when they are compared with more traditional candidates, at least during the 1960s and 1970s. My results suggest that even in this relatively early era of LGBT political representation, LGBT candidates do not face a clear electoral roadblock. If one accepts the notion that LGBT candidates are being highly selective in terms of when and where they run for state legislative seats, one can then conclude that the model results simply indicate that LGBT Democratic candidates are more successful than their heterosexual counterparts in targeting districts and years in which they have an electoral advantage.

Meanwhile, the model that predicts electoral victory for Republicans (second column) provides some additional evidence. The results indicate that Republicans benefit from incumbency, a higher district income, and more Protestant fundamentalists. Those characteristics that tend to benefit Democrats do not benefit Republicans—candidates are less likely to be elected in districts with higher levels of education, more African Americans, and more Hispanics. Neither the percentage of same-sex couple households nor a candidate's sexual orientation appears to play a role in the likelihood of a Republican being elected.

At a minimum, the results suggest that LGBT Republican candidates are no more or less likely than their heterosexual peers to achieve victory. LGBT Republican candidates, like LGBT Democratic candidates, may avoid running in a district or during election cycles when their sexual orientation would be a more significant factor. It seems reasonable to conclude that for LGBT Democrats or Republicans, sexual orientation is not a systematic negative on electoral outcomes. This finding confirms the qualitative analysis from chapter 2 and is consistent with the experimental and survey data analysis, which indicate that sexual orientation is not a serious impediment to electoral victory.

To determine how robust these findings are, I estimated a number of additional models including independent variables where data for all years or districts were not available. Although not shown here, the results for these models are substantively similar to the results shown in table 3.3. Some of the more interesting findings suggest that (1) higher Democratic registration increases the likelihood of a Democratic victory, but including Democratic registration of a district also decreases the (positive) influence of a candidate's sexual orientation on the likelihood of Democratic victory; (2) Democratic female candidates in this sample are slightly more likely to be elected than their male peers; (3) spending by Democratic candidates positively increases the likelihood of their electoral victory but has no significant effect for Republicans; and (4) being a gay-versus-lesbian Democratic candidate has no significant influence on the likelihood of being elected.

In sum, a candidate's sexual orientation does not appear to decrease the likelihood of being elected to a state legislative seat and may even increase the likelihood of election for Democrats. Indeed, of the 182 LGBT Democrats in the data set, 76 percent won their races, compared with 62 percent of the heterosexual Democrats. This suggests that disentangling the impact of sexual orientation on electoral victory is not a simple story.

On the basis of the analysis in chapter 2 and the analysis in this chapter, the high rate of success for LGBT candidates suggests that potential LGBT candidates who run for state legislative seats go forward with a campaign only when they are very well positioned to win elections. If we presume that the common wisdom is consistent with the experimental research findings—that LGBT candidates are rated somewhat lower than heterosexual candidates and are somewhat less likely to receive support—potential LGBT candidates may take this "fact" into account and only pursue office when the odds appear to be in their favor. Additionally, as the poll results discussed in chapter 2 made clear, although about 25 percent of adults at the national level might not vote for a gay or lesbian candidate even if they agree on issues, this population of voters is relatively easy to identify and therefore possible to avoid. This means that some potential LGBT candidates simply see too many barriers and choose not to run. Those who perceive fewer barriers are running and are more likely to be successful. Thus, the observable bias against LGBT persons does not translate into significantly lower electoral support in the available real-world data.

The results given in table 3.4 for the final set of models support this supposition. The dependent variable is simply the percentage of the two-party vote received by major party candidates. The results mirror those displayed in table 3.3. On average, lower average income in the district, higher education, more minorities, more same-sex households, and fewer Protestant fundamentalists are associated with greater electoral support for Democratic state legislative candidates. In addition, the results for these models continue to suggest that LGBT Democratic candidates may actually have an electoral advantage, whereas LGBT Republican candidates do not face significantly less support than their heterosexual counterparts. Indeed, on average and with all other factors controlled for, LGBT Democratic candidates appear to receive higher than 7 percentage points more of the two-party vote than their heterosexual peers. Meanwhile, LGBT Republicans do not significantly differ from their heterosexual peers in terms of vote percentage achieved. Also note the influence of specific populations within a district. As the proportion of Protestant fundamentalists increases 1 percentage point, support for Democrats declines by nearly 0.5 percent, whereas support for Republicans increases by nearly 0.8 percent. And as same-sex households in a district increase by 1 percentage point, support for Democrats increases by nearly 1 percent.

To assess the robustness of these findings, I estimated a number of additional models that include independent variables where data for all years or districts were not available. Although not shown here, the results for these models are substantively similar to the results shown in table 3.4. Some of the more interesting findings indicate that (1) Democrats perform slightly better in single-member districts versus multimember districts (about 1.6 percentage points); (2) although Democratic female candidates in this sample are slightly more likely to be elected than their male peers, male candidates receive, on average, about 0.78 percent more of the two-party vote; (3) the gender of Republican candidates has no significant influence on vote percentage; (4) while minority Democrats perform somewhat better than

Table 3.4 Influences on the Percentage of the Two-Party Vote Received by State
Legislative Candidates in General Elections, by Party, 1992–2006

Independent Variable	Democratic Candidate	Republican Candidate
LGBT candidate	7.338**	−3.341
	(2.044)	(5.432)
Incumbent candidate	30.023**	25.417**
	(.470)	(.423)
Average income	−.0001**	.00005**
	(.00002)	(.00001)
% college educated	.036*	−.005
	(.017)	(.016)
% African American	.447**	−.530**
	(.013)	(.015)
% Hispanic	.173**	−.245**
	(.020)	(.018)
% Protestant fundamentalist	−.479**	.781**
	(.028)	(.027)
Same-sex households	.922**	.061
	(.271)	(.219)
Year counter	−.253**	−.297**
	(.060)	(.056)
Constant	554.662**	635.427**
	(120.354)	(110.963)
R^2	.42	.48
F	880.58	871.35
Probability F	.000	.000
No. of cases	10,773	8,375

Note: Coefficients are ordinary-least-squares regression coefficients. Standard errors are in parentheses.
Significance levels: ** < .01; * < .05; # < .10.

their white peers, race and ethnicity have no significant influence on voting percentage for Republicans; and (5) being a gay-versus-lesbian Democratic candidate has no significant influence on the percentage of the two-party vote a candidate receives.

Conclusions

In this chapter I have systematically explored the role of a candidate's sexual orientation in state legislative elections. The discussion and analysis from chapter 2 suggest that although a significant portion of the population is unlikely to support LGBT candidates, potential candidates strategically select where and when to run and thereby reduce, and perhaps negate, the role of sexual orientation in elections.

The analysis in this chapter focuses on where and when LGBT candidates run, as well as the role of candidate sexual orientation in election outcomes and electoral support by examining district-level data from state legislative general elections in ten states between 1992 and 2006. The findings allow me to draw five important conclusions.

First, the findings suggest that the distribution of LGBT candidates across state legislative districts is not random—LGBT candidates are more likely to run for state legislative office in some types of districts than others. LGBT candidates are more likely to run for office in districts where more citizens have a college education, more residents are Hispanic or LGBT, average income is somewhat lower, and there are fewer African Americans and Protestant fundamentalists. In addition there is some evidence that candidates are more likely to run in more urban districts with high Democratic Party registration. Although the data do not allow for conclusions about the extent to which LGBT candidates "select" districts, the analysis in chapter 2 and the pattern revealed here suggest that some selection process is occurring, either through the decision making of potential candidates or those who recruit them. Potential candidates likely avoid those districts that have the greatest concentration of voters who are likely to be opposed to their candidacy because of their sexual orientation.

One case illustrates this point, even though it is not in the data analysis. Utah has three openly gay or lesbian state legislators, although it is one of the most conservative Republican states in the union and seemingly one of the least likely places for LGBT candidates to run for office. All three LGBT legislators there ran as Democrats in relatively diverse urban districts that include portions of Salt Lake City. It seems likely that these legislators would not have been successful in other parts of the state or even in nearby states. But in and around Salt Lake City, they clearly saw fewer barriers to election and capitalized on the opportunity.

Second, although the historical experience of female and minority candidates suggests that LGBT candidates should also be less likely to win elections relative to their heterosexual peers, the results for models that predict election outcomes suggest that LGBT candidates are not less likely to be elected. In fact, LGBT Democratic candidates may even have a slight edge over their opponents in a general election contest. For LGBT Republicans there does not appear to be an electoral advantage or disadvantage. This does not mean that voters necessarily prefer LGBT candidates over heterosexual candidates, but it may indicate that when LGBT candidates run for state legislative office, they are in a stronger position than their heterosexual counterparts because of where they choose to run, when they run, and how they run, such as holding a lower-level office or enlisting more support before a campaign. The discussion in chapter 2 supports this perspective. Of course, this means that some potential LGBT candidates are simply not running for office because they do not perceive a favorable electoral environment or have not yet become a "quality" candidate. In this sense sexual orientation has an impact on election outcomes; it is just not the significant barrier that many have assumed it to be.

Third, this pattern also appears in an analysis of the share of the two-party vote received by candidates. Overall, LGBT candidates do not receive a lower percentage of the vote than do their heterosexual peers, and LGBT Democrats tend to receive about 7 percentage points more of the two-party vote than their heterosexual counterparts, controlling for all other factors. Interestingly, gay male candidates do not receive more support than do lesbian candidates, which suggests that there is little combined bias toward sexual orientation and gender.

Fourth, my results would likely be viewed in a positive manner by the LGBT community. Even if LGBT candidates are not particularly advantaged in the electoral process, it also appears that they are not particularly disadvantaged. This indicates that the LGBT community will not be especially disadvantaged if it seeks the political representation of its interests through the election of LGBT candidates. However, descriptive representation does not guarantee substantive representation in the policy process. We turn to this question in chapters 4 and 5.

However, a few caveats are in order. Ideally an analysis of election outcomes would examine both primary and general elections, simply because in many state legislative districts the most competitive election is the primary election. My analysis is limited to general state legislative elections and does not cover all fifty states. However, the interviews with candidates in chapter 2 suggest that for most candidates, the role of sexual orientation is similar in both primary and general elections. Nevertheless, no firm conclusions should be drawn from this analysis of primary elections or general elections outside state legislative races in the ten states examined.

In addition, my analysis does not suggest that LGBT candidates can simply run for office in any state legislative district in any state in the country; far from it. Instead, my analysis suggests that the candidates who choose to run appear to be making solid strategic choices on when, where, and how to run. And this appears to account for a higher degree of success when compared with their heterosexual peers. But this also means that some potential candidates are choosing not to run. For some potential candidates, the perceptions of voter bias might be exaggerated, while for others the perception of voter bias is real and unavoidable. Thus many potential candidates face real or exaggerated barriers to election. Because some potential candidates choose not to run, it means that LGBT representation is simply not going to occur in many places around the country.

Notes

1. Unless otherwise noted, all election data are from the respective secretaries of state and all district demographic data are from Lilley et al. (1998, 2008).

2. New Hampshire is the outlier, with 400 seats in its lower chamber.

3. The final database therefore included more states and candidates than are actually included for the analysis.

4. These data are from the respective secretaries of state or state election websites.

5. These data are from Lilley et al. (1998, 2008).

6. Ibid.

7. The data on Protestant fundamentalists are from Glenmary Research Center (2004) and cover 1990 and 2000 (all other years are imputed). Following Haider-Markel and Meier (1996), the denominations classified as Protestant fundamentalist were Churches of God,

Latter-Day Saints, Churches of Christ, Church of the Nazarene, Mennonites, Conservative Baptist Association, Missouri Synod Lutherans, Pentecostal Holiness, the Salvation Army, Seventh-Day Adventists, Southern Baptists, and Wisconsin Synod Lutherans.

8. Same-sex partner household data are from the U.S. Bureau of the Census (2003) and only measure same-sex couples living in households. The 1990 Census measure is not used because it was widely viewed as failing to count many same-sex households.

9. It is also possible that the sampling of districts for which party registration data are available is biased or has confounding effects on other variables in the model.

CHAPTER FOUR

In the Legislature: Case Studies on Political Representation and LGBT State Legislators

It is impossible to not relate to hate crimes issues, GLBT issues. It's impossible to not relate to it from sexual orientation. While it's legislation that somebody out there needs, it's also legislation that I need, that I want. In the same way that a small business person will stand up and say this is how it affects small business, I'm going to be able to stand up and say this is how it's going to affect me and my life and my sister and friends. So I will speak up to that which affects me.

—Openly lesbian Arizona state senator Paula Aboud (D)
on her role as an LGBT legislator

I think being there and being a gay legislator made a lot of people think about things that they have never had to think about in the past. . . . There were some people who came up and told me they were glad they met my partner and how nice she was. I think something like that helps people overcome, maybe a preconceived notion that they had. I hope (the session) did raise some awareness among legislators who maybe hadn't had the opportunity to work with somebody who was an openly gay person and see that I wasn't, you know, some horrible person.

—Arkansas freshman state representative Kathy Webb

A S THE QUOTATIONS ABOVE make clear, LGBT legislators believe that increased descriptive representation has a real and enduring impact on the policy process in the policymaking process. And at least some LGBT legislators believe that they play a special role in advocating for the interests of the LGBT community—that their constituents include more than simply the residents of their district. In this chapter we begin to examine LGBT substantive representation in the state policy process through the political context of several states in which LGBT legislators have been elected. The states examined in a mini-case-study format are

California, Massachusetts, Minnesota, Oregon, Virginia, and Washington. These states were selected because each has experienced the election of at least one LGBT legislator in the past fifteen years, but also because, together, they represent all regions of the country, and they differ in terms of LGBT political history, composition of the legislature, and socioeconomic characteristics. These case studies are meant to illustrate the history of LGBT politics in each of these states and to highlight the role of LGBT legislators. However, this form of analysis limits my ability to draw general conclusions, and some details about the influence of LGBT legislators on particular bills are inferred from media reports and, in some cases, interviews with legislators.

Political Representation and State Legislatures

Recall that if an elected official clearly belongs to or identifies with a particular ethnic, racial, or religious group, it can be argued that the group has achieved descriptive representation (Bratton 2002; Eulau and Karps 1977; Fox 1997; Swain 1993). If a group achieves descriptive representation, many infer that the elected official will pursue the policy interests of the group with which he or she identifies, thus achieving substantive representation (Bratton 2002; Fox 1997; Saltzstein 1989; Swain 1993; Thomas 1994). Although substantive representation also may be achieved by electing sympathetic elites (Browning, Marshall, and Tabb 1984; Haider-Markel, Joslyn, and Kniss 2000), descriptive representation is often viewed as the most reliable way to achieve substantive representation in government (Gerber, Morton, and Rietz 1998).

A considerable body of research has accumulated on the substantive representation of group interests in the policy process. For example, research on the election of blacks in urban areas has uncovered fairly consistent links between black representation and increased policy benefits to the black community, including employment and appointment opportunities as well as favorable police department policies (Browning, Marshall, and Tabb 1984; Campbell and Feagin 1977; Cole 1976; Eisinger 1982; Keech 1968; Levine 1974; Mladenka 1989; Saltzstein 1989). Research on Hispanic officials has uncovered similar patterns of substantive representation (Browning, Marshall, and Tabb 1984; Mladenka 1989), and studies of women in state legislatures suggest that increased female representation leads to an increased number and types of policy proposals relating to women (Berkman and O'Connor 1993; Bratton 2002; Norrander and Wilcox 1999; Thomas 1994).

However, one should not assume that descriptive representation leads to substantive representation simply because elected representatives that identify with a group are introducing and championing proposals that benefit the group—there may be additional dynamics at play. Indeed, simply having representatives of a group in a policymaking body may influence other decision makers' attitudes about the group and subsequent support for policy proposals related to the group (Barrett 1995, 1997; Bratton 2002; Browning, Marshall, and Tabb 1984; Hawkesworth 2003; Rayside 1998; Wahlke 1971; Yoder 1991). In a role model capacity, the elected representatives of a group may likewise influence public perceptions of the group, and public and legislator preferences concerning policies related to the group (Barrett 1995, 1997; Hawkesworth 2003; Pitkin 1967; Smith and Haider-Markel 2002). Thus, descriptive representation may increase substantive representation not only through the policy entrepreneurship activities and political skills of the official representing the group but also because that official's mere presence may influence the attitudes and behavior of other policymakers.

Interestingly, descriptive representation and its connection to substantive representation may be especially relevant to policies of concern to the LGBT community. In this policy area the debate is often peppered with moral perspectives, with political actors lobbying to gain government approval of core secular or religious values, thereby solidifying the importance of symbolism (Haider-Markel and Meier 1996; Wald, Button, and Rienzo 1996). Furthermore, as with representatives of other groups, the presence of LGBT officials may serve to undermine the arguments of opponents that are based on overblown stereotypes of LGBT people. Without the articulation of these arguments, officials may be less inclined to make decisions that oppose the policy goals of the LGBT community. This phenomenon may occur even without the direct presence of LGBT officials in public office. Indeed, Wald, Button, and Rienzo (1996) find that localities where LGBTs had simply run for public office, but failed, were more likely to adopt antidiscrimination policies. Furthermore, at least 80 percent of all local ordinances that ban discrimination based on sexual orientation were introduced and championed by heterosexual officials that sympathized with the LGBT community (Button, Rienzo, and Wald 1997).

But whether officials are descriptive representatives of a group or sympathizers with a group, they are all constrained in their policymaking roles by the context in which they operate and their individual preferences and characteristics (Fox 1997; Kingdon 1989; Sharp 1997). For example, state legislator behavior will also be driven by legislator partisan affiliation and ideology, the composition of the legislature, district and state characteristics, and public preferences, among other things (Bratton 2002; Berkman and O'Connor 1993; Cammisa and Reingold 2004). Thus, any examination of substantive representation must also account for broader forces in the policymaking process.

LGBT State Legislators and Representation

At the state level the number of LGBT legislative officials has shown a steady increase since the late 1990s. The first openly LGBT state legislators were Elaine Noble (Massachusetts House) and Allan Spear (Minnesota Senate). Noble ran for office in 1974 as an out lesbian and served two terms. Spear was first elected to the State Senate in 1972 and came out in 1974, serving until he retired in 2000. Both Spear and Noble took incredible political risks by coming out, but voters were not deterred. In addition, the first transgender state legislator in the county was Althea Garrison, elected in 1992 to the Massachusetts House of Representatives.

In 1988 there were only three sitting openly LGBT state legislators, but by 1998 there were twenty-six openly LGBT officials in sixteen states. During the November 1998 elections, sixty-one LGBT candidates ran for a variety of state and local offices around the county. Of these candidates, sixteen were incumbents seeking reelection to state offices, and twenty were LGBT candidates challenging incumbents for state offices (Freiberg 1998). By 2001 there were forty-three openly LGBT state legislators in twenty-one states, a historic high. The number jumped to seventy-eight in 2009, but this is still only 1 percent of the 7,382 seats in state legislatures. In some states, such as Rhode Island, Utah, and Montana, these officials are the only openly LGBT officials in the state, but in most states LGBT legislators emerge from a "farm team" of local elected officials.

Overall there have been more than two hundred openly gay or lesbian state legislators since 1974. Most of these officials have served in the lower legislative chamber (usually called the House or Assembly), which tends to have members from smaller districts. Furthermore, nearly all these legislators have served in urban districts, in more conservative states such as Montana, Virginia, and Utah, as well as in more liberal states such as California and Minnesota. In other states, such as Wisconsin, LGBT legislators have tended to represent areas that include major colleges and universities.

Of course, some states have seen a greater increase in LGBT legislators than others. In politically moderate New Hampshire, openly LGBT legislators formed the country's first state legislative caucus of gay and gay-friendly legislators in 1999, and these officials made a concerted effort to recruit more LGBT candidates for the 2000 election cycle. A result of these efforts was that five openly LGBT legislators sought reelection and seven more LGBT persons ran for state legislative seats. In addition, state legislator Ray Buckley claimed that four Republicans who were running were closeted (Freiberg 2000b). And in neighboring Vermont, six LGBT challenger candidates ran for the state legislature in 2000; three won their races. Conservative Utah and Montana each have had three openly LGBT legislators, with all three Utahans still serving in the 2009 legislature. In Maryland the three LGBT members of the House and one LGBT member of the Senate formed an informal LGBT caucus in 2006 to better strategize on the pursuit of LGBT civil rights legislation as well as to recruit LGBT candidates to run for office. Historically, New Hampshire has had the most LGBT legislators with ten; California, Connecticut, Massachusetts, and Maine follow with eight; Arizona, Oregon, Vermont, and Washington with seven; Rhode Island with six; and New York with five.[1]

But once they are elected, are these officials having an impact on LGBT-related policy? The anecdotal evidences suggest yes. For example, in Illinois, gay representative Larry McKeon (D-Chicago) sponsored bills in 1997 and 1998 that would have banned discrimination in employment and housing based on sexual orientation. McKeon testified before legislative committees and built a nonpartisan coalition of supportive legislators for the measures. His annual nondiscrimination measures did not pass until 2005 but throughout the legislative debate fellow legislators remarked on how his presence in the chamber over the years had made them realize how important the measure was (Victory Fund 2005).

In 2006 a number of LGBT legislators played significant roles in the consideration of LGBT-related legislation. A group of three LGBT legislators in the Maryland House of Delegates helped to defeat a constitutional amendment that would have banned same-sex marriage. In Utah Senator Scott McCoy, Representative Jackie Biskupski, and Representative Christine Johnson helped to ensure that a bill that would have banned domestic partner benefits did not move out of committee and assisted in blocking the worst anti-LGBT portions of another bill on student clubs in public schools; and in Idaho Representative Nicole LeFavour worked with other legislators to effectively block a bill that would have limited student access to gay and lesbian clubs in high schools (Stone 2006).

Colorado state senator Jennifer Veiga (D-Denver) consistently sponsored legislation to ban sexual orientation discrimination in the 2000s, and a measure concerning sexual orientation discrimination in employment eventually passed in 2007 (SB 25), whereas a measure to expand discrimination protection to housing and public accommodations (SB 200) was codified in 2008 (Barna 2008). Freshman representative Kathy Webb effectively used her position on the State House Judiciary Committee to convince her colleagues to vote against a 2007 bill that would have banned same-sex couples from adopting children in Arkansas. Webb argues that her role is not to introduce pro-LGBT legislation because she has seen such bills get nowhere in the legislature; instead she says her role is to stall or defeat anti-LGBT bills (Wiest 2007).

Iowa state senator Matt McCoy sponsored successful legislation that banned discrimination based on sexual orientation, passing the Senate by thirty-four to sixteen, and sponsored another bill that protected LGBT students in public schools in 2007. Montana's only openly LGBT legislator, State Senator Christine Kaufmann (D-Helena), sponsored bills in 2005 and 2007 to include sexual orientation in the state's antidiscrimination statutes. Both measures were supported by the governor but failed to reach his desk. And New Hampshire's historic and successful 2007 Civil Union Bill was sponsored in the House by openly gay representative James R. Splaine (D).

Although these examples are illustrative, LGBT legislators do not always pursue direct efforts at policy representation, such as sponsoring legislation or lobbying other legislators to defeat an anti-LGBT bill. In Alabama, for example, Representative Patricia Todd (D-Jefferson) participated in a "stealth campaign" to pass bills on hate crimes and reduce the bullying of LGBT students. As the House came to consider the hate crime measure, Todd says that supporters did not go to the floor to discuss the measure. Instead the bill's sponsor, Representative Alvin Holmes, had quietly informed supporters just before its consideration that it was coming, and in order to avoid mobilizing conservative opponents, they were asked not to discuss the bill on the floor. The measure passed forty-six to forty-four (Lee 2008).

Likewise in Connecticut, lesbian state representative Beth Bye chose a nonsponsorship strategy. The state began to allow civil unions in 2005 with the help of several LGBT legislators, but in 2007 Bye chose not to sponsor a measure legalizing same-sex marriage whereas two other LGBT legislators did (Senator Andrew McDonald and Representative Michael Lawlor); instead she testified before the joint House-Senate Judiciary Committee on the measure. Her tearful testimony covered her thankfulness that her devout Catholic father participated in her civil union ceremony but that when she went to complete a health care form, her choices were "married," "divorced," "widowed," "single," or "other." She said: "Forgive me if I'm not patient. I don't want to be 'other' anymore. I want to be married" (Price 2007). The bill passed the committee overwhelmingly (twenty-seven to fifteen) but was never brought up for a vote on the floor (Price 2007).[2] Bye's strategy appeared to help pass the bill from committee but it was clearly not an influential factor in the chamber.

In New York State two LGBT officials have tried to represent the LGBT community in different ways. In 2007 Senator Thomas Duane introduced his own bill to legalize same-sex marriage. Meanwhile, two LGBT legislators in the lower chamber, Representative Deborah Glick and Representative Daniel O'Donnell, decided to wait for a gubernatorial bill on the issue, which is known in New York as a program bill. Glick and O'Donnell argued that Duane's bill had been introduced every year for four years and had not made much progress. Therefore, it was time to allow the governor to set the agenda (Eleveld 2007). The disagreement on strategy points to a view of representing issues regardless of outcome versus a view of allowing others, who may have more status or a greater ability to set the agenda, to lead.

Although neither bill was ultimately successful, O'Donnell's strategy seemed to be effective in garnering support in the Assembly. He introduced the governor's program bill on same-sex marriage on May 21, 2007. At the time he had confirmed fifty-five cosponsors and seventy-one legislators pinned down as yes votes. But unless he could get eighty or more yes votes, the measure would not be allowed on the floor for a vote. All three LGBT legislators in the Assembly (O'Donnell, Glick, and Matthew Titone) worked together to line up votes (Straube 2007). Based on their efforts, the governor's program bill on same-sex marriage did eventually pass the Assembly by a wide margin but it never received a floor vote in the Senate.

In addition, sympathetic LGBT supporters, including closeted legislators, can also advocate for the interests of the LGBT community. Such actions may even lead to a reversal of events—such as when a legislator pursuing pro-LGBT policies reveals that she is a lesbian. Since the late 1990s these cases have become more frequent as state legislators have faced more bills on divisive issues such as same-sex marriage. For example, in New Jersey Assemblyman Reed Gusciora (D-Mercer) decided to reveal that he was gay after rumors circulated based on his sponsorship of a bill to allow same-sex couples government-sanctioned "civil marriage" in the state. Representative Gusciora was first elected in 1995. Of his sexual orientation he said, "I've just never made an issue of it. If someone asks me, I tell them. No one ever asked me publicly before." New Jersey Assembly speaker Joseph J. Roberts Jr. (D-Camden) said he "doubted Gusciora's acknowledgment would affect his standing in the Statehouse or his relationship with other lawmakers" (Howlett 2006).

Still, and as we saw with the candidates who are discussed in chapter 2, LGBT legislators try to avoid being seen as one-issue legislators. As Representative Karla Drenner, an environmental activist but also the only openly LGBT legislator in Georgia, explains: "That's been the most disheartening thing. I traded in the title of 'representative' for 'lesbian legislator.' . . . I don't really fit in anywhere . . . I'm still an outcast." Drenner says that some legislators in Georgia refuse to ride in the elevator with her: "I think it's especially hard in the South" (Gelineau 2005).

These vignettes reveal that although many LGBT legislators may attempt to represent the interests of the LGBT community once elected, the institutional and political context in which they operate may limit or prohibit their opportunities to represent the interests of the LGBT community. To better explain the representation process, we turn to more detailed case studies, beginning with California.

California

California is frequently viewed as a progressive policy innovator, and it is also nationally known for its politically active gay community. Its legislature is one of the most professionalized in the country; it has a long session, high legislator compensation, and a high degree of staff support. Legislators are also more diverse than in most parts of the country; about 5 percent are African American, 25 percent are female, and 25 percent are Latino.

California is one of the first states to address gay rights questions through the ballot initiative process, and the only state to propose restrictive, even draconian, measures for persons with AIDS. The state leads the nation with the most elected and appointed LGBT officials, with 116 in 2008 (Pennsylvania is a distant second, with 37) (La Corte 2008). But before the 1990s the state legislature considered little gay-related legislation, gay activists had only a few legislative successes, and no gay or lesbian official was elected to the state legislature.[3] One notable success was the early passage of a hate crime measure in 1984, which was strengthened based on law enforcement support and lobbying by local officials in 1987. By 2008 California had seen more pro- and anti-LGBT legislative activity than perhaps any other state in the country—between 1992 and 2007, at least 303 pro-LGBT bills and 92 anti-LGBT bills were introduced.

In 1993 and 1994, the number of progay bills introduced in California increased from one or two per year to more than ten per year. As the first LGBT legislator in the state, Representative Sheila Kuehl (D) played a significant role in this increase, sponsoring or cosponsoring many gay-related bills, and lobbying for others that she did not introduce. She was the first LGBT person elected to the San Diego City Council, and she used that position as a springboard to the state legislature. As she had done on the San Diego City Council, she immediately began to introduce legislation that would expand LGBT rights in the state but several conservative legislators made sure that those bills died and publicly "denounced her 'unnatural' lifestyle" (Warren 2001).

Conservative Republicans also began to pursue a same-sex marriage ban after Kuehl entered the legislature. The first ban attempt began in late 1995, when Assembly member Pete Knight (R-Palmdale) introduced AB 1982. Before key committee votes were taken, religious conservatives heavily lobbied Republican legislators to pass the ban (Haider-Markel 2001b). AB 1982 did pass the Assembly, forty-one to thirty-one, and only Democrats voted against it. In the Senate Judiciary Committee, the bill was all but killed by Kuehl and other Democrats when a "poison pill" amendment was attached that would have provided gay couples with domestic partner status (Gunnison 1996; Keen 1996). With the amendment attached, Democratic leaders and gay groups were convinced that Republican legislators would not support the bill (Keen 1996) but it passed through committee (Gunnison 1996). On the Senate floor Republicans tried to strip the amendment but failed; the bill was then sent to the "inactive" file (Keen 1996).

Immediately following the death of AB 1982, Republicans began pushing SB 2075, another bill intended to ban same-sex marriages. This bill had originally passed the Senate without the ban but in the Assembly Republicans removed the original, unrelated language and added the ban in committee (Keen 1996). In a largely party-line vote, the bill passed the Assembly forty-two to thirty-one but Kuehl worked with other Democrats to stall its return to the Senate for concurrence by using a parliamentary device (Times Staff 1996). The bill reached the Senate Judiciary Committee in August but it saw no action and died with the end of the session. In 1997 two measures to ban same-sex marriage failed in committee votes (Haider-Markel 2001).[4]

But Representative Kuehl's first major battle on pro-LGBT legislation came in 1997, when she introduced AB 101, which would have banned discrimination bias based on sexual orientation in school employment, curricula, and the treatment of students on campus. Conservative legislators had defeated a similar bill sponsored by Kuehl in 1996 (AB 1001), and in 1997 they coordinated their efforts with conservative religious groups such as the Traditional Values Coalition (Weintraub 1997). Kuehl was able to steer the bill through the Assembly Education Committee before it failed in a vote on the Assembly floor, by thirty-six to forty (Weintraub 1997).[5] Kuehl also sponsored a historic 1999 antibullying bill that provided protection for LGBT students in elementary and high schools. The measure was opposed by the Traditional Values Coalition, which provided the governor's office with 20,000 signatures against it. During the legislative debate Assembly Republicans held up the Bible and declared "homosexuality an abomination" (Warren 2001). However, Kuehl's influence in the now-Democratic-controlled chamber helped to ensure eventual passage.

Kuehl was assisted in her 1996 and 1997 legislative efforts by openly lesbian representative Carol Migden, who had been elected in a special May 1996 election. Migden represented a San Francisco district until term limits forced her out in 2002. Throughout her tenure she sponsored or cosponsored a series of bills that would protect the rights of gays and lesbians, including a 1999 bill to cement antidiscrimination laws in employment and housing and establish a state domestic partner registry.

In 1998 the state replaced its Republican governor with a pro-LGBT Democrat, Governor Gray Davis. Kuehl and Migden capitalized on these changes by introducing and passing more LGBT-friendly legislation than ever before. When Kuehl ran for and was elected to a seat in the State Senate in 2000, two additional out lesbians, Jackie Goldberg (D-45) and Christine Kehoe (D-76), were elected to seats in the State Assembly. During the 2000 primary election, California voters adopted an initiative that would ban same-sex marriage (Proposition 22). This event led LGBT legislators to pursue a statutory change that would allow civil unions for same-sex partners. In 2001 the growing number of LGBT legislators, lead by Migden, spearheaded the adoption of AB 25, which provided more benefits for domestic partners than any law except Vermont's civil unions law (Warren 2001).

In office Kehoe consistently cosponsored legislation that would allow same-sex marriages. And she took an active role in establishing the first formal gay caucus in any state legislature in the country. But she developed an image that allowed her to be viewed as a legislator rather than a lesbian legislator; as one observer saw it, "she takes as much pride in pushing legislation to create the San Diego River Conservancy as she does in helping secure a new policy that requires state contractors to provide benefits to same-sex domestic partners" (Gardner 2004). She served as speaker pro tempore in the Assembly and ran for the Senate in 2004. She won the 23rd District seat and was reelected in 2008.

As Migden stepped down from her Assembly seat in 2002 because of term limits, the first two openly gay men were elected to the State Assembly, John Laird (D–Sacramento) and Mark Leno (D-3). Laird served as chairman of the Assembly Budget Committee until term limits forced him out at the end of 2008, and he focused much of his energy there. Of the eighty-two bills he sponsored that were signed into law, only five expanded protections for the LGBT community but he considered these to be important accomplishments (Henshaw 2008).

In late 2003 the same-sex marriage debate resurfaced as the State Supreme Judicial Court of Massachusetts issued a decision that allowed same-sex marriages or the legal equivalent. In part as a reaction to this decision, San Francisco mayor Gavin Newsome began to grant marriage licenses to same-sex couples in the city. When these licenses were nullified by the courts in 2004, LGBT legislators began to pursue a statutory change that would allow same-sex marriages. When it was first introduced by Representative Leno, he had lined up support for the measure (AB 19) from Assembly speaker Fabian Nuñez, thirty other legislators, and a number of high-profile statewide Democratic officeholders. Leno had been able to push the bill through two legislative committees in 2004 but set the bill aside until after the November elections (Matier and Ross 2004). However, a nearly identical 2005 measure (AB 849) received a bare majority in both chambers, only to be vetoed by Governor Arnold Schwarzenegger. Leno had built a coalition of some 250 organizations to support the bill and lobbied his fellow legislators. He used the same strategy in 2006 and 2007 but he picked up forty-one coauthors across both chambers and more votes because he was able to argue effectively that none of the 2005 supporters had suffered electorally in 2006. The 2007 measure passed both chambers but was again vetoed by Governor Schwarzenegger (Perry 2007).

In 2006 the future of California's LGBT Legislative Caucus began to look bleak. Legislative term limits for sitting legislators were about to force a decline in LGBT representation. The caucus chair, Representative Jackie Goldberg (D–Los Angeles), was being forced out by term limits in 2006, and the lesbian candidate she recruited to run for her seat, Elena Popp, lost her Democratic primary race (Bajko 2006). Three other members of the caucus would be term-limited out of office in 2008. Other LGBT candidates in 2006 were also doing poorly—for instance, Ron Oden, the gay mayor of Palm Springs, lost a close race for the 80th Assembly District seat.

In 2007 LGBT legislators were still dominating the debate over LGBT issues in the legislature. Of the fourteen pro-LGBT related bills in 2007, eight were sponsored by LGBT legislators. These included SB 518, Migden's bill to protect LGBT youth in the criminal justice system; SB 777, Kuehl's proposal to protect LGBT students in public schools and ban curricula that discriminate against LGBT people; AB 43, Leno's same-sex marriage measure; SB 105, Migden's measure to allow California registered domestic partners to file joint tax returns; SB 559, Kehoe's bill to reverse discriminatory tax increases for domestic partners; AB 14, Laird's proposal to strengthen fifty-one existing state antibias laws for LGBT people; and SJR 6, Kehoe's resolution urging Congress and the president to repeal the federal "Don't Ask, Don't Tell" policy for the military. Of the fourteen measures, eleven became state policy. The pattern was similar in 2008, with nine pro-LGBT bills introduced. Of these, six were introduced by LGBT legislators and five became state policy. Of the bills that failed, two passed the legislature but were vetoed by the governor. Meanwhile, the four anti-LGBT bills introduced in 2007 and three anti-LGBT bills introduced in 2008 never received a floor vote in either chamber.

LGBT legislators in California have also held important posts in the legislature, and some have built strong alliances with the governor's office. Migden served as chairwoman of the powerful Assembly Appropriations Committee, and she was annually named "one of the hardest-working and most influential legislators" by *California Journal*. Kuehl built strong relationships with the governor and quickly won the trust of Senate leader John Burton. Kehoe held the post of assistant speaker pro tempore, which meant that she was often able to run Assembly floor sessions. The three become known as the "Lavender Caucus," and their influence was spread across a range of issues, including energy and crime, not simply LGBT-related legislation (Warren 2001).

In 2008 Leno was term-limited out of office and challenged Migden (D-3) for her seat. Leno won but there was no net LGBT representation gain in the Senate. For the Assembly races, Tom Ammiano (D-13) captured Leno's former seat, and John Perez (D) took the seat in the 46th District.[6] Kehoe was reelected to the State Senate. Thus, following the 2008 elections, there were only four LGBT legislators but they were divided between the Senate and Assembly, which brought an end to the LGBT Caucus in the Assembly (four members are required for an official caucus).

As the 2009 session began, the passage of Proposition 8 the previous November, which is a constitutional amendment that bans same-sex marriage, weighed heavily on the remaining legislators. Early in the session only three pro-LGBT bills had been introduced but the future of each was uncertain. Having been elected to the Senate in November 2008, Leno reintroduced a bill to declare May 22 as Harvey Milk Day in the state. Leno had sponsored the bill in the Assembly in 2008 only to see it vetoed by the governor. Leno and Representative Ammiano also each introduced identical, nonbinding resolutions (SR 7 and HR 5) that "would make it official state policy that Proposition 8 was an invalid revision to the California Constitution. It would also set forth that any change to the Constitution that would eliminate a fundamental right from a minority group must be passed by the Legislature before being placed on the ballot" (Rojas 2009). Leno also introduced a late bill that would officially recognize the marriages performed for same-sex couples in other states before the passage of Proposition 8. His Harvey Milk Day bill and his same-sex marriage bill were signed by the governor in October 2009.

Overall, the number of progay bills introduced in the California legislature increased significantly, rising from two in 1990, to seven in 1994, to twenty-seven in 1997, to thirty-two in 1999, to eleven in 2001, to twenty-four in 2003, and to fourteen in 2007. The number of progay bills introduced, as well as the number that passed, coincide directly with the increasing number of openly LGBT legislators who were elected in the 1990s and early 2000s.

However, increasing descriptive representation for the gay community has not come without a price. Even representatives who have worked directly with legislators, such as Kuehl, worried about the increase in LGBT legislators (Warren 2001). Before the 1990s the number of anti-LGBT bills introduced in the state legislature did not average even one per year. But following the election of Kuehl in 1992 and Migden in 1996, the number of anti-LGBT bills introduced began to dramatically increase—one was introduced in 1995, ten in 1996, twelve in 1997, seventeen in 1998, and six and seven in 1999 and 2000, respectively. The number of anti-LGBT bills decreased to two in 2001 but jumped back to nine in 2002. In 2003 and 2004 only three anti-LGBT measures were introduced but the number jumped to seven for each year from 2005 to 2007 as legislators returned to the issues of same-sex marriage and topics such as homosexuality in the public school systems. The pattern suggests that there is a connection between LGBT electoral victories and legislation but this pattern indicates that increases in gay representation are associated with increases in anti-LGBT legislation. This pattern will be explored systematically as backlash in chapter 6.

In summary, for the case of California, the evidence suggests that openly LGBT legislators can achieve substantive representation of the LGBT community by sponsoring or cosponsoring LGBT-related legislation and by advocating for the LGBT community on pro-LGBT legislation introduced by other legislators. LGBT legislators also represent the LGBT community in California by blocking or reducing the impact of anti-LGBT legislation. However, an increased presence of LGBT legislators also appears to be associated with an increase in anti-LGBT legislation, which suggests a pattern of backlash. In addition, LGBT legislators in California must contend with a nonlegislative institution, the initiative process, which can thwart their representation efforts.

Massachusetts

For decades Massachusetts has been viewed as a very liberal enclave in a generally liberal region of the country. The legislature is also highly professionalized, ranking number four in the country (Hamm and Moncrief 2008). Female representation in the legislature is high at around 25 percent but minority groups are not well represented. Massachusetts would seem to be a prime location for LGBT candidates for state office. Indeed, two gay members of Congress have hailed from Massachusetts, former representative Gerry Studds and current representative Barney Frank. Both men were elected to the U.S. House and later came out while in office. As of the 2008 elections, nine LGBT legislators have served in the state, with five still serving in 2009. Although Massachusetts was not an early leader on LGBT rights at the state level, beginning in the 1989, when the state added sexual orientation to its antidiscrimination laws, state action on LGBT issues occurred more rapidly than it did in most other states. With a scattering of pro-LGBT bills before 1995 and no anti-LGBT bills introduced in more than a decade, twelve pro-LGBT bills were introduced in 1995. In 1996 two bills, HB 5191 and SB 165, were introduced to expand the state's 1979 hate crimes law to include sexual orientation. The measure also added protection for persons with HIV/AIDS to the relatively comprehensive law. A final version was signed by the governor in July 1996. Following this action it would be almost ten years before any pro-LGBT legislation became law.

Each subsequent session saw several pro-LGBT bills introduced, with an explosion of twenty-nine in 2001. The number of bills dropped to a steady stream of a half dozen through the first decade of the 2000s. But anti-LGBT legislation also grew, with no bills before 1995, two in 1995, eight in 1999, and fifteen in 2001. In the following years anti-LGBT bills focused on same-sex marriage, especially in 2004 and 2005. As was the case in California, both pro- and anti-LGBT legislation increased as more LGBT candidates were elected to the legislature. Notably, in November 2003 Massachusetts became the first state in the country to allow, and not rescind, same-sex marriage when the Supreme Judicial Court ruled (*Goodridge v. Department of Public Health*) that the state could not legally deny marriage licenses to same-sex couples and gave the legislature 180 days to change state statutes.[7] The *Goodridge* decision drove much of the LGBT-related legislation from 2004 to 2007.

Massachusetts was home to the first openly LGBT person directly elected to a state legislature in the country. Elaine Noble, a community activist from Boston, ran as an out lesbian in 1974 and won. In a 2007 interview she described the campaign and taking a seat in the state legislature:

> I was emotionally and physically exhausted. . . . There were people all over the country calling and asking if I would come and speak. They'd say "Well, you have a responsibility to a bigger constituency." I was pulled a thousand different ways. . . . [In the legislature] it really got harder in terms of the threats and being a target that was readily available to people. One day, I was walking to the State House and there was a guy, 85 years old, and he walked up and said, "Representative Noble." And I reached up to shake his hand and he spit on me. And then I turned around and he started doing his diatribe. I walked all the way home and showered and changed my clothes. So even walking to work or riding my bike to work was not terribly safe. (Nichols 2007)

Noble did little to advocate for the LGBT community in terms of formal legislative activity, in part because she became overwhelmed with the position. In fact, her stress over the position, and perhaps the assassination of Harvey Milk (of the San

Francisco Board of Supervisors), led her to retire her seat after two terms (Nichols 2007).

The next LGBT legislator to serve in the state was also a first. In 1992 Althea Garrison (R-5) became the first transgender person to be elected to a state legislature, and she appears to have been the first LGBT Republican elected to a state legislature. However, she was not entirely open about being transgender and appears to have been outed in a *Boston Globe* article. She did not have a notable term in the legislature and lost her seat to a Democrat in 1994 (Smith and Haider-Markel 2002).

In 1998 Elizabeth Malia (D-11) was first elected to the State House in a special March election after her boss, the current seat holder, resigned to take a teaching position. Then in November Jarrett Barrios was also elected to the State House (D-28), making him the first openly gay man elected to the legislature. Malia was reelected to her seat through the 2008 election. Malia led a legislative fight to obtain domestic partner benefits in 2001, but she is probably best known for her work on children's health and crime issues. In fact, some have suggested that she did not really come out as a lesbian legislator until 2004, following the first round of voting on three constitutional amendments to ban same-sex marriage, which the constitutional convention established because of the *Goodridge* decision (Kiritsy 2004).

In 2007 and 2008 Malia was in the forefront of a push to pass the MassHealth Equality bill, a measure that requires equal treatment of same-sex and opposite-sex married couples in the administration of the MassHealth insurance program (Jacobs 2008b). Aided by the mobilization of the LGBT community on same-sex marriage in 2005 and 2006, Malia was able to move the bill forward in 2008, having failed in 2007. In the last months of the 2008 session, she convinced House speaker Sal DiMasi to prioritize the measure and obtained a floor vote. One observer suggested that several factors contributed to the successful adoption of the bill, one being "Liz Malia making it her number one commitment." Malia herself attributed part of the success on the MassHealth measure, as well as the repeal of a law banning marriages of nonresidents, to the visible profile of LGBT legislators. She said, "I think we've humanized [the issue in] the legislature in the past few years, and with us being LGBT folks a lot of the mythology has been lost and buried in the same way it has in society at large and in Massachusetts" (Jacobs 2008b).

Meanwhile, Barrios served two terms in the House and ran for the Senate in 2002. During his tenure in the House he played a central role in blocking Representative John Rogers's (R) legislative proposals to ban same-sex marriage in the state (HB 472 and SB 3375). Barrios also played key roles in moving domestic partner legislation out of committee in 2001 and 2002 but he did not sponsor any of the legislation (Kiritsy 2002). However, in the House he took positions that sometimes differed from those of LGBT activists, including providing political support to the speaker of the House, who often refused to allow LGBT-related legislation to reach the House floor, and in pursuing a strategy of revising domestic partner legislation to include more than same-sex couples, but also opposite-sex couples and blood relatives (Kiritsy 2002), a strategy that has been pursued in many other states.

In June 2000 state senator Cheryl Jacques (D) came out as a lesbian. She had first been elected in 1992, and she continued to be reelected after coming out. She has been credited with the inclusion of sexual orientation in the state hate crimes law in 1996, but at the time she was not public about her sexual orientation. She has also been noted for her work on children's issues, AIDS, and gun control. In 2001 she ran unsuccessfully for the U.S. House in the 9th District. From 2000 to 2003 she sponsored or cosponsored a number of bills that address the needs of LGBT youth and of persons with HIV/AIDS. She has been described as "a prominent advocate for gay rights" in the legislature, and in 2003 she sponsored the first bill ever introduced in the state to legalize same-sex marriage. At the same time she used her position on the Joint Committee on the Judiciary to oppose attempts to ban same-sex marriage. In April 2003 she made a personal appeal to her colleagues on the committee, arguing that "we serve side by side. Many of you are friends of mine. Explain to me how in any way my partner Jenn and our two little boys Tommy and Timmy threaten your family." The impact of her appeal is unclear, but the ban did not pass. She served through 2003, when she left to head the Human Rights Campaign, the largest national LGBT group in the country (Rapp 2003).

Barrios became the first Latino and LGBT person elected to the State Senate in 2001. He served until 2007, when he resigned to become president and chief executive officer of the Blue Cross Blue Shield of Massachusetts Foundation (Kiritsy 2007). Throughout his time in the legislature, he was a highly visible advocate for LGBT rights, public safety issues, health care for poor people, and the rights of immigrants.

As a member of the Senate Barrios worked with a small group to develop and implement a strategy to first comply with the court decision on same-sex marriage and also thwart legislators and activists who wanted to overturn the decision.[8] The initial legislative response was a joint convening of both chambers during the 2003–4 session to consider a constitutional change. The joint meeting resulted in a proposal for a constitutional amendment that would have banned same-sex marriage and allowed civil unions. However, the state constitution requires that constitutional amendments must be approved by a joint session in two consecutive sessions. When the joint session convened during the 2005–6 legislative session, Barrios and others were able to maneuver a procedural defeat of the proposal—putting the convention in recess without taking a final vote on the measure—and ensure that the measure did not go to voters for final approval or defeat (Kiritsy 2007). Representative Carl Sciortino gave an impassioned speech against the amendment during the debate and relayed his own story of coming out to his family and the broader struggle for LGBT rights. He added in reference to his own presence in the legislature: "I would not be here if my own district had not said no to discrimination" (Dower 2005).

Before the recess vote, hesitant but sympathetic legislators were provided with political cover in a procedural maneuver. Rather than vote on the citizen-proposed main constitutional measure, which would only take 50 votes to pass, the convention first considered a different amendment to ban same-sex marriage that had been introduced in 2005 by a legislator. Because the measure had been introduced by a legislator and not by a citizen group, it would take 101 votes to pass. That measure was defeated. Arline Isaacson, cochairwoman of the Massachusetts Gay and Lesbian Political Caucus, said the strategy was to provide a means that legislators "can all point to the fact that they fully debated same-sex marriage and took a vote on it," but the main measure could still be defeated on the procedural move for a recess rather than an actual vote on substance (Belluck 2006). The final blow for the attempt to overturn *Goodridge* came in 2007. The marriage amendment was defeated by a vote of 151 to 45 (with 50 needed) in the June 14, 2007, second joint session of the state legislature meeting in a constitutional convention.

In reference to Barrios's role in defeating legislative efforts to overturn the 2003 *Goodridge* decision in 2007, his colleagues referred to him as "one of the leaders in a historic fight in the building and in the Commonwealth." Phil Johnston, the former chair of the state Democratic Party said: "I can tell you this, as somebody who served in the legislature for a long time, I don't think that gay and lesbian citizens would have the right to be married had it not been for Senator Jarrett Barrios" (Kiritsy 2007).

One of Senator Barrios's final successes in the 2008 legislative session was to sponsor SB 800, which repealed a state law that bans nonresidents from being able to legally marry within Massachusetts. LGBT activists had been pushing for the change because LGBT nonresidents were unable to take advantage of the state's legalization of same-sex marriage. Barrios secured passage by voice vote in the Senate, and the House passed the measure by a roll call vote of 119 to 36 in July at the end of the legislative session.

Another LGBT legislator, Carl M. Sciortino Jr. (D-34), was first elected to the State House in 2004. In the primary he barely eked out a win against the incumbent, Vincent Ciampa, an opponent of same-sex marriage. In fact, Sciortino ran for the seat because his sitting representative refused to support same-sex marriage following the *Goodridge* decision. The victory was an indication of support for same-sex marriage in the state (Kiritsy 2008). He was reelected in 2006 and 2008.[9]

In 2005 Sciortino was able to speak to his fellow legislators on the floor for the state constitutional convention on same-sex marriage. Although that first vote put the measure forward, he fulfilled a central goal of running for the office. From 2005 to 2008 he was a strong advocate in the legislature for strengthening youth LGBT programs and ensuring funding for HIV/AIDS. Of particular importance, he cosponsored the first transgender civil rights legislation in the state during the 2008 session. The bill (HB 1722), which died in committee but had twenty-five cosponsors, would have added transgender-inclusive language to the state's antidiscrimination and hate crimes laws. In March 2008 he "organized testimony for the Judiciary Committee hearing on the bill, the first legislative hearing focused on trans issues in the state's history" (*Bay Windows* 2008).

Sarah K. Peake (D-4) also first ran for the legislature in 2004 in large part because the incumbent refused to support the *Goodridge* decision, but her bid against an incumbent was unsuccessful (Kiritsy 2008). In 2006 the incumbent stepped down and Peake was able to defeat opponents in the primary and general election in what is a traditionally Republican district. Peake has focused on affordable housing, veterans' affairs, and home rule designations for local government (Desroches 2007). She was able to vote against the constitutional amendment banning same-sex marriage in 2007 and a vote for repeal of the law banning nonresident marriages in 2008. During her 2008 race voters were more concerned with the economy than with LGBT issues but she accused her opponent of trying to make an issue of her sexual orientation during the contest (Jacobs 2008a). She was reelected in 2008.

Finally, the most recent freshman LGBT legislator in the Massachusetts House is Kate Hogan, who ran for the 3rd District seat when the incumbent stepped down in 2008. With the endorsement of the former incumbent, Hogan was able to overcome her Republican opponent in a fairly conservative district. As she took office in 2009, the central LGBT issues in the legislature were the passage of a bill to add gender identity and expression to the state's nondiscrimination and hate crimes laws (similar measures had died in the 2007–8 session) and to ensure that LGBT and HIV/AIDS programs were not cut. Hogan did not sponsor the transgender bill; instead, it was again sponsored by the openly gay Sciortino. As in many states for the 2009 session, severe budget cuts greatly reduced the expansion of any laws or programs that would increase costs (Jacobs 2009).

Recent history in Massachusetts suggests that as LGBT descriptive representation increases, LGBT legislators are able to effectively translate that presence into substantive representation in the policy process. The events surrounding the *Goodridge* decision and the efforts by LGBT legislators to ensure that the decision was not overturned through a constitutional amendment provide one of the most dramatic examples of how substantive representation can occur. In addition, while increases in anti-LGBT legislation were also associated with the increase in LGBT legislators in the state, backlash to the *Goodridge* decision appears to have been the main driver. The Massachusetts case also makes it clear that LGBT legislators take different paths to pursuing substantive representation, with some legislators acting as bill sponsors and others operating in the background.

Minnesota

Minnesota is a medium-sized midwestern state notable for progressive politics and progressive leaders on both sides of the political aisle. Its legislature is considered to be a hybrid, between citizen and professional. Female representation in the legislature is very high, at about 35 percent, but minority groups are not well represented. Like its neighbor, Wisconsin, Minnesota was a relatively early adopter of laws protecting LGBT civil rights, and the LGBT community has a long history in local politics. Minnesota's position as an earlier adopter of LGBT legislation was possible partly because of notable LGBT legislators, including Senator Allen Spear and Representative Karen Clark, both Democrats, but the state also has seen a relatively rare Republican LGBT legislator in Senator Paul Koering.[10]

The trends in LGBT-related legislation follow the legislative careers of Spear and Clark, but also the national battles over same-sex marriage in the mid-1990s and early 2000s. Minnesota had some significant LGBT legislation considered before the 1990s, but following the national pattern, LGBT-related legislation increased considerably during the 1990s. There was a significant burst in LGBT-related legislation in 1996, with six pro-LGBT bills and three anti-LGBT bills introduced before the legislature. In 1997 the number of pro-LGBT bills increased to twelve, with seven passing, and anti-LGBT bills increased to thirteen, mostly focused on banning same-sex marriage. From 1997 on, the LGBT-related legislation stabilized until 2001, when another burst occurred, with twenty pro-LGBT bills and ten anti-LGBT introduced. Throughout the early 2000s the number of LGBT-related bills steadied at about four on either side per session, with a brief burst at thirteen both pro and anti in 2006. These patterns are based in large part on the activities of LGBT legislators in the state, the emergence of same-sex marriage as a national issue, and, apparently for some of the anti-LGBT legislation, in reaction to the legislative activities of the state's LGBT legislators.

There have been two towering LGBT legislators in Minnesota—Spear and Clark. First elected in 1972, Spear (D) retired in 2000 after serving for twenty-six years in the State Senate. He publicly announced his sexual orientation in 1974 while serving his first term. At the time there was only one other openly LGBT state legislator in the country, Elaine Noble in Massachusetts. Spear served as a liberal member of the Minnesota Democratic Farmer-Labor Party (DFL) but had the respect of all legislators. When he came out in 1974, he told a newspaper reporter how "lousy" he had felt in 1973 as the legislature debated a gay civil rights bill and he remained silent (Grow 2000). He served for twenty-six years as an openly LGBT state senator, which makes him the longest-serving elected LGBT official in the country thus far. He was perhaps best known for witty and educational speeches, and he became a policy wonk in the area of criminal justice, but throughout his career he was a key advocate in the legislature for LGBT rights. In fact, he began his initial attempts to amend the state's Human Rights Act to include sexual orientation in the late 1970s following the efforts of others (Dunbar 2008).

Senator Spear was joined in the legislature in 1981 by lesbian representative Karen Clark, following her election as a DFL candidate for the State Assembly 61a seat. She did not hide her sexual orientation during the 1980 election and has continued to be reelected in every cycle through 2008. She is now the longest-serving lesbian state legislator in the country. She worked on many local and progressive issues through the 1980s, but in 1987 Spear joined forces with her to repeal Minnesota's sodomy law. But even though the effort had a full-time lobbyist, it failed.

In 1988 Spear was the primary sponsor of S 2183, which would have added sexual orientation to the state's 1983 hate crimes law. He had included sexual orientation in the original 1983 bill but the language was stripped before it passed both chambers. During the 1988 legislative session he pushed for a law that would require Minnesota police departments to collect statistics on bias crimes and a separate law to enhance criminal penalties for bias crimes. The hate crime statistics bills, H 2340 and S 2124, were cosponsored by Spear and Representative Howard Orenstein (Berrill 1992). Facing opposition from several conservative legislators, the bills' sexual orientation clause was changed to "characteristics identified as sexual orientation." After the compromise S 2124 passed sixty-four to zero and H 2324 passed 125 to 1.

However, Spear's and Clark's hate crimes bills to enhance criminal penalties and include sexual orientation (H 2368 and S 2183) faced more serious opposition. A right-wing group called the Berean League convinced a number of conservative legislators that the bills provided "special rights" to gays and lesbians. Nevertheless, S 2183 passed easily in the Senate by forty-seven to seven. The House voted to remove the sexual orientation clause but the motion failed in a vote of sixty-one to sixty. In an effort to appease House conservatives, attempts were made to extend the groups protected, including prolife persons and National Rifle Association members. House conservatives responded by introducing an amendment that removed all categories and substituted the phrase "with hatred or prejudice against the person assaulted." Spear and others considered the language too vague and withdrew the bill even though it had passed. In 1989 Spear pursued the original 1988 bills, which were reintroduced and quickly passed when much of the opposition was diffused in a nonelection year (Berrill 1992). Spear also used his committee chair position to expand police training programs on hate crimes and even allow for hate crimes civil suits by 1996.

Spear's position was enhanced in 1993 when his colleagues elected him president of the Senate. But he thought that one of his greatest victories was the passage of a comprehensive civil rights law in 1993 that included sexual orientation as well as gender orientation. He sponsored the bill in the Senate, and Clark sponsored the bill in the House. During debate on the bill, some state senators continued to argue that the law was unnecessary because "homosexuality is a choice, not a condition of birth." Spear responded with a speech on the Senate floor in which he pointed out: "Let me tell you, I'm a 55-year-old gay man and I am not just going through a phase. I can also assure you that my sexual orientation is not something I chose, like choosing to wear a blue shirt and a red tie today" (Grow 2000).

Some suggest that Spear's greatest contribution was as a role model of a gay person. As one legislator described it, Spear "did a great job in the educating process. Homosexuality was something I'd barely heard of in my little town. It wasn't talked about. Here we had Allan Spear. He was a good person, no different from the rest of us. We all needed that education" (Grow 2000). Clark had worked closely with Spear on the bill, and after his death in 2008 she recalled working with him:

> For twenty years Allan and I served together in the Minnesota legislature, the only openly gay state legislators in the country for the first six. Allan was a good friend and also a trusted legislative ally I could go to for thoughtful advice. His unwavering commitment to civil rights and to economic and social justice for all ran deep, reflected Allan's own high standards for personal and professional integrity, and earned him the respect not only of his constituents and colleagues here, but also throughout the nation. Time and again we teamed up, especially for those who lacked a voice at the Minnesota Capitol. One of my proudest moments was emerging victorious from the House Chamber in the spring of 1993, hand in hand with Allan after the House voted to outlaw discrimination against LGBT people in Minnesota.[11]

Spear and Clark were also active in opposing anti-LGBT legislation. Clark helped to remove antigay language from an education bill (HF 1000) in 1995, and Spear and Clark played a role in defeating 1996 bills that would have limited damages sought for discrimination based on sexual orientation, along with a bill that would have banned homosexuals from 4-H clubs.

Although they were unable to defeat it, Spear and Clark were also effective in delaying the state's adoption of a ban on same-sex marriage over a two-year period. The main proponent of a ban in 1996, Representative Tom Van Engen, successfully attached an amendment (SF 2067) in committee, but the bill failed to reach the House floor. In a final effort, Van Engen tried to attach an amendment to SF 1996 that would ban same-sex marriage. However, the majority DFL Party killed the amendment in a party-line vote of sixty-eight to sixty-three. In 1997 Republicans successfully passed a same-sex marriage ban but only after ten failed attempts. In April the deadline for all bills to pass their first committee had been reached, meaning that proponents of a ban could only amend existing bills. The Republicans in the House were able to successfully amend the ban to a Democrat-supported health and human services appropriations bill, SF 1908. The Democrats had a difficult time opposing their own social welfare bill, and their effort to remove the amendment on the House floor failed. Without the efforts of Spear and Clark, a ban on same-sex marriage would have likely passed in 1996.

In 2007 Clark cosponsored legislation (HF 1618) that would have allowed state employees to provide health care benefits to their domestic partners. The bill never received a floor vote in the House. However, a version of her cosponsored bill (HF 1589) to allow hospital visitation rights for domestic partners did eventually pass. In 2008 she cosponsored legislation (HF 4248) that would have effectively recognized same-sex marriages. The bill never made it out of committee. She also cosponsored HF 3478, which would have enhanced the ability of aggrieved parties of discrimination to engage in civil law suits. She also worked to pass HF 219 and HF 1812, which would have provided some domestic partner benefits, but both measures stalled under a threatened gubernatorial veto. Likewise, her cosponsored measure (HF 615) to enhance sex education in public schools, especially for LGBT youth, died under the threat of a gubernatorial veto. She was reelected in 2008, and she is now the longest-serving openly lesbian official in any office in the country.

As Spear retired from the Senate, Scott Dribble (DFL-60B) was elected to the Assembly in 2000. After one term Dribble ran for Spear's District 60 seat in the Senate and was elected; he was reelected in 2006. Dribble has focused much of his attention on economic development, health, poverty, and environmental issues, but he has also taken some notable actions on LGBT issues. During the 2004 to 2006 sessions he played a key role to block an attempt to amend the state Constitution to ban same-sex marriage. Clark, who also worked hard to block the bans, said of the measure following its first hearing in 2004: "It hurts GLBT families, who are an important part of our community here in Minnesota. . . . It's a very dangerous bill, and would enshrine bigotry in the Minnesota Constitution" (Scheck 2004). She went on to compare the ban to laws that banned interracial marriage.

Dibble said the fight over same-sex marriage bans had created policy gridlock because the governor wanted the legislation before consideration of bills on major policy areas such as health care and education. Dibble explained the situation: "For the past three years, we haven't managed to get anything done on behalf of this state because this issue has divided us so profoundly." But Dibble said the election results suggest that an amendment banning same-sex marriage would now likely be "DOA in Minnesota," arguing that "the chief anti-gay politicians who really put that front and center in their rhetoric and ran hard on those issues were defeated. And folks who were targeted on [gay] issues—and it was a brutal campaign—were affirmed and went on to be elected" (Eleveld 2006).

Aided by Clark in the House, Dribble had been a key player in the battle, and once it was over he expressed his belief that more pro-LGBT legislation could be pursued: "I think we are ready to start talking about the things that make up the civil, legal and economic parts of our relationships—whether that's emergency medical decision making, hospital visitation, extending health-care benefits, rights of inheritance" (Eleveld 2006). Nevertheless, similar attempts to push a constitutional ban on same-sex marriage and domestic partnerships were pursued by Republicans in 2007 and 2008 but those measures were easily defeated by the Democratic leadership in both chambers.

In 2007 Dribble helped push certain benefits, such as hospital visitation rights, for domestic partners through both chambers but the governor vetoed most of the bills, except a limited version of the hospital visitation measure. Likewise, when Dribble pushed measures (SF 960 and SF 1128) in 2008 that would have provided sick leave and health care benefits for state employees with domestic partners, the legislation passed both chambers only to be vetoed by the Republican governor. Dribble also cosponsored a 2008 measure (SF 3880) to recognize same-sex marriages. In the 2009 session he cosponsored a bill (SF 120) that would allow same-sex marriages to be recognized in the state and sponsored a bill (SF 204) to improve HIV education programs.

The only Republican LGBT legislator in Minnesota is Paul Koering. Koering held a Senate seat from a rural corner of the state since 2003 and publicly announced that he was gay in April 2005 after he was the only Republican in the Senate to oppose an effort to force a floor vote on a constitutional gay marriage ban. The debate led him to reveal his sexual orientation. Polling suggests that the revelation hurt him with voters in his relatively conservative district, but he was reelected in 2006 after appearing to switch gears to allow a vote on a constitutional ban of same-sex marriage.

By 2009 LGBT legislators in Minnesota were ready to try a strong push for a bill that would allow same-sex marriage and another bill that would require the state to recognize same-sex marriages established elsewhere. However, the Republican governor's promise to veto any same-sex relationship bills virtually assured the defeat of the same-sex marriage measures. LGBT legislators viewed the introduction of the bills as a means to educate legislations over a multiyear process, with hopes that such measures might pass by 2013 (Johnson 2009).

Minnesota's role as an early adopter of many LGBT civil rights measures likely would not have occurred without the efforts of LGBT legislators. As appears to be the pattern in other states, LGBT legislators in the state focus much of their attention on non-LGBT-related issues. But on key issues for the LGBT community, such as civil rights, hate crimes, HIV/AIDS, and relationship equality, LGBT legislators have advocated for the LGBT community.

Oregon

Like California, Oregon has developed a reputation for progressive politics, but this reputation tends to stem from environmental politics rather than from social issues such as LGBT equality. The Oregon legislature is a hybrid of a professionalized and a citizen body. Its racial and ethnic diversity is low but female representation is often close to 30 percent. The history of LGBT equality in the state has been less than a linear expansion.[12] LGBT activists in Oregon have attempted to pass a gay civil rights law in nearly every legislative session since 1973 (in Oregon the legislature only meets in odd-numbered years). In an effort to reduce the salience of the issue, gays changed strategies and successfully lobbied the governor to sign an executive order in 1987 that bans discrimination because of sexual orientation in state employment. In reaction a new conservative group, called the Oregon Citizens' Alliance, mobilized to repeal the order at the ballot box. An LGBT group called Oregonians for Fairness formed to fight the 1988 initiative (Measure 8) but its campaign failed. In the wake of the ballot campaign, activists formed the first permanent statewide group, Right to Privacy, which lobbied to pass gay civil rights legislation in each legislative session following the 1988 defeat. It achieved limited success in 1991, when a progay rights bill passed the Senate with the support of the governor, but the bill stalled in the House (Bull and Gallagher 1996, 44). Meanwhile, in 1992 and 1994 Oregon's voters defeated measures that would have blocked the passage of local and state gay civil rights laws.

Overall, LGBT-related legislation in Oregon has been haphazard. When LGBT legislators reached office in the early and mid-1990s, at least eight pro-LGBT measures were introduced and two of them passed. In 2001 there was a flurry of pro-LGBT bills introduced based on lobbying by Right to Privacy. These measures addressed antidiscrimination, hate crimes, and domestic partner issues. Of fifteen measures, only a hate crimes measure became law. There was almost no pro-LGBT legislation until 2005, when eleven pro-LGBT bills were introduced that addressed the same primary issues from 2001. These measures failed and were scaled back to three distinct bills in 2007. In terms of anti-LGBT legislation, Oregon has only seen twenty measures since 1992, and only two of these passed the legislature. In large part this is likely because the most sweeping LGBT measures, dealing with civil rights and same-sex marriage, were considered at the ballot box through citizen initiatives.

During these ballot battles in the early 1990s, Gail Shibley (D-66) was appointed to the Oregon House of Representatives. She won a full term in 1992 to become the first out lesbian official in the state. During her tenure she sponsored several gay-related bills, including a bill to ban sexual orientation discrimination in employment, a resolution asking Congress to repeal the ban on gays in the military, and a bill to ban sexual orientation discrimination in public accommodations and housing (Shibley 1994, 97). She also led the legislative effort to block the continued efforts of the Oregon Citizens' Alliance to pass local laws to preempt bans on sexual orientation discrimination with HB 3600, which simply stated that state law trumps local laws that limit the rights of people based on sexual orientation. Representative Shibley served through 1997.

In 1994 there was an influx of LGBT candidates for the legislature, and they all won. The incoming legislators were representatives Chuck Carpenter (R-7), Gail Shibley (D-66), Kate Brown (D-13), George Eighmey (D-14), and Cynthia Wooten (D-41). Nearly all these candidates had been motivated to run because of the divisive gay rights battles at the ballot box. Carpenter was the only Republican in the bunch, and all were reelected in 1996.

In 1997 a limited gay civil rights bill came closer to becoming law than any gay civil rights bill in Oregon during the twenty-five-year period when they had been introduced. The bill was supported by many high-profile companies in the business community and by all the LGBT members of the legislature. But it was Republican representative Chuck Carpenter, who was openly gay, who was the chief sponsor of the bill (HB 2734). Carpenter scaled back the scope and focused only on employment discrimination. When the Republican leadership failed to give the bill a hearing in committee, Carpenter used a rare procedural maneuver—a motion to have the bill go directly to the House floor. The Republican leadership called a recess to avoid voting on the bill (Esteve 1997). Carpenter reached a compromise with the leadership, whereby HB 2734 was allowed to die in committee and a new bill was drafted and sent to a different committee. The new bill (HB 3719) was given "priority" status. Even with significant lobbying by opponents, Carpenter was able to ensure that HB 3719 quickly passed the House Commerce Committee by eight to one and the full House by forty to twenty (Chibbaro 1997).

In the Senate, Carpenter testified before committees and built bipartisan support, but the bill was again stalled in committee by the Republican leadership. Carpenter teamed up with Democrats in the Senate, who threatened to block activity on any legislation until the bill was put to a floor vote. However, he was unable to replicate his House victory and the bill failed one vote short of a majority (Gay and Lesbian Victory Fund 1998).

The Republican leadership, still furious with Carpenter, demanded that he resign from the party. When he refused, conservatives recruited an ultraconservative candidate, Bill Witt, to challenge Carpenter in the 1998 Republican primary. Witt was a founding member of the Oregon Christian Coalition and a major donor to the Oregon Citizens' Alliance (Gay and Lesbian Victory Fund 1998). During the campaign Witt was able to energize antigay sentiment in the electorate on the issues of same-sex marriage and "special rights" for LGBT persons. Outmaneuvered at the grassroots, Carpenter outspent Witt by a large margin, raising more than $256,000, which is the most money raised by any House candidate in Oregon history (Esteve 1998). In the end, Carpenter lost by only fifty-four votes (Ivers 1998). Carpenter clearly provided a lightning rod for antigay sentiment in Oregon, a fact that appears to have significantly contributed to his defeat at the ballot box.

Carpenter's defeat came just after Shibley lost her seat in 1997, and lesbian representative Elli Work was defeated after one term in 1998. In addition, bisexual representative Kate Brown moved from the House to the Senate (D-21) in 1997 and

LGBT representatives Cynthia Wooten (D-41) and George Eighmey (D-14) were term-limited out of office in 1998. This meant that Senator Brown was the only LGBT state legislator until after the 2006 election. However, in 2004 Brown became the Senate majority leader, which placed her in a good position to push pro-LGBT legislation until she stepped down at the end of 2008.

Following the 2003 *Goodridge* decision in Massachusetts, Multnomah and Benton counties in Oregon briefly legalized gay marriage in 2004. In reaction to these events, an Oregon group was formed to push a ballot initiative, Measure 36, to constitutionally ban same-sex marriage in the state, which passed to the dismay of LGBT activists. Interestingly, during the 2004 election Oregon voters also chose to elect the first openly LGBT person to a state supreme court, Rives Kistler, in a retention election (Kistler had been appointed to the seat in 2003). Judge Kistler was joined by lesbian Virginia Linder following the 2006 elections.

LGBT activists in Oregon had been used to waiting a long time for success but rights for same-sex couples came rather quickly once a serious push began. A wide-ranging bill that would have provided domestic partner benefits and antidiscrimination protections for LGBT residents passed the Senate in 2005 with the force of the Democratic majority and the governor's support. But once the bill reached the Republican-controlled House, it was refused even a floor vote. The 2006 elections provided a boost to the Democrats and provided the leverage for renewed action on these measures.

Oregon adopted a law banning discrimination based on sexual orientation in 2007. It happened with an LGBT legislator playing a key role. In fact, the state's only LGBT legislator, Representative Tina Kotek (D-Portland) helped to ensure that the House adopted the ban on discrimination based on sexual orientation and a domestic partner registration on the same day. The antidiscrimination law is the Oregon Equality Act, which amended the state's nondiscrimination laws to ban sexual orientation discrimination in housing, employment, public accommodations, education, and public services. The bill passed thirty-five to twenty-five. The domestic partner bill is called the Family Fairness Act (HB 2007-A) and does not use the term "civil unions" to avoid a legal challenge under the same-sex marriage ban. The compromise proved to be adroit—because it created a separate legal construct from marriage, social conservatives declined to move forward with a ballot measure that might have overturned the policy (Law 2007).[13]

Both bills passed the Senate and were signed by the governor. Due in part to the efforts of bisexual Senate majority leader Kate Brown (D-21), in the Senate the debate on the domestic partner measure only took 30 minutes, and the only legislator who spoke against the bill simply complained that the legislation did not list all that statutes that would need to be amended with the approved law.[14] Senator Brown called the passage a "giant step forward for gay and lesbian citizens in Oregon." Representative Kotek spoke at an LGBT rally after the vote, saying "now we can just get on with our lives" (Law 2007). Senator Brown took her own advice. In 2008 she declined to run for her Senate seat again and ran for secretary of state. She won in November and became the highest-ranking bisexual official in the country.

Oregon fits with a set of states, including Maine and Vermont, where many LGBT candidates successfully ran for the legislature in the 1990s. And in both Maine and Oregon most candidates were motivated by grueling ballot initiative battles over LGBT rights. In all three states the surge in LGBT legislators was not maintained because once these legislators left office (often because of term limits) there was no ready group of LGBT candidates to run for their seats. Thus Oregon has a pattern of strong LGBT representation for a period during the 1990s followed by a significant gap, and a return to LGBT issues after the 2003 nationwide same-sex marriage debate began. Nevertheless, the case of Oregon does make clear that descriptive representation was translated into substantive representation, even in the face of a well-coordinated anti-LGBT civil rights movement.

Virginia

As part of the former Confederacy, Virginia represents the South in this sampling of states. The state has increasingly leaned toward Democratic interests and more liberal attitudes as its northern portion has effectively become a suburb of Washington. Yet even with these recent trends, Virginia politics has traditionally been conservative, and in 2009 it again elected a Republican governor. Before 2010 the last two governors were moderate-to-conservative Democrats, and most of the recent congressional delegation has been Republican. The state legislature follows a citizen legislature model, providing little compensation and a fairly short session. In the 1990s conservative Republicans gained control of the legislature but Democrats gained back some of these seats in the 2000s.

Not surprisingly, only few LGBT candidates have emerged in local or state races. Those who have been elected have spent more time fighting anti-LGBT legislation than pursing pro-LGBT legislation. Only one LGBT state legislator has been elected, and there is not a strong correlation between LGBT-related legislation and the presence of an LGBT legislator. From 1992 to 2007 there were eighty-six pro-LGBT measures introduced and sixty anti-LGBT measures. Only seven of the pro-LGBT measures passed, while eight of the anti-LGBT measures passed. Since 1997 at least two pro-LGBT measures have been introduced in each session, with peaks in 2000 and 2001. Anti-LGBT legislation has been the highest in each session following 2000.

Delegate Adam Ebbin (D-Alexandria), the first LGBT legislator in the state, got his start in Virginia politics by working for local campaigns and as the Alexandria coordinator for incumbent Virginia Democrat Charles S. Robb during his 1994 U.S. Senate race. After serving as chief deputy commissioner of labor and industry through a 2002 gubernatorial appointment, Ebbin ran for a seat in the House of Delegates in the most diverse district in the state during the 2003 election cycle (Gelineau 2005).

In 2005 Ebbin faced a gauntlet of anti-LGBT legislation, from constitutional bans on same-sex marriage, to legislation that sought to ban gay–straight alliances in public schools, to a law that would make it more difficult for LGBT people to adopt children. The adoption measure failed in a State Senate committee after passing the

House of Delegates, but a constitutional ban on same-sex marriage did pass. Ebbin could do little but vote against the measures and voice his opposition. Of the session, he said: "People say, 'Isn't it discouraging?' . . . and I disagree totally. I know that any time that people are gonna tell lies about gays and lesbians on the House floor, that I can grab my mike and speak—and that's really empowering" (Gelineau 2005). Even as the chamber adopted more anti-LGBT legislation than ever before, Ebbin decided that he had to pick and choose his battles, and he remained optimistic:

> I feel good. You sit here and listen to the bad legislation—which is not just targeted to gays and lesbians—but the things we do, to immigrants and others. . . . It is difficult not to speak up all the time because freshmen don't talk too much. I said I was going to stand up against anti-gay, anti-immigrant, and anti-common sense legislation but you have to pick and choose. I knew this [constitutional amendment] was coming up and I had time to think about what I was saying. There's something very empowering having that microphone on the House floor and being able to speak. I'm naturally talkative but it takes a lot of discipline not to stand up and shout every time there is an absurdity. And there is a lot of it. (Crea 2005)

Dyana Mason, the executive director of Equality Virginia, agrees, arguing that Ebbin "brings a real voice and face for our community to the General Assembly and that is invaluable. I believe it does change the debate for some people" (Gelineau 2005). Indeed, during the 2005 Virginia House consideration of a constitutional amendment banning gay marriage, Ebbin made a passionate speech, arguing that passage of the ban was akin to discrimination and the harsh treatment of blacks and American Indians in the past:

> Today is one of those moments for which we shall one day be ashamed. I cannot stand by as this body continues to use gays and lesbians as scapegoats for what has happened to the institution of marriage. What are we defending marriage from? Are we defending it from the high heterosexual divorce rate by seeing that we will never grant civil unions? Are we defending marriage from the criminal offense of adultery? No, we are not. . . . This is all about politics and reelection campaigns. The measure before us addresses none of the threats or challenges that husbands and wives face today. (Crea 2005).

Known for more than simply being the gay representative, Ebbin's work in the legislature has been praised by friends and political foes alike. Delegate Ward L. Armstrong, a supporter of the constitutional ban on same-sex marriage, said of Ebbin: "I suppose that one of the concerns was that since he is the only openly gay member of the legislature, is whether or not that would be the only issue that he would . . . talk about. That clearly has not been the case. He is a very versatile delegate" (Gelineau 2005).

In the 2007 and 2008 sessions, Ebbin was more proactive on LGBT issues and had the advantage of working with a larger Democratic margin in the chamber as well as a Democratic governor. In 2007 he sponsored legislation to ban discrimination because of sexual orientation for state employees. The bill (HB 2550) had dozens of cosponsors but failed to pass out of subcommittee. Ebbin also sponsored legislation to modify the language of the state's ban on same-sex marriage with the intent of making sure that domestic partner benefits could be provided by both public and private employers. He helped push legislation that allows individuals to designate any person with hospital visitation rights, including same-sex partners. He was able to help pull a bipartisan coalition together and pass the measure. In 2008 he pushed, but did not sponsor, a bill (HB 805) that would establish a domestic partner registry with the Department of Health. Registered partners would then be able to make medical decisions for each other in emergencies. That measure passed the House ninety-five to four (Johnson 2008).

Also in the 2007 and 2008 sessions, Ebbin sponsored a measure, HB 865, that would allow private employers to provide life insurance to same-sex partners of employees, and a measure prohibiting discrimination for Virginia's public employees. Both measures failed in subcommittee. In 2008 three other bills—one to prohibit sexual orientation discrimination in housing, one that would allow Fairfax County to add sexual orientation to its Human Rights Ordinance, and another to allow local governments to provide health insurance benefits to same-sex couples—were also introduced. Ebbin did not sponsor these bills but instead allowed other Democratic legislators to sponsor the measures in the House (Johnson 2008). None of these bills were passed by the House.

In the 2009 session only three pro-LGBT bills were introduced, and no anti-LGBT bills were immediately introduced. Ebbin reintroduced his bill to ban sexual orientation or gender identity discrimination for public employees (HB 2385). In addition House and Senate versions of a measure to allow private companies to provide health insurance to domestic partners of their employees were also introduced—HB 1726, by Delegate Tom Rust (R); and SB 945, by Senator Janet D. Howell (D).

Ebbin's presence in the legislature has made an impact on the institution and increased the number and diversity of LGBT-related bills introduced. His efforts, along with several Democrats in the House and Senate, have decreased the likelihood of anti-LGBT bills from passing and increased the likelihood of pro-LGBT legislation becoming law. However, as appears to be true in other conservative states, more often than not the strategy pursued has been one of "degaying" legislation—focusing less on the potential benefits to LGBT residents and more on the politically neutral elements of legislation—and keeping LGBT activists on the outside of committee hearings and other legislative activities.

Washington

The state of Washington shares similarities with California in terms of being a policy innovator, but outside its urban areas is not nearly so diverse. The legislature typically has one of the highest levels of female representation in the country (around 33 percent), but fewer than 3 percent of the legislators are African American or

Latino. In terms of professionalization, the legislature is a hybrid, so some elements of a citizen legislature, such as length of the session, remain. And although the state has a history of being progressive on social issues, LGBT issues have only moved forward in fits and starts. In terms of all local and state elected and appointed LGBT officials, Washington ranks third in the country, with thirty-five in 2008 (La Corte 2008). Because most of these officials are in local offices, Washington likely has a steady stream of experienced LGBT politicians who will be able to run for the legislature in the near future.

Washington first saw measures to protect LGBT residents from discrimination introduced in the legislature in 1976, and in 1985 Governor Booth Gardner issued an executive order banning discrimination against gays and lesbians in state hiring (Friederich 2003), but little action on LGBT-related issues took place at the state level before the 1990s. Between 1992 and 2007 some seventy pro-LGBT-related measures were introduced in the legislature. These measures numbered two or three a year until 1997, when the average shifted to about five. With peaks in 2001 and 2002, the average has settled at around four per year. There were limited successful measures but these included a hate crimes law in 1993. The pattern follows the increase in LGBT legislators in the late 1990s and early 2000s. Meanwhile, anti-LGBT legislation followed a similar pattern, with little activity before 1997. From that point on, there was a steady stream of bills until 2006; and between 2006 and 2010, no anti-LGBT bills were introduced. Of the sixty-five anti-LGBT measures introduced, only two passed the legislature.

Although Washington's LGBT legislators have grown to be one of the largest contingents in the country, perhaps the largest symbolic figure in the state was Senator Calvin (Cal) Anderson, Washington State's first openly gay legislator, who died of AIDS in 1995. Denis Dison of the Victory Fund, a national political action committee for LGBT candidates, called Anderson (D-43) a "towering figure in the gay community" (La Corte 2008). Anderson first served in the House from 1987 to 1994, and that year he was elected to the State Senate. As a representative, Anderson was eventually able to move an antidiscrimination bill to the floor, and at times he orchestrated a majority vote in favor of these measures.[15] However, the antidiscrimination bills would most often die in a Senate committee. This was the case in 1993, when Representative Anderson and other Democrats were unable to convince conservative Democratic colleagues on the Senate's Ways and Means Committee to forward a gay civil rights bill to the Senate floor (Penhale and Williams 1993). This pattern of pro-LGBT bills passing the House only to be bottled up in Senate committee largely held through the mid-2000s. Although a similar antidiscrimination bill again passed the House in 1994, this did not occur again until 2003. The bottleneck convinced four LGBT candidates to run for the legislature in 1994 but all faced LGBT-friendly incumbents and lost their races.

After Anderson's death, Representative Ed Murray (D-43) carried his mantle for years as the only LGBT legislator in the state, and it was Murray who was finally successful on a LGBT civil rights bill in 2006 (La Corte 2008). During the 1997 Washington legislative session, Murray introduced several progay measures, including a bill to allow same-sex marriages, a bill banning employment discrimination based on sexual orientation, and a bill giving domestic partnership benefits tor state employees (Haider-Markel 2000). In addition, the state faced a ballot initiative campaign for Initiative 677 that would have enacted an antidiscrimination law for sexual orientation. The measure only garnered 40 percent support in November and mobilized LGBT opponents for several years. When LGBT advocates had begun pursuing a ballot measure in 1995, then–senator Cal Anderson had argued "I don't think we should be putting people's rights on the ballot" (Maier 1995).

In 1998 the LGBT community faced a setback when the state passed a ban on same-sex marriage. The law was in reaction to a 1993 court ruling in Hawaii, which convinced many conservatives that other states would be forced to recognize same-sex marriages sanctioned in Hawaii. And in fact the passage of the ban was delayed for two years because of the efforts of Murray and other Democrats in the Senate and House to thwart conservative Republicans by taking advantage of institutional rules and the presence of a progressive Democratic governor. The first bill (HB 2262) passed the Republican-controlled House by sixty to thirty-six in February 1996. With the help of Senate Democrats and a sympathetic committee chair, gay groups were able to delay the bill in committee until the end of the session.

In 1997 Republicans, who now controlled both the House and Senate, introduced three bills banning same-sex marriage. The main anti-same-sex-marriage bill, SB 5398, passed the Senate. The House quickly followed with passage in a vote of sixty-three to thirty-five. However, Governor Gary Locke vetoed the bill and the Senate failed (twenty-six to twenty to three) to override his veto (Ammons 1997). Faced with the defeat of SB 5398, Republicans revived another marriage ban (HB 1130) in the House and amended it to place the question before the voters as a ballot referendum. The House passed the measure by fifty to forty-eight but in the Senate moderate Republicans focused efforts to have its ballot language removed. The amendment was removed by voice vote, and the Senate then passed the amended bill. But with the removal of the ballot requirement, the House refused to concur with the Senate amendment and the bill died with the end of the session. However, in 1998 conservative Republicans were able to effectively use the legislative amendment process and the threat of a ballot referendum to pass a ban (Savage 1998).

In fact, the 1998 measure, HB 1130, had something of a strange history. Once the measure passed the House and Senate, some suggested that the governor should avert a potentially divisive ballot imitative fight on the issue by allowing the measure to become law without his signature (Foster 1998). If the governor vetoed the measure, proponents threatened an initiative. When openly gay representative Murray heard of the governor's dilemma, he publicly urged the governor to allow the bill to become law without his signature rather than veto it. LGBT activists railed against Murray for this tactic, and he suffered politically; the next day he flipped his position and supported a veto (Mapes 1998). The final action on the bill occurred with the support of Democrats to avoid a ballot fight: "In a series of carefully orchestrated maneuvers, the ban flew through both houses, went to Locke for a veto and was overridden in both houses in less than five hours" (Foster 1998).

Murray was dismayed, but he thought that passage of the ban might mobilize the LGBT committee for future actions (Mapes 1998).

Murray expanded his repertoire of pro-LGBT legislation in 1999. He introduced a bill (HB 1765) that was designed to reduce bullying in public schools, with the intention of reducing the harassment of LGBT students. Religious conservatives opposed the measure, and although the bill had sixty-three cosponsors, the strategy was to educate legislators about the issue rather than force the measure through both chambers in 1999 (Searcey 1999).

Events that occurred outside the legislature began to shape some of the debate over LGBT rights. For example, the state Public Employees Benefits Board (composed of gubernatorial appointees) voted to extend health insurance coverage to the same-sex partners of state employees in May 2000. After some resistance, but under pressure from Democratic leaders and LGBT legislators, Democratic governor Locke supported the state Public Employees' Benefits Board decision to provide health care benefits to the live-in partners of gay and lesbian state employees (Davila 2001). Even though conservatives in the legislature objected to the move, the decision appears to have eased the full consideration of domestic partner measures in the legislature down the road.

In 2001 the legislature was fairly evenly divided. In fact, the House was tied between forty-nine Republicans and forty-nine Democrats, which made it difficult for controversial bills to even reach the floor for a vote. Murray was joined in the legislature by openly gay representatives Joe McDermott (D-34) and Dave Upthegrove (D-33), and continued to introduce antidiscrimination legislation such as HB 1524.[16] And even though fiery testimony during committee hearings had disappeared relative to the 1990s, the measures still were defeated (Postman 2001). Conservative legislators continued to suggest that any LGBT-positive legislation was part of a "gay agenda" and killed a bill, sponsored by Murray, that was intended to block bullying in public schools, including the bullying of LGBT students. In special elections the Democrats picked up seats, and Murray reintroduced the measure in 2002. Once it passed committee the measure easily passed a floor vote (eighty-one to sixteen) and was signed by Governor Locke (Staff 2002).[17] And although Murray had introduced bills to legalize same-sex marriage from 1998 to 2000, in 2001 he changed tactics and introduced legislation to create civil unions in the state. The initial effort failed but it would bear fruit as similar measures were introduced in the following years.

The 2003 legislature opened with another openly gay legislator, Representative Jim Moeller (D-49). Murray, along with McDermott, again introduced a bill (HB 1809) to ban sexual orientation discrimination in housing, employment, and financial transactions in 2003. After passing the House fifty-nine to thirty-nine with bipartisan support, the measure was held up in committee by a Republican chair.[18] Murray failed in his effort to convince his Senate colleagues to suspend the rules and pull the bill from the committee to the floor (Friederich 2003). However, even with the House victory, the four LGBT members of the House were unable to obtain even a committee vote on their bill (HB 1939) that would have legalized same-sex civil unions, even with twenty-two other cosponsors and the support of the Demo-cratic governor. Murray said that the measure likely required "a longer conversa-tion, a longer struggle" (Ammons 2003).

In the 2006 election a number of LGBT legislators were elected and reelected. First, Murray ran for the State Senate and won. Second, following an expensive campaign, openly gay Jamie Pedersen (D-43) was elected to replace Murray in the State House. Meanwhile, openly gay representatives McDermott, Moeller, and Upthegrove were all reelected. Pedersen is a lawyer who was chair of the board of Lambda Legal, an LGBT civil rights legal group. Pedersen also served as Lambda Legal's lead volunteer lawyer on the unsuccessful case that challenged the Washing-ton state ban on same-sex marriage. Pederson lists this information on his website as well as information about his partner and their adopted son.

During 2006 the legislature passed a bill that bans discrimination on the basis of sexual orientation in housing, lending, and employment (HB 2661). The effort had taken almost thirty years from the first time a similar bill was introduced and was eased by a Democrat-controlled legislature and governor's office. The Senate and the House passed the measure with only a few Republicans voting in the affirmative. The measure had been introduced by Murray, who had introduced a similar mea-sure for almost ten years. In 2005 Murray's bill had failed by one vote in the Senate. The difference in 2006 was that one Republican changed his vote (McGann 2006).[19]

In his first session in the House in 2007, Pedersen was able to sponsor or cospon-sor six significant bills that passed. In large part this was due to the fact that Ped-ersen was from the same district as the speaker of the House, and subsequently received assistance from the speaker. But Pedersen was most pleased with his role in passing the 2007 domestic partner bill (McGann 2007a). Also in 2007, Represen-tative Brian Sullivan stepped down from his legislative seat to take another position. The Democratic precinct committee officers for the 21st District voted to appoint an openly gay man, twenty-six-year-old Marko Liias (D-21), to fill the remainder of the term. The appointment gave Washington the second-largest LGBT legislative caucus in the country (La Corte 2008).

During the 2007 session the five LGBT legislators in Washington had clearly coalesced around the goal of legalizing same-sex marriage, but they also understood that they would be unsuccessful if they focused their efforts on the final goal without trying first to find an incremental method to achieve it. They chose to pursue the provision of some of the benefits of marriage by establishing a domestic partner registry and providing some benefits to registered partners. They also introduced a bill that allowed same-sex marriage, but they did not expend resources trying to pursue its passage. Of the strategy, McDermott said that marriage equality was the goal but that domestic partnerships could serve as a bridge to "provide some rem-edy, some relief and some humanity to couples until they can marry and enjoy the full rights and benefits" (La Corte 2007). So, while a same-sex marriage bill was tabled in committee without even receiving a hearing in 2007, that same year Wash-ington adopted a historic domestic partnership law that gives registered same-sex and opposite-sex unmarried couples hospital visitation rights and inheritance rights.[20] The measure (SB 5336) was sponsored by Senator Murray and pushed through the House by McDermott. Murray attended the governor's signing ceremony and said the law was a "beginning and not an end" (Cockerham 2007).

Going into the 2008 legislative session, the LGBT community was optimistic as to what could be accomplished. As the session began, the Washington legislature had the second-largest gay caucus in the country, at six members, trailing New Hampshire's seven members. This caucus hoped to expand the domestic partnership law to include retirement and pension benefits for same-sex couples (McGann 2007b). Liias and Pedersen were cosponsors of the House measure, HB 3104, whose main elements were incorporated into the Senate version, SB 6716, which was cosponsored by Murray. The final version expanded the existing domestic partner law to give same-sex partners 170 rights and responsibilities to which married couples are entitled, including community property, the guardianship of adopted children, and the right to refuse to testify against partners in court. The measure passed the House twenty-nine to twenty and the Senate by sixty-two to thirty-two.

Governor Chris Gregoire signed the measure into law on March 12. Following the governor's signing ceremony, Representative Pederson said: "Less than two years ago, the Washington Supreme Court said that it was up to the Legislature to decide whether same-sex couples and their families enjoyed any legal recognition or protection. . . . I am amazed and proud at how far we have come since then." And Representative Liias commented that "today Washington has taken another step towards recognizing equality for all; this is a great day for civil rights, and a great day for families across the state" (Liias 2008).

In 2009 all five LGBT legislators in the state were pushing a 110-page bill to further expand domestic partner rights in the state so that registered domestic partners would effectively have all the rights and responsibilities of heterosexual married couples. The effort was being led by Senator Murray, who described the previous measures and the 2009 measure as a "multiyear process to engage the citizens and the Legislature in a discussion about what our families are about and what the issues are about. . . . We haven't settled yet on a bill and a strategy." This quotation helps to make it clear that each piece of LGBT-related legislation introduced, even in a relatively progressive state, needs to have a strategy for passage. And although he did not plan to push it through to a vote, Murray was also introducing a bill to legalize same-sex marriage (Shannon 2009). The domestic partner measure was sponsored in the Senate by Murray (SB 5674) and in the House by Pederson (HB 1727). The measure had twenty cosponsors in the Senate and sixty in the House, making its passage very likely. Murray said that "the bill finishes and completes domestic partnership legislation, and gives gay and lesbian couples all the rights and responsibilities the state confers to married people" (Fairbanks 2009). Pederson also sponsored a same-sex marriage bill, but he said that "there's no way the marriage bill would pass because Washington state does not have the infrastructure to fight a referendum on the bill, should it be challenged" through the initiative process (Johnson 2009).

The case of Washington is especially interesting for a variety of reasons. From one perspective Washington has a long history of LGBT activism and appears to be a relatively progressive state on LGBT issues. However, much of that activism was traditionally focused on the local level, and especially in Seattle. Although representative and later senator Anderson played an important role at the state level in LGBT-related policy, the state did not begin to adopt significant pro-LGBT legislation until several LGBT legislators were elected. Once several LGBT legislators were in office, the state leapfrogged ahead of other states in terms of LGBT equality legislation in the 2000s. Clearly, increased descriptive representation made a significant difference in Washington. It is also clear from this case that LGBT legislators perceive their roles in different ways. But the basic concept of pursuing incremental change toward a broader final goal is perhaps the most successful in the legislative process. Legislators seem to need education and time to become comfortable with new ideas and the notion that some existing conditions are real problems that should be addressed.

Discussion and Conclusion

This chapter has examined several states in historical detail to better explore the question of whether increased descriptive representation results in substantive representation. My case study approach in this chapter limits my ability to generalize about all states and all state legislators. News media reports, interviews, and bill histories have provided significant detail to inform my discussion, but some details were inferred and the roles of particular actors may be overstated or understated. But some reliable conclusions can be drawn from this analysis. The cases illustrate that although description representation can translate into substantive representation, the pattern differs across states. Likewise, the strategies of LGBT legislators differ, even within the same state. Although this finding is not surprising by itself, it does highlight the fact that like other politicians, LGBT politicians are strategic in terms of how and when they engage in substantive representation of the LGBT community. And it also demonstrates that even for LGBT legislators who have actively pursued LGBT issues in the legislature over multiple legislative sessions, these bills are still often a relatively small percentage of the total number of bills a legislator might sponsor or cosponsor and invest considerable time in pursuing.

In some states legislators clearly feel constrained in actively pursuing pro-LGBT legislation through sponsorship or cosponsorship. In fact, some legislators appeared to have realized that it can be advantageous to allow others to be the central proponents of pro-LGBT bills. If the LGBT legislator is the one to sponsor a given bill, it may shape who chooses to support or oppose the measure. In addition, allowing more seasoned legislators to introduce a given bill might attract more cosponsors, help passage in committee, and provide benefits in that legislator's own district.

Indeed, one clear pattern across all the cases is that LGBT legislators believe that part of their representation role is simply to educate other legislators on LGBT issues. Part of this occurs simply through their presence in the institution but also through the pursuit of incremental policy change. The cases highlight many examples of LGBT legislators who introduce bills that are assured of defeat with the goal of educating other legislators on issues so that a future version of the bill might pass down the road. Some observers refer to this process as "softening up."

We can also see that although individual legislators can be quite effective in pursing the interests of the LGBT community, there is certainly additional leverage within legislative institutions when there are multiple LGBT legislators present, especially when they are in each chamber. This finding is consistent with the research from chapter 2 on women and minorities in legislatures, and is consistent with the quantitative analysis in the next chapter.

Notes

1. In this count, legislators serving in more than one chamber are only counted once.

2. In November 2008 the Connecticut State Supreme Court legalized same-sex marriage.

3. Unless otherwise noted, information on California is based on correspondence with Jennifer L. Richard, a legislative assistant, and Laurie McBride of (now defunct) LIFE Lobby.

4. Proponents of same-sex marriage bans moved from the legislative arena to the ballot box with a citizen initiative, which passed in 2000. California's constitutional ban on same-sex marriage passed in 2008.

5. At one point during the debate, Assemblyman Peter Frusetta (R), a lifelong rancher, said: "I've seen thousands and thousands of cattle . . . I've probably seen three . . . maybe four that had the hormone imbalance of being odd, unnatural. We called the heifers hermaphrodites. . . . [They would] shy away from bulls and take up with other heifers. . . . We're going down a very dangerous path here" (Skelton 1997).

6. In December 2009 Representative Perez became speaker-elect of the State Assembly, making him one of the most prominent LGBT politicians in the country and one of only a few LGBT legislators to hold a leadership position in a state legislature.

7. The Hawaii Supreme Court had taken a similar step in 1993 but that decision was reversed through a constitutional amendment.

8. Senator Barrios also married his partner following the decision in *Goodridge*.

9. Another LGBT legislator, Representative Cheryl A. Coakley-Rivera (previously Cheryl A. Rivera), was first elected to the 10th District in 1998 but she did not reveal her sexual orientation until February 2004. She was reelected that fall. Her highest position has been serving as chair of the Committee on Children, Families, and Persons with Disabilities. She was reelected in 2006 and 2008.

10. Unless otherwise noted, information on Minnesota is from the state legislature website and correspondence with Representative Clark's office.

11. Representative Karen Clark as quoted following Spear's death at www.senate.leg.state .mn.us/members/member_pr_display.php?ls = 86&id = 1932.

12. Unless otherwise noted, all information on Oregon comes from Haider-Markel (2000) and Smith and Haider-Markel (2002).

13. There was a state legal challenge but it failed.

14. Senator Brown is an out bisexual but is married to an opposite-sex partner.

15. As the House considered the 1993 antidiscrimination bill in committee, more than 700 people tried to attend the hearing. Given the number of people, the hearing was moved into the full House chamber (Friederich 2003).

16. Upthegrove was appointed just before the 2001 session when the sitting legislator stepped down.

17. In an additional minor victory, LGBT members of the legislature had their same-sex partners listed in the legislative phone directory in 2002 (Galloway 2002).

18. Following the House vote, Representative McDermott was quoted as saying: "This is one of the biggest votes I've ever taken and the one that made me the proudest. . . . The signs in the shop windows used to say 'Irish need not apply.' I was thinking about that the other day when I was signing papers to buy a house with my boyfriend, and thinking that they could just reject the whole thing after seeing two gay men sign the papers" (Ammons 2003).

19. Opponents attempted to collect enough signatures to repeal the law at the ballot box, but they failed.

20. For opposite-sex couples, one partner would have to be age sixty-two years or older. This component of the bill helped to diffuse some of the opposition.

CHAPTER FIVE

Translating Descriptive Representation into Substantive Representation

There has been notice statewide that some of the LGBT representatives in Sacramento are terming out and being replaced by straight representatives who in many cases are very strong allies. The fact they are strong allies makes it certainly more palatable. At the same time there is no substitute for having a seat at the table. When you are talking about marriage equality, I think having LGBT representatives telling their own stories to other representatives must be very powerful. You could only achieve that by putting LGBT representatives into office.

—Stephen Whitburn, president of the San Diego Democratic Club (Bajko 2006)

It was a big thrill to stand in the state reception room with the governor and my colleagues in the gay caucus and a lot of our colleagues in the Legislature and see that signed into law. . . . It's very satisfying to make some forward progress on that issue.

—Washington representative Jamie Pedersen, following
the passage of his domestic partner bill (McGann 2007b).

I N THIS CHAPTER I build on the analysis presented in chapter 4 by systematically exploring whether the presence of LGBT state legislators produces substantive representation in state legislatures. The evidence from chapter 4 suggests that even though LGBT legislators hold a small percentage of state legislative seats, their presence has the potential to increase substantive representation in the state policymaking process. However, the cases explored may not fully represent the patterns in all states and may overstate the substantive representation observed. Recall that, based on my count, more than 200 LGBT state legislators have served since 1974. As of 2009 there were 78 sitting LGBT members of state legislatures out of 7,382 total seats, for 1.06 percent of all seats. Although this number is small, descriptive LGBT representation in state legislatures has been dramatically increasing since 1996, as have the number of LGBT-related issues on state political agendas

(Smith and Haider-Markel 2002). Thus we can begin to systematically explore empirical questions relating to LGBT representation in the states.

I examine the influence of openly LGBT elected officials on the number and type of LGBT-related bills introduced in state legislatures, the legislative outcome of these bills, and the adoption of specific LGBT-related policies in the states. The analysis proceeds in two parts. First, I revisit theoretical arguments concerning political representation and outline the processes by which descriptive representation might engender positive outcomes in the policy process for the represented group. Second, I make use of a broader theory of state policy consideration and adoption in quantitative models of legislative bill introduction and policy adoption to examine the impact of descriptive representation.

The findings from the quantitative analyses support the findings from chapter 4 and suggest that LGBT representation in state legislatures is more than simply descriptive. Even when accounting for the state legislature ideology, interest group strength, and public opinion, among other factors, the presence of LGBT state legislators influences the number and type of LGBT-related bills introduced in state legislatures, the legislative outcome of these bills, and the adoption of specific LGBT-related policies in the states. For those who argue that a seat at the table is important for achieving policy goals, the evidence here is quite supportive. However, the influence of other factors, such as legislature ideology and interest groups, also makes it clear that descriptive representation is simply part of the story.

Political Representation: A Multivariate Analysis

My review of the literature on female and minority political representation in chapter 1 suggests that increased descriptive representation often leads to increased substantive representation in the policy process. When groups such as African Americans have achieved greater levels of political incorporation, especially at the local and state levels, policy benefits for the black community have followed. Similar patterns have been uncovered for women and ethnic minorities, such as Latinos. However, there are limitations to much of this research—including the fact that identifying policies that are of central importance to a particular community is not always straightforward because some of the purported policy goals of the community may not be universally shared. For the LGBT community this problem does not loom nearly so large. For one thing, there is considerable agreement in the community regarding policy goals (Haider-Markel, Querze, and Lindaman 2007; Schaffner and Senic 2006). In addition, it is frequently quite simple to identify legislation that has direct relevance to the LGBT community because key terms, such as sexual orientation, are often used.

So what is the connection between descriptive representation and substantive representation? As the case studies in chapter 4 demonstrate, we might simply expect that elected representatives who identify with a group are introducing and championing bills that benefit this group, and are actively working to defeat those bills that their community opposes. But the case studies also reveal that descriptive representation may influence substantive representation through other means. In several states it was clear that the simple presence of representatives of a group in a policymaking body influenced the attitudes and behavior of other legislators. This pattern has been observed with female and minority legislators as well (Barrett 1995, 1997; Bratton 2001, 2002; Browning, Marshall, and Tabb 1984; Hawkesworth 2003; Rayside 1998; Wahlke 1971; Yoder 1991). In what we might call a role model capacity, elected representatives of a group may broadly influence public perceptions of the group, and the public's and legislators' preferences concerning policies related to the group (Barrett 1995, 1997; Hawkesworth 2003; Pitkin 1967; Smith and Haider-Markel 2002). Thus descriptive representation may increase substantive representation not only through the direct or indirect policy entrepreneurship activities of the official representing the group but also because that official's presence may influence the behavior of other policymakers as well as the general public.

We also know that the presence of LGBT legislators in the states is not random. The electoral environment for LGBT candidates varies across the states; it is therefore not surprising that some states have had more LGBT candidates and legislators than others. For example, in the Republican-dominated state of New Hampshire, Democratic leaders successfully recruited five openly LGBT legislators to seek reelection and another seven LGBT candidates to run for state legislative seats in 2000 (Freiberg 2000a). In Vermont, six LGBT candidates ran for the state legislature in 2000. Interestingly, New Hampshire has had the most LGBT legislators, with nine; Oregon and Maine follow, with six; and California and Massachusetts both had five. Some of the factors that shape when and where LGBT candidates run, as well as their success, are also likely to shape the broader policymaking context in which LGBT-related legislation is introduced and considered. These forces include interest groups and public opinion, and they can be accounted for along with the presence of LGBT legislators. And as the number of LGBT legislators has grown in the past fifteen years, we can now carry out a unique systematic test of the influence of descriptive representation in the policy process and account for other forces in the political environment.

Dependent Variables

Because my central question concerns the policy impact of descriptive political representation of the LGBT community, each dependent variable must concern policy related to LGBTs. I measure policy actions with a count of the annual number of pro-LGBT bills introduced in each state, as well as the number of pro-LGBT bills that passed each year from 1992 to 2007.[1] Pro-LGBT bills include those that would expand antidiscrimination protections, enhance penalties for hate crimes, allow for same-sex civil unions, and the like. Over the period of study, the general trend in bills introduced and passed was generally upward (see the descriptive statistics given in appendix B).[2]

Bill counts, although simplistic, have clear face validity as measures of legislative activity (Edwards, Barrett, and Peake 1997). However, the measures are limited because they do not weight legislation according to its potential impact on the LGBT community (Bratton 2002), nor do I count only those bills sponsored or cosponsored by LGBT legislators. I chose not to count only LGBT-sponsored and LGBT-related legislation because although such a measure would ensure that I captured the most extreme form of substantive political representation, it would miss the possible political nuances of legislative sponsorship. For example, at times it may be more advantageous to build political support if the actual sponsor of the bill is someone who is perceived as less partisan, more detached from the issue, or simply as someone with more political experience (Schiller 1995). The case studies presented in chapter 4 provided plenty of examples of this type of legislative strategy. My measures, therefore, should be the best measures of potential substantive political representation by LGBT legislators.

To account for some of the limitations of these policy measures, I make use of one additional dependent variable—the passage of state laws that ban discrimination on the basis of sexual orientation. LGBT activists have focused more attention on passing these types of laws at the local, state, and national levels than on any other LGBT-related policy. Although many such laws have been passed at the local level, only twenty states adopted such policies between 1982 and 2008.[3] Thus it seems appropriate to examine whether LGBT legislators increase the likelihood of adopting antidiscrimination laws. My data set for this analysis is composed of state years, with each state's data starting in 1982, the year the first law was passed.[4] Each state has a case for each year through 2008, unless it adopted the policy. In that instance the dependent variable is coded as 1, and no additional case years are included in the data set for that state. For all other cases, the dependent variable is coded as 0. The descriptive statistics for each of the dependent variables and each independent variable are displayed in appendix B.

Independent Variables

This section outlines the logic behind my independent variables and their operationalization. Although the key variable is my measure of political representation, the theoretical discussion above as well as previous research suggest that a number of forces will likely influence legislative activity on LGBT issues, including public opinion, the preferences of elites, state population characteristics, and the characteristics and rules of the legislature (Haider-Markel 1999b).

Descriptive Representation

Recall that central to my analysis is the notion that the election of openly LGBT legislators will increase the substantive representation of LGBT concerns. To assess this influence I first identified all openly LGBT legislators who had ever held office in each state and their terms of service.[5] Second, I created a simple count variable of the number of openly LGBT legislators who served in each state for each year from 1992 to 2007. Thus, this variable captures the potential for LGBT legislators to sponsor LGBT-related legislation or to simply support or oppose LGBT-related legislation introduced by another legislator. I expect representation to be positively related to the introduction and passage of pro-LGBT bills, as well as to the adoption of antidiscrimination laws.

Population Characteristics

Across the states, some LGBT groups have considerable strength and can exercise significant influence in the policymaking process, especially in states with a larger gay community (Haider-Markel 2000). Likewise, elected officials are attuned to the social and demographic composition of their consistencies. For LGBT groups and elected officials, the relative size of a LGBT constituency could be important in shaping policymaking. The relative size of a LGBT community is also a resource for LGBT groups that would lobby state government—the larger the community, the more potential resources for LGBT groups (Haider-Markel 1997, 2007). To account for this I include a measure of the percentage of households that are composed of same-sex unmarried partners.[6]

On the other side of the issue are conservative religious groups that tend to oppose the positive legal recognition of homosexuals or homosexuality. Because most religions have explicit moral codes, orthodox followers will often have strong views on issues they perceive to involve morality, which often includes homosexuality. Persons with conservative religious beliefs in a state are a potential resource for conservative religious groups. Those religious denominations that are likely to have the strongest opposition to homosexuality are Protestant fundamentalists and conservative evangelicals because their religious doctrines oppose homosexuality (Layman and Carmines 1997). Similar to past research (Mooney and Lee 1995; Wald, Button, and Rienzo 1996), I capture the conservative religious population by including a measure of the percentage of a state's population that belongs to Protestant fundamentalist denominations.[7]

Legislature Ideology and Public Opinion

As legislators debate policy issues related to LGBTs, the preferences of the public and political elites shape legislative outcomes. Research suggests that liberal-leaning legislators are more supportive of LGBT civil rights issues, and that legislators are more supportive when their constituents support LGBT civil rights (Haider-Markel 1999b). I control for the ideological preferences of legislators with the measure of liberal/conservative ideology in the legislature developed by Berry and his colleagues (1998).[8] Higher scores for this measure indicate greater liberalism, and I expect liberalism to be associated with pro-LGBT legislation as well as legislative outcomes. Public preferences toward LGBT civil rights are accounted for with Lewis and Edelson's (2000) measure of average state public support for hiring homosexuals across five job categories. Higher scores for this measure indicate greater support for hiring LGBTs, and I expect higher support to be associated with more pro-LGBT legislation as well as more pro-LGBT legislative outcomes.

Additionally, competition between political parties may influence the policy process. As parties become more competitive, the demands of appealing to voting and building electoral coalitions may result in more liberal policies. I control for party competition using Holbrook and Van Dunk's (1993) district-level measure of party competition.[9]

Institutional Characteristics

In my preliminary analysis I included several variables to capture institutional characteristics that might influence the legislative process and outcomes, including session length, professionalization, and the number of bills introduced and enacted. I expected that each of these variables might increase the total number of LGBT-related bills considered, and perhaps those adopted. However, the only consistently performing variables were the simple counts of the number of bills introduced and enacted. This measure seems to be a reasonable indicator of each legislature's agenda size. As such, in the models of bills introduced I include a control variable for the total number of bills introduced, and in the models of bills passed I include the total number of bills passed.[10] Each variable is coded "missing" for the years in which legislative sessions were not held. As a measure of agenda size I expect the number of bills introduced to be positively associated with the number LGBT bills passed. Likewise, I expect that as more bills are adopted, more LGBT bills will be adopted.

Results and Discussion

Because the dependent variables in my models that examine bills that are introduced and passed are simple count variables, I estimated each equation using a random-effects Poisson regression (Lindsey 1999).[11] The results for the models that predict the introduction and adoption of pro-LGBT legislation are shown in table 5.1.[12]

The results in the first column of table 5.1 suggest a number of important findings. Overall, the number of pro-LGBT bills that were introduced in state legislatures is a function of legislature ideology, LGBT population, Protestant fundamentalist population, party competition, the total number of bills introduced, and the number of openly LGBT legislators. As the Protestant fundamentalist population increases, pro-LGBT bills decrease, which suggests that legislators are responsive to the size of the Protestant fundamentalist community or that the population serves as a resource for groups that lobby against pro-LGBT legislation. Conversely, pro-LGBT bills increase as the LGBT population increases, which suggests here, too, that either legislators respond to the size of this constituency or that interest groups are able to make use of this potential resource.

The results also indicate that as legislative ideology becomes more liberal, pro-LGBT bill introduction increases. Although not surprising, this result indicates that the LGBT community can rely, to some extent, on more liberal legislators to support its interests, regardless of their sexual orientation. Counter to expectations, as party competition increases, pro-LGBT bills tend to decrease. Although the literature suggests that party competition increases the likelihood of liberal policies, this finding indicates that higher party competition may persuade legislators to avoid controversial topics, and therefore introduce fewer LGBT-related bills. However, the influence of party competition is only marginally significant in the model.

Most important, the results indicate that as the number of LGBT legislators increases, the number of pro-LGBT bills introduced increases. This appears to be clear systematic evidence to suggest that the LGBT community can achieve

Table 5.1 Determinants of State Introduction and Adoption of Pro-LGBT Legislation, 1992–2007

Independent Variable	Introduction Model	Adoption Model
LGBT legislators	.166**	.183**
	(.017)	(.040)
Legislature ideology > liberal	.006**	.008*
	(.001)	(.003)
Protestant fundamentalists	−.028**	−.011
	(.009)	(.013)
LGBT households	1.198#	1.516#
	(.691)	(1.089)
Public support for LGBT rights	.015	.018
	(.015)	(.017)
Party competition	−.019#	.008
	(.010)	(.011)
Total bills considered or adopted	.0001*	.0007**
	(.0000)	(.0002)
Constant	1.666*	−2.819**
	(.615)	(.774)
Log likelihood	−2,279.184	−666.826
Wald chi-square	169.46	106.62
Probability chi-square	.000	.000
No. of cases	740	742

Note: Dependent variables are raw counts of pro-LGBT bills introduced or passed. Coefficients are random-effects Poisson regression coefficients. Standard errors are in parentheses. Significance levels for two-tailed tests: ** $< .01$; * $< .05$; # $< .10$.

substantive representation in state legislatures by electing openly LGBT candidates to the legislature. When this is considered in conjunction with the evidence from the case studies that appear in chapter 4, one can make a compelling case to support a link between descriptive representation and substantive representation.

The last column of table 5.1 displays the results for the model that explain the adoption of pro-LGBT policy. The results indicate that the adoption of pro-LGBT legislation is associated with a similar set of forces as bill introduction, including the number of openly LGBT legislators, population characteristics, legislature ideology, and the total number of bills enacted each year. Higher rates of bill adoption are associated with a larger LGBT community but not significantly related to the size of the Protestant fundamentalist community. This suggests that the Protestant fundamentalist population appears to deter the introduction of pro-LGBT-related bills, but once introduced does not play a significant role in the outcome, accounting for all other factors. Meanwhile, the LGBT population has some role to play in both the introduction and adoption processes.

Elite and mass preferences find mixed influence. Legislature ideology influenced bill introduction and influences adoption as well, with more liberal legislatures seeing more pro-LGBT bills introduced as well as adopted. Meanwhile, my measure of public opinion on antidiscrimination measures does not appear to be associated with the number of bills introduced or adopted. This is not to suggest that public opinion plays no role on LGBT-related policy. Instead the influence of public opinion appears to partly depend on the specific issue under consideration (see Haider-Markel and Kaufman 2006; Lax and Phillips 2009), and the measure used here includes a broad array of LGBT-related issues.

But most important, the influence of openly LGBT legislators is statistically significant, is positive, and endures even under alternative model specifications, such as including alternative measures of legislative ideology and public opinion.[13] These results provide strong evidence that substantive political representation can be achieved for the LGBT community by increasing description representation.

One additional point is relevant to the influence of descriptive representation. It would seem that the influence of LGBT legislators on substantive representation might differ between more liberal and more conservative legislatures. All things being equal, for example, we might expect that the LGBT legislator sitting in a more liberal chamber is more likely to introduce or champion pro-LGBT legislation relative to the LGBT legislator sitting in a more conservative legislature. I examined this proposition by creating an interaction variable. Simply put, I multiplied the number of LGBT legislators by legislature ideology. This interaction term was not statistically significant for either of the reestimated models. I also created a dichotomous variable for conservative legislatures. Legislatures were coded 1, as conservative, if the legislative ideology score was below the mean for all states and all years, and they were coded 0 otherwise. This allowed me to separately estimate each model for liberal and for conservative legislatures. The results of this analysis revealed that legislative context has little influence on the relationship between LGBT legislators and the amount of pro-LGBT legislation. However, because there were few LGBT legislators in very conservative legislatures, this result is not conclusive. I return to the issue of context in chapter 6.

Adopting Antidiscrimination Laws

The dependent variables (bills introduced and adopted) cover an array of issues, some of which might not be considered significant policy changes by all observers. To establish that there is a linkage between descriptive representation and *significant* policy change in LGBT-related issues, I conducted an additional test to examine the factors associated with the probability that a state will legislatively adopt an antidiscrimination policy including sexual orientation. Because I coded the passage of antidiscrimination laws as a dichotomous dependent variable, logistic regression was used to estimate the model parameters in an event history analysis model. The results are reported in table 5.2.

The results indicate that a state is more likely to adopt sexual orientation antidiscrimination laws in employment when public opinion is more supportive of antidiscrimination laws. Most of the rest of the variables do not achieve statistical

Table 5.2   Determinants of State Adoption of Antidiscrimination Laws Covering Sexual
Orientation, 1982–2008

Independent Variable	Adoption Model
LGBT legislators	.802**
	(.202)
Legislature ideology	.012
	(.011)
Protestant fundamentalists	−.058
	(.045)
LGBT households	.001
	(.002)
Public support for LGBT rights	.112*
	(.047)
Party competition	−.009
	(.028)
Constant	−5.281**
	(1.452)
Log likelihood	−75.0833
% correctly predicted	98.15
Chi-square	51.13
Probability chi-square	.000
Pseudo R^2	.25
No. of cases	1,198

Note: The dependent variable is coded 1 for the year in which a state adopts a sexual orientation antidiscrimination law and 0 otherwise. Coefficients are logistic regression coefficients. Standard errors are in parentheses. Significance levels for two-tailed tests: ** $< .01$; * $< .05$; # $< .10$.

significance. Clearly, for a policy that is a major policy goal of the LGBT community, public opinion plays a more significant role than other factors in a state, including potential interest group resources and legislature ideology. This finding suggests that for a significant LGBT policy area, constituency preferences may matter more than other forces.

Higher numbers of LGBT legislators increase the probability that states will adopt policies that ban discrimination on the basis of sexual orientation. This test confirms the findings considered above and strongly suggests that descriptive representation of the LGBT community can lead to significant policy victories for the LGBT community. Combined with the finding that public preferences matter on this issue, it suggests that the LGBT community would find an easier path to policy success if there were more descriptive representation and favorable public opinion. Given that the election of LGBT officials is also partially dependent on tolerant political attitudes, it is clear that significant LGBT-related policy is unlikely without public support. This finding is consistent with recent work by Lax and Phillips (2009), who suggest, without accounting for descriptive representation, that in many states it would be difficult to adopt pro-LGBT policies without levels of public support approaching 65 percent.

Conclusions

In this chapter I have systematically examined the question of whether descriptive political representation in state legislatures can lead to positive substantive political representation. I suggest that LGBT citizens are more likely to see their issues on the political agenda and achieve legislative success if they elect LGBT officials. To test these hypotheses I conducted analyses of pro-LGBT and anti-LGBT bill introduction and bill adoption using 1992 to 2007 data from the American states. In addition, I examined whether increased LGBT representation increases the likelihood of significant policy change by using event history analysis to predict the adoption of sexual orientation antidiscrimination laws between 1982 and 2008.

My empirical results suggest that the LGBT population, conservative religious population, public support for LGBT civil rights, the ideology of political elites, and institutional characteristics all play a role in the introduction and adoption of LGBT-related legislation. However, the adoption of significant policies, such as antidiscrimination laws, is driven more by public preferences.

On the central question the results clearly indicate that as more LGBTs are elected to a state's legislature, the number of pro-LGBT bills introduced increases, as does the number of pro-LGBT bills adopted. Likewise, LGBT representation increases the probability that a state will adopt significant antidiscrimination policies.

Although this systematic analysis confirms the pattern observed in chapter 4, the findings also allow for some general conclusions. The overall importance of public preferences in the election of LGBT officials and the adoption of pro-LGBT policy was confirmed in this analysis and suggests that the process of LGBT-related policy change is unlikely unless public opinion in a state is tolerant. Other forces, such as potential interest group resources and legislature ideology, have an important role to play, but pro-LGBT policy change appears to hinge indirectly or directly on public support.

With this in mind, LGBT activists seeking policy change must consider a broader strategy of grassroots mobilization that involves a "changing hearts and minds" strategy versus a dominance of backroom politicking in state legislatures. Interestingly, and as we will see in the next chapter, backroom procedural maneuvering may matter more for blocking anti-LGBT legislation, but it is not a long-term strategy for winning.

Notes

1. These data are from the National Gay and Lesbian Task Force, Human Rights Campaign, state LGBT interest groups, and searches of state legislative websites and the Lexis-Nexis state government universe by the author.

2. For a detailed description of the types of bills included for a variety of years, see the National Gay and Lesbian Task Force Reports, www.thetaskforce.org/reslibrary/list.cfm? pubTypeID = 2.

3. Maine adopted an antidiscrimination policy in 1997 only to have it repealed at the ballot box. But because the legislature did pass the law and gain the governor's approval, Maine is counted here as an adopting state.

4. The data on state antidiscrimination law adoption are from the National LGBT Task Force.

5. These data are from the National LGBT Task Force, the LGBT Victory Fund, and newspaper searches of LexisNexis using the keywords "gay," "lesbian," and "candidate." In a preliminary analysis I also included a measure of the number of LGBT candidates who had run for state legislative office. At no point did this measure approach statistical significance, so it was removed from the final models.

6. These data are from the U.S. Bureau of the Census (2003). In the 2000 census respondents were asked if they lived with an unmarried partner. Only respondents who said they lived with a same-sex partner are counted here. Although it is clear that this only counts those gays and lesbians who live with a partner and are willing to signify it, the measure is a reasonable surrogate of the size of the LGBT community (see Haider-Markel 1997; Wald, Button, and Rienzo 1996).

7. Following Haider-Markel and Meier (1996), the denominations classified as Protestant fundamentalist are Churches of God, Latter-Day Saints, Churches of Christ, Church of the Nazarene, Mennonites, Conservative Baptist Association, Missouri Synod Lutherans, Pentecostal Holiness, the Salvation Army, Seventh-Day Adventists, Southern Baptists, and Wisconsin Synod Lutherans. These data are from the Glenmary Research Center (2004) and exclude independent churches. The Catholic population was included in early models but dropped because of a lack of theoretical or empirical support.

8. Additional annual data are from the Berry et al. (1998) data update on the website of the Interuniversity Consortium for Political and Social Research, www.icpsr.umich.edu.

9. Because Louisiana is missing from the Holbrook and Van Dunk (1993) measure, I used other measures of partisanship and competition to estimate Louisiana's score as 17.07.

10. These data are from the Council of State Governments (various years).

11. The models estimated here were also estimated with a heteroskedastic corrected liner regression model, a fixed-effects model, and a random-effects regression model (Diggle et al. 2002). The results from these estimation techniques produce similar results to those presented here, indicating that the models are quite robust.

12. In my preliminary analysis I also created interaction variables with several variables in the model but no interactions produced significantly different or substantively interesting results.

13. Democrats tend to be more supportive of gay civil rights than Republicans (Haider-Markel and Joslyn 2008). Thus, a related measure would be partisan control of the state legislature. However, my preliminary analysis found that the inclusion of a percent Democrat variable was not statistically significant, nor did it improve the models. Furthermore, given the high number of conservative Democrats in southern legislatures, a partisan control variable should be expected to perform poorly. An additional consideration for these models was the party of the governor. Including a variable to capture party control of the governor's office, as well as divided government, does not substantively improve the models presented here. To reduce collinearity problems, these variables were removed from the models.

CHAPTER SIX

Descriptive Representation and Backlash

It seems that those who announce their sexual orientation to the world are trying to get all of us to say their relationships are legitimate. . . . I like [lesbian legislator] Sheila [Kuehl]. She's a nice lady. But I'll never believe that sort of sexual behavior is acceptable.

—California senator Ray Haynes (R-Riverside)

I saw where that [gay rights] bill went two years ago, and I would have to say at this point, you know, I'll fight bad bills, but that's probably what my best role is right now, to fight bad bills.

—Arkansas representative Kathy Webb on her role as an LGBT legislator

It's just been very intense. . . . I spend as much time and energy as I can talking to my colleagues, talking to my community, organizing a larger coalition response, really trying hard to cultivate other kinds of voices to help participate in this whole conversation. . . . Meanwhile, I'm trying to work on quite a few other issues. It really does distract from our creative energy, our time, the work that goes into crafting the kind of solutions I'm working on for other issues.

—Openly gay Minnesota state senator Scott Dibble (R)
regarding his efforts to block a state constitutional amendment
that would have banned same-sex marriages

THE RESULTS ANALYZED in chapters 4 and 5 clearly indicate that increased LGBT descriptive representation is associated with increased substantive representation. This conclusion is consistent with a considerable amount of research on ethnic and racial minorities as well as women in elected office. The other side of this coin is an exploration of the influence of LGBT descriptive representation on anti-LGBT legislative efforts. If LGBT legislators can serve to promote LGBT interests by pursuing pro-LGBT legislation, they can also serve to promote the interests of the community by blocking anti-LGBT legislation.

However, in considering anti-LGBT legislation we also need to consider that LGBT legislators might indirectly contribute to the amount and success of this type of legislation. A few scholars have explicitly discussed the potentially negative implications of increased descriptive representation for a minority group (Bratton 2002; Kanter 1977, 1994; Preuhs 2002). Many scholars and political observers frequently suggest that as groups that have been traditionally relatively powerless begin to gain political, social, or economic power, they may engender a counterreaction or backlash (Blalock 1967; Faludi 1991; Francisco 1996; Hawkesworth 2003; Lublin and Voss 2000; Yoder 1991), but as Thomas (2008) makes clear, little existing research has systematically explored the notion of backlash in the context of political representation (but see Barrett 1995, 1997; Bratton 2002; Cammisa and Reingold 2004; Haider-Markel 2007; Studlar and McAllister 2002; Thomas 1994).

Anecdotally, the notion of a backlash against the successes of the LGBT movement generally seems to be evident. Much of the politics around LGBT issues appears to involve a backlash against the successes of the LGBT movement—beginning with Anita Bryant's "Save Our Children Campaign" to repeal a Dade County, Florida, ordinance that banned sexual orientation discrimination; running through the late 1980s and early 1990s in Oregon, Colorado, and Idaho ballot measures to repeal and/or block antidiscrimination laws; to the wave of constitutional referenda measures to block same-sex marriage following the *Goodridge* decision in 2003; to the 2008 direct constitutional repeal of the California's Supreme Court's legalization of same-sex marriage. However, in this chapter I focus on actions taken within state legislatures with a particular focus on the potential backlash by some legislators against the election of LGBT legislators. Chapter 4 suggests some limited evidence of this phenomenon.

Thus, this chapter outlines what is meant by a backlash hypothesis and systematically tests for the phenomenon. Specifically, I examine the influence of openly LGBT elected officials on the number and type of LGBT-related bills introduced in state legislatures, the legislative outcomes of these bills, and the adoption of specific LGBT-related policies in the states. The analysis proceeds in two parts. First, I revisit theoretical arguments concerning political representation and outline the processes by which descriptive representation might engender both positive and negative policy for the represented group. Second, as I did in chapter 5, I make use of a broader theory of state policy consideration and adoption in quantitative models of legislative bill introduction and policy adoption to examine potential backlash against descriptive representation.

My analysis indicates that increased descriptive representation may in fact engender a backlash within legislatures. The results of statistical models examining bill introduction and passage suggest that as the number of LGBT legislators increases, so too does the amount of anti-LGBT legislation. I conclude that the net effect of LGBT political representation is positive legislative outcomes for the LGBT community.

Descriptive Representation and Backlash

Although both democratic theory and empirical evidence suggest that groups can achieve positive substantive policy representation through descriptive representation, some scholars have suggested that there may be a backlash, or negative reaction, as a politically marginal group achieves social, economic, or political gains (Blalock 1967; Bratton 2002; Cammisa and Reingold 2004; Crowley 2004; Preuhs 2007; Studlar and McAllister 2002; Yoder 1991). For example, many have argued that the women's movement, while accomplishing many significant goals in the 1970s, created a backlash of antiwoman, or at least antifeminist, sentiment in the 1980s (Banaszac 1996; Faludi 1991; Haas-Wilson 1993; Thomas 1994, 1997; Yoder 1991).

Similar arguments have been made concerning the white response to the black civil rights movement, increased black political participation, and the election of black officials (see Blalock 1967; Klarman 1994; Hedge, Button, and Spear 1996; Guerrero 1997; Lublin and Voss 2000; Krueger and Mueller 2001; Voss and Lublin 2001; Preuhs 2002).[1] Some empirical evidence supports these claims. Bratton's (2002) analysis of state legislative bills found that an increase in black descriptive representation was associated with an increase in legislation counter to the interests of the black community.

Furthermore, research has found evidence of a backlash, or a negative counterresponse, in a variety of social and organizational contexts (Francisco 1995, 1996; Rudman and Glick 1999). Thus, it seems clear that political actors may feel threatened by the political successes of groups that previously had little voice in public arenas, including the policy process (Blalock 1967; Thomas 1994, 2008; Yoder 1991). The reaction to this perceived threat might change individual preferences or behavior in a variety of social or political contexts, including political institutions such as legislatures (Blalock 1967; Bratton 2002; Thomas 1994, 2008; Yoder 1991). And if enough individuals respond to the perceived threat in a consistent manner, the result of these individual changes in behavior should be observable in aggregate-level analysis (Bratton 2002; Francisco 1995, 1996; Studlar and McAllister 2002; Voss and Miller 2001).

Thus, one narrow definition of a backlash would be any political reaction that attempts to curtail or reverse the political gains, including electoral and policy gains, of a previously weaker group or coalition (Haider-Markel 2007). Indeed, Mansbridge and Shames (2008, 627) argue that three elements are necessary for a backlash: "First, the action must be a reaction. A backlash lashes *back* at something another has done. Second, the reaction must involve coercive power. Third, the reaction must involve trying to reinstate part or all of one's former power in the most general meaning of capacity to turn preferences or interests into outcomes." The reaction can be an actual loss or simply the threat of a loss. Mansbridge and Shames do not highlight political or governmental elements as I have, but they are focused on a more general definition. For the purposes of this chapter, the thrusts of the definitions are parallel.

Sanbonmatsu (2008) argues that the increased representation of women in elective office might invoke a backlash and lead some voters to be less supportive of female candidates because they believe increased female representation is a threat to their position in society or politics, or at least the policy status quo. However, the backlash might also result from an individual perception that female officials threaten one's identity, male or female, which is built around traditional gender roles.

Whether the definition is broad or narrow, does backlash occur in legislatures? Recall the examination of California in chapter 4. As LGBT candidates, including Representative Sheila Kuehl (1992) and Representative Carol Migden (May 1996), took seats in the state legislature in the 1990s, the number of pro-LGBT bills introduced and adopted in the legislature began to increase. The pattern continued as more LGBT candidates were elected to the legislature in the early 2000s. However, the election of these officials also coincided with an increase in the number of anti-LGBT bills that were introduced. Before the 1990s the number of antigay bills introduced in the state legislature did not average even one per year. But following the election of Kuehl and Migden, the number of antigay bills introduced began to dramatically increase—one was introduced in 1995, ten in 1996, twelve in 1997, seventeen in 1998, and six and seven in 1999 and 2000, respectively. The number of antigay bills decreased to two in 2001 but jumped back to nine in 2002. During the 2003 and 2004 sessions there were only three anti-LGBT bills introduced, but the number again jumped to seven in 2005 and 2006. Thus, the pattern suggests a potential connection between LGBT descriptive representation and anti-LGBT legislation.

The cases of Minnesota, Oregon, and Washington follow a similar pattern to California. In addition, a number of the individual legislators' experiences described in chapter 4 point to the suggestion that at least some legislators might choose to show their displeasure with the presence of LGBT representatives by introducing anti-LGBT legislation. Representative Chuck Carpenter in Oregon certainly invoked the ire of conservatives in 1997, and the number of anti-LGBT bills jumped to three.

Of particular importance, several researchers have found systematic evidence of backlash or at least a marginalization of legislators from traditionally underrepresented groups. In legislatures where there are very few African American representatives, black legislators tend to find themselves and their proposals marginalized by the white majority (Barrett 1995, 1997; Button and Hedge 1996; Carroll and Strimling 1983; Githens and Prestage 1977; Hedge, Button, and Spear 1996). Haynie's (2000) analysis suggests that black representatives were viewed as less effective than their white counterparts. Female legislators have faced some of same patterns of social isolation in legislatures (Carroll and Strimling 1983; Githens and Prestage 1977). In addition, an analysis of female incorporation in local government legislatures concludes that increased female representation enhances trust in government among female constituents but is associated with declines in trust among men (Ulbig 2007), which might be considered a backlash by male constituents.

Bratton (2002) found that an increase in the number of female state legislators is associated with a legislative backlash—an increase in antiwoman legislation. Crowley (2004) found evidence of a decline in the impact of female legislators once female representation reaches 15 percent, which she interprets as a potential backlash (see also Thomas 1997; Yoder 1991). Heath, Schwindt-Bayer, and Taylor-Robinson (2005) found that female legislators in Latin America are marginalized after election by being denied access to key legislative committees. Kathlene's (1994) analysis of state legislative committee hearings suggests that male legislators tend to become more verbally aggressive when there are more female legislators on a committee. Kathlene argues that this behavior is evidence of a backlash against female representation within a masculine institution.

Preuhs's (2005) analysis of states' adoption of English-only laws suggests that although greater numbers of Latinos in legislative leadership positions decreases the likelihood that a state will adopt an English-only law, the presence of the citizen initiative process leads to a policy backlash—the combination of the initiative and higher levels of Latino incorporation into legislative leadership positions makes the likelihood of adoption more likely. And Bratton and Haynie's (1999) analysis of state legislation sponsored by African Americans was significantly less likely to pass in half the states they examined. Likewise, Bratton's (2006) analysis of Latino state legislators found that in some states, such as California, Latino legislators were more likely to see their bills fail.

However, Bratton and Ray's (2002) analysis of female representation in Norway did not find evidence that increased representation leads to a backlash. And analysis of the success of female legislators on bills they have sponsored shows that women are at least as successful as men in seeing their bills passed (Saint-Germain 1989; Thomas 1994).

Even if there is increased descriptive representation that engenders a backlash (more anti-LGBT bills introduced), the end result could still be increased substantive representation as LGBT legislators are able to defeat anti-LGBT legislation or the net result is more pro-LGBT legislation than anti-LGBT legislation. Indeed, many of the examples from chapter 4 make this clear. In 2006 LGBT legislators were able to block significant anti-LGBT legislation in the states. In the Maryland House of Delegates three gay legislators helped to successfully block a constitutional amendment to ban same-sex marriage from going to the voters; in Idaho Representative Nicole LeFavour blocked a bill that would have restricted student access to LGBT clubs in high schools; and in Utah Representative Jackie Biskupski and Senator Scott McCoy played a role in preventing a bill banning domestic partner benefits from coming to a floor vote (Stone 2006).

In an effort to isolate and identify manifestations of political backlash, I focus on state legislative backlash against electoral gains, with special attention given to backlash against increased descriptive representation of LGBT legislators. The notion of backlash seems especially relevant in LGBT politics because scholars in the 1990s began to argue that the mobilization of the LGBT civil rights movement in the 1970s also created a backlash, or a countermobilization of religious conservative forces. Evidence for such a backlash seems to abound, with the passage of ballot initiatives (Witt and McCorkle 1997), legislation, and policy-relevant court cases that repealed or limited the policy achievements of the LGBT movement (Smith and Haider-Markel 2002). And if one considers that the election of an openly LGBT legislator is a relatively novel event that is likely to receive considerable media coverage, it is important to note that Haider-Markel and Meier (1996) found that the increased salience of LGBT issues makes the adoption of pro-LGBT policy less likely (see also Lax and Phillips 2009), which is consistent with the backlash hypothesis. However, no existing studies have systematically tested for a backlash in LGBT politics and policy.

On the basis of this overview I hypothesize that increased LGBT descriptive representation will engender a legislative backlash in the form of greater numbers of anti-LGBT bills being introduced, and perhaps adopted, in state legislatures.[2] Next I examine the negative—backlash—implications of descriptive political representation by employing statistical models to explain the number and type of LGBT-related legislative proposals and policies adopted.

Dependent Variables

Because my central question concerns the policy impact of descriptive political representation of the LGBT community, each dependent variable must concern policy related to LGBTs. I measure policy actions with a count of the annual number of anti-LGBT bills introduced in each state, as well as the number of anti-LGBT bills that passed each year from 1992 to 2007.[3] Anti-LGBT bills include those that would ban same-sex marriage, prevent LGBT student clubs in public schools, ban homosexuals from being foster parents, and prevent positive discussions of homosexuality in sex education courses. Throughout the period under study, pro-LGBT bills tended to outnumber anti-LGBT bills. However, between 1995 and 1999 there was a significant increase in the number of bills banning same-sex marriage based on a coordinated national response by religious conservative groups to a Hawaii court ruling on same-sex marriage (Haider-Markel 2001). A similar pattern followed a 2003 Massachusetts court ruling in 2004 to 2005 (see the descriptive statistics given in appendix B).[4]

Additionally, I model the difference between the number of pro-LGBT bills introduced and the number of anti-LGBT bills introduced, as well as the difference between the number of pro-LGBT bills passed and the number of anti-LGBT bills passed. The difference variables allow me to capture the relative impact of the independent variables on pro-LGBT versus anti-LGBT legislation. Bill counts, although simplistic, have clear face validity as measures of legislative activity (Edwards, Barrett, and Peake 1997). However, the measures are limited because they do not weight legislation according to its potential impact on the LGBT community (Bratton 2002).

Independent Variables

This section outlines the logic behind my independent variables and their operationalization. Although the key variable is my measure of descriptive representation, the theoretical discussion above as well as previous research suggest that a number of forces will likely influence legislative activity on LGBT issues, including public opinion, the preferences of elites, state population characteristics, and the characteristics and rules of the particular legislature (Haider-Markel 1999b, 2007).

Descriptive Representation

Recall that central to my analysis is the backlash hypothesis, which suggests that descriptive representation will increase the likelihood of negative policy proposals being introduced. To capture these influences, I first identified all the openly LGBT legislators who had ever held office in each state and their terms of service.[5] Second, I created a simple count variable of the number of openly LGBT legislators who served in each state for each year from 1992 to 2007. Thus, this variable captures the potential for LGBT legislators to sponsor LGBT-related legislation or to simply support or oppose LGBT-related legislation introduced by another legislator. I expect representation to be positively related to the introduction and passage of pro-LGBT bills, as well as to the adoption of antidiscrimination laws.

And although one might expect representation to be negatively related to the introduction and passage of anti-LGBT bills, recall that the backlash hypothesis suggests that the relationship will in fact be positive if openly LGBT legislators increase the visibility of LGBT issues in a state (Haider-Markel and Meier 1996). Increased salience in the legislative arena may lead to a legislative backlash in which perceived LGBT electoral successes lead legislators and interest groups to mobilize and then introduce and pass anti-LGBT legislation. Thus, representation should be positively associated with both anti-LGBT legislation and pro-LGBT legislation.

State Population Characteristics as Group Resources

Across the states, some LGBT groups have considerable strength and can exercise significant influence in the policymaking process, especially in states with a larger gay community (Haider-Markel 1997). Likewise, elected officials are attuned to the social and demographic composition of their consistencies. For LGBT groups and elected officials, the relative size of a LGBT constituency could be important in shaping policymaking. To account for this I include a measure of the percentage of households that are made up of same-sex unmarried partners.[6]

On the other side of the issue are conservative religious groups that oppose the positive legal recognition of homosexuals or homosexuality. Because most religions have explicit moral codes, orthodox followers will often have strong views on issues that they perceive involve morality, which often includes homosexuality. As such, persons with conservative religious beliefs in a state are a potential resource for conservative religious groups. Those religious denominations that likely have the strongest opposition to homosexuality are Protestant fundamentalists and conservative evangelicals because their religious doctrines oppose homosexuality (Layman and Carmines 1997). Similar to past research (Mooney and Lee 1995; Wald, Button, and Rienzo 1996), I capture the conservative religious population by including a measure of the percentage of a state's population that belongs to Protestant fundamentalist denominations.[7]

Legislature Ideology and Public Opinion

As legislators debate policy issues related to LGBTs, the preferences of the public and political elites shape legislative outcomes. Research suggests that liberal-leaning legislators are more supportive of LGBT civil rights issues, and that legislators are more supportive when their constituents support LGBT civil rights (Haider-Markel 1999b). I control for the ideological preferences of legislators with the measure of liberal/conservative ideology in the legislature developed by Berry and his colleagues (1998).[8] Higher scores for this measure indicate greater liberalism, and I expect liberalism to be associated with pro-LGBT legislation as well as legislative outcomes.[9] Public preferences towards LGBT civil rights are accounted for by using Lewis and Edelson's (2000) measure of average state public support for hiring homosexuals across five job categories. Higher scores for this measure indicate greater support for hiring LGBTs, and I expect that public support will be associated with fewer anti-LGBT measures being introduced and adopted.

Additionally, competition between political parties may influence the policy process. As parties become more competitive, the demands of appealing to voting and building electoral coalitions may result in more liberal policies. I control for party competition using Holbrook and Van Dunk's (1993) district-level measure of party competition.[10]

Institutional Characteristics

In my preliminary analysis I included several variables to capture institutional characteristics that might influence the legislative process and outcomes, including session length, professionalization, and the number of bills introduced and enacted. I expected that each of these variables might increase the total number of LGBT-related bills considered, and perhaps those adopted. However, the only consistently performing variables were the simple counts of the number of bills introduced and enacted. As such, in the models of bills introduced I include a control variable for the total number of bills introduced, and in the models of bills passed I include the total number of bills passed.[11] Each variable is coded "missing" for the years in which legislative sessions were not held.

Results and Discussion

Because the dependent variables in my models that examine bills introduced and passed are simple count variables, I estimated each equation using a random-effects Poisson regression (Lindsey 1999).[12] I first replicate the analysis in Haider-Markel (2007). The results for the models predicting the introduction (the first column) and the adoption of anti-LGBT legislation (second column) from 1992 to 2002 are shown in table 6.1.

Table 6.1   Determinants of State Introduction and Adoption of Anti-LGBT Legislation: Legislative Backlash Models, 1992–2002

Independent Variable	Introduction Model	Adoption Model
LGBT legislators	.412**	.296**
	(.041)	(.083)
Legislature ideology	−.019**	−.014**
	(.002)	(.004)
Protestant fundamentalists	.034**	.003
	(.012)	(.011)
LGBT households	−1.510	−.590
	(1.071)	(1.124)
Public support for LGBT rights	−3.958#	−1.037
	(2.226)	(2.578)
Party competition	−.028*	−.009
	(.013)	(.012)
Total bills considered or adopted	.000	.001
	(.000)	(.000)
Constant	3.155**	.045
	(.774)	(.791)
Log likelihood	−1,323.503	−396.901
Wald chi-square	152.79	25.31
Probabilty chi-square	.000	.000
No. of cases	509	509

Note: Dependent variables are raw counts of anti-LGBT bills introduced or passed. Coefficients are random-effects Poisson regression coefficients. Standard errors are in parentheses.
Significance levels for two-tailed tests: ** $< .01$; * $< .05$; # $< .10$.

The results indicate that number of anti-LGBT bills introduced is a function of population characteristics, legislature ideology, party competition, and public support for LGBT rights, which plays a more significant role than it did in the chapter 5 models for pro-LGBT legislation. The results suggest that as public support for LGBT rights increases, legislators may be less likely to introduce anti-LGBT bills. Additionally, legislature ideology plays a significant role here, with more liberal legislatures experiencing the introduction of fewer anti-LGBT bills. Interestingly, party competition is negatively related to bills in this model, which suggests that higher party competition might restrain legislators from introducing anti-LGBT legislation (as well as pro-LGBT legislation, as noted in chapter 5). For many legislators the issue may simply be too controversial to address in competitive political environments. The model of legislature adoption of anti-LGBT policies reveals a similar pattern, but population characteristics and public opinion appear to matter somewhat less for anti-LGBT policy adoption. This finding suggests that once bills are introduced, legislators might be less inclined to cater to constituency interests.

The population characteristics and legislative agenda play a role as well. Higher proportions of Protestant fundamentalists are associated with more anti-LGBT legislation being introduced. Meanwhile, the size of the LGBT population appears to have little influence on the number of anti-LGBT bills introduced, all other factors being considered. Interestingly, the size of the legislative agenda (i.e., total bills introduced) does not appear to influence the number of anti-LGBT bills introduced, even though chapter 5 noted a relationship between agenda size and pro-LGBT bills introduced. This finding simply suggests that the number of anti-LGBT bills introduced is not either enhanced or constrained by the overall legislative agenda.

However, the results of the bill adoption model do differ from the introduction model. Here legislature ideology and descriptive representation appear to be key drivers, and public opinion, party competition, and population characteristics play less of a role. This suggests that the success of anti-LGBT legislation is determined primarily by the context of the institution, and only indirectly by external forces.

But it is particularly important, and as predicted by the backlash hypothesis, that the number of LGBT legislators appears to increase the number of anti-LGBT bills introduced and passed. This finding conflicts with our traditional understanding of the theory of political representation, which suggests that the presence of representatives of a group will lead not only to increased substantive representation with more progroup legislation but also that increased descriptive representation should decrease the amount of antigroup legislation (Hedge, Button, and Spear 1996).

In sum, the evidence supporting the backlash hypothesis suggests that although political representation theory is partially correct—more descriptive representation is associated with more group-favorable legislation (chapter 5)—increased descriptive representation does not always reduce antigroup legislation, and instead appears to be associated with an increase in antigroup legislation (see also Bratton 2002). So even though chapter 4 provided plenty of examples of LGBT legislators who played a role in delaying or blocking anti-LGBT legislation, the systematic evidence would suggest that this representational role may be limited.

Nevertheless, one still must wonder how consistent this pattern of backlash is likely to be and whether or not we should reassess the importance of descriptive representation. This pattern could simply reflect the early gains of the LGBT movement in legislatures during the 1990s. To assess this potential, I expand the years under study to 1992 to 2007. These results are displayed in table 6.2.

The results for the expanded data set review that the influence of population characteristics (Protestant fundamentalists and LGBT households) may have declined during the 2000s because the size of these groups in each state is not associated with the introduction or adoption of anti-LGBT legislation. Likewise the influence of public opinion and party competition appears to have declined. Interestingly, the size of the legislative agenda appears to have become more important, as a significant positive influence on bill introduction and adoption. Thus during the 2000s the size of a state's legislative agenda served both to constrain and to enhance the number of anti-LGBT bills introduced and adopted.

Table 6.2   Determinants of State Introduction and Adoption of Anti-LGBT Legislation: Legislative Backlash Models, 1992–2007

Independent Variable	Introduction Model	Adoption Model
LGBT legislators	.075*	.111#
	(.026)	(.067)
Legislature ideology	−.007**	−.009*
	(.002)	(.003)
Protestant fundamentalists	−.012	.012
	(.009)	(.008)
LGBT households	.957	−.776
	(.789)	(.880)
Public support for LGBT rights	−1.845	.163
	(1.749)	(2.042)
Party competition	−.011	−.004
	(.009)	(.010)
Total bills considered or adopted	.0001*	.0008**
	(.0000)	(.0002)
Constant	1.487*	−.956
	(.587)	(.605)
Log likelihood	−1,972.210	−521.167
Wald chi-square	34.42	28.50
Probability chi-square	.000	.000
No. of cases	740	742

Note: Dependent variables are raw counts of anti-LGBT bills introduced or passed. Coefficients are random-effects Poisson regression coefficients. Standard errors are in parentheses.
Significance levels for two-tailed tests: ** < .01; * < .05; # < .10.

Interestingly, the results indicate that descriptive representation may have become less important for predicting legislation over time. This is evidenced by a much smaller coefficient in the expanded introduction model and the fact that the coefficient did not achieve traditional levels of statistical significance in the expanded adoption model. Thus, although some evidence for a backlash continues to exist, it appears to have declined since 2002. Given the pattern of events we observed in chapter 4, it seems that national trends, such as the Supreme Court decision in *Lawrence v. Texas* and the same-sex marriage debate following *Goodridge*, might be driving much of the post-2002 state legislative activity. The evidence from chapter 4 also suggests that the broader pattern we observe in these results—a decline in backlash against descriptive representation—could be occurring because the overall number of LGBT legislators has dramatically increased. This dramatic increase in descriptive representation coincides with an increase in pro-LGBT legislation as well, and this fact might be shaping the amount of anti-LGBT legislation introduced. This issue deserves more exploration, to which I move below.

Additional Analysis

Recall that although I narrowly defined backlash, the broader idea behind the hypothesis was that general social, political, and economic victories, not just electoral victories, for a previously marginalized group might lead to a backlash against the group in a variety of venues (Blalock 1967; Bratton 2002; Cammisa and Reingold 2004; Yoder 1991). Furthermore, I noted that the election of LGBT officials might serve to increase the salience of LGBT issues, and this in itself might invoke a counterresponse. If this more general principle is true, then perhaps other measures of successful LGBT political activity, such as consideration of more pro-LGBT policies, will also be associated with an increase in anti-LGBT legislation. To test this notion I reestimated the anti-LGBT legislation models and included the number of pro-LGBT bills introduced and passed as additional independent variables. If a backlash occurs because the election of LGBTs to the legislature makes some legislators introduce more anti-LGBT bills as a reaction to the perceived gains or threats of LGBT activists, then so too should any increase in the pro-LGBT agenda of the legislature.

In addition, I estimated the models with an interaction term for the number of LGBT legislators multiplied by the number of pro-LGBT bills passed or adopted. Although I hypothesized that increased LGBT victories in elections or on legislation might generate more anti-LGBT legislation, in combination it seems likely that a backlash might be overwhelmed, and the amount of anti-LGBT legislation might decline. The results of these models are displayed in table 6.3.

Although the pattern of backlash discovered above suggests that a broader application of the concept of backlash can be applied, a political backlash may also simply be a function of the institutional context in which LGBT legislators serve. In other words, it could be that a backlash only tends to occur when LGBT legislators are elected to relatively conservative legislative bodies. If this is the case, then the combination of liberal legislatures and LGBT legislators should lead to less anti-LGBT legislation, but the combination of conservative legislatures and LGBT legislators should lead to more anti-LGBT legislation. Thus, the influence of LGBT legislators would be context dependent. To test this hypothesis I reestimated the same models of anti-LGBT legislation but first created a dichotomous variable for conservative legislatures. Legislatures were coded 1, as conservative, if the legislative ideology score was below the mean for all states and all years, and were coded 0 otherwise.

Next I included an additional interaction variable, which is the sum of LGBT legislators multiplied by the conservative legislature ideology variable. If LGBT legislators have a negative influence on anti-LGBT legislation in liberal legislatures, but a positive influence in conservative legislatures, then the interaction variable should be positive and statistically significant. The first two rows in table 6.3 test the notion that a backlash occurs because some political actors perceive that LGBTs are making political gains, while the second two rows test the notion that the impact of descriptive representation is contextually determined.

The results appear to support the backlash hypothesis over the legislature ideology or context hypothesis. The number of pro-LGBT bills introduced has a positive

Table 6.3 Determinants of State Introduction and Adoption of Anti-LGBT Legislation, Backlash and Context, 1992–2007

Independent Variable	Introduction Model	Adoption Model
All variables plus:		
Pro-LGBT bills introduced or passed	.051**	.210**
	(.003)	(.041)
Interaction: pro-LGBT bills introduced or passed * LGBT legislators	−.016**	−.037#
	(.002)	(.020)
All variables plus:		
Conservative legislature ideology	.208**	.317*
	(.061)	(.161)
Interaction: LGBT legislators * conservative legislature ideology	−.182**	−.231#
	(.048)	(.143)

Note: Dependent variables are raw counts of anti-LGBT bills introduced or passed, 1992–2007. Coefficients are random-effects Poisson regression coefficients. Standard errors are in parentheses. All variables from the original models are included for the analysis, except that legislature ideology is modified. Conservative legislatures are coded 1 if the ideology score is below the mean ideology for all states and years and 0 otherwise. Significance levels for two-tailed tests: ** < .01; * < .05; # < .10.

influence on the number of anti-LGBT bills introduced, and the number of pro-LGBT bills adopted influences the number of anti-LGBT bills adopted. This suggests that a backlash does in fact occur when legislators, and perhaps other political actors, observe an increase in the legislature's pro-LGBT agenda. However, the results for the interaction variable between pro-LGBT legislation and LGBT legislators suggest that as both increase, anti-LGBT legislation tends to decrease, indicating that the backlash may be overwhelmed by large LGBT political gains. As pointed out in cases such as the state of Washington and Massachusetts, once several LGBT legislators are in office and major pro-LGBT legislation (e.g., antidiscrimination laws and domestic partner or marriage laws) has been adopted, it seems fairly pointless for conservative legislators to continue to introduce bills that might, for example, prevent the formation of LGBT clubs in public schools.

Conversely, there is somewhat less support for the context hypothesis as outlined. First, the dichotomized variable for conservative legislatures performs in a similar manner to that of the original interval level measure—more conservative legislatures are associated with more anti-LGBT bills introduced and adopted. Second, the interaction variable for context (LGBT legislators multiplied by conservative legislatures) is significant in the introduction model but is barely significant in the adoption model. However, the sign is negative, suggesting that conservative legislatures respond *more positively to the presence of LGBT legislators than do more liberal legislatures*, relative to the overall mean.

Indeed, if the relationship is broken down according to the actual number of LGBT legislators, at 0 legislators, legislature ideology is significant and positive (b = .415, $p <$ .000), but it becomes insignificant and negative as 1 and 2 LGBT legislators are added (b = .111, $p <$ .505; b = −.035, $p <$ .823). This is counter to the expectations of the context hypothesis, and suggests that *the backlash against LGBT legislators may in fact be greater in more liberal legislators.* There is support for this notion; states that tend to have more LGBT legislators, and more liberal ideologies, such as California, also tend to see a greater number of anti-LGBT bills introduced. This pattern could result because these legislatures also tend to have more ideological polarization between members, but the data do not allow for a clear test of this proposition.

Although these results are inconclusive, the evidence provides the strongest support for the political gains backlash hypothesis. However, both sets of results clearly indicate that the political context within legislatures can condition the influence of LGBT legislators, and even in those cases where increased descriptive representation creates a backlash, when it is combined with greater substantive representation (i.e., pro-LGBT bills introduced), the number of anti-LGBT bills declines. Nevertheless, as the quotation from Arkansas representative Kathy Webb at the beginning of this chapter suggests, legislative context may play a role. When LGBT legislators are elected to conservative legislatures, their influence may come in terms of decreasing anti-LGBT legislation, at least relative to what it would be predicted at given the ideology of the legislature. In more liberal legislatures, LGBT legislators appear to increase the amount of anti-LGBT legislation, relative to what would be predicted.

Assessing the Overall Representational Benefit

The analysis thus far clearly suggests that there can be a negative component of descriptive representation. If LGBTs increase representation through the election of LGBT officials and increasing the pro-LGBT agenda of legislatures, they also will also likely face an increasing anti-LGBT agenda in state legislatures. Recall that Bratton (2002) found similar results for increased black descriptive representation. Should we conclude that underrepresented groups should consider forgoing descriptive representation?

Perhaps most observers would be unlikely to argue for less descriptive representation, but the question indicates that we should evaluate the negative influence of descriptive representation relative to the positive influence. To determine if the net effect of increased descriptive political representation might in fact be positive rather than negative, I estimated two additional models, which are displayed in tables 6.4 and 6.5. For these models I simply subtracted the number of anti-LGBT bills from the number of pro-LGBT bills introduced (the first column) and adopted (second column). Thus, each dependent variable is still a simple count, with a higher positive number indicating a higher pro-LGBT legislative agenda.

The results in table 6.4 replicate the original analysis from Haider-Markel (2007) and cover the years 1992 to 2002. The pattern is similar to that found in chapter 5 and suggests that increases in legislature liberal ideology, LGBT households, and the

Table 6.4 Determinants of the Difference between Pro-LGBT Legislation and Anti-LGBT Legislation Considered and Adopted: Overall Pro-LGBT Policy Benefit, 1992–2002

Independent Variable	Pro-Anti Introduction Model	Pro-Anti Adoption Model
LGBT legislators	.492**	.200**
	(.162)	(.053)
Legislature ideology	.005	.004#
	(.007)	(.002)
Protestant fundamentalists	−.029*	−.014**
	(.011)	(.004)
LGBT households	3.602#	1.090*
	(2.082)	(.508)
Public support for LGBT rights	1.256	.666
	(2.891)	(.700)
Party competition	.001	.009
	(.017)	(.006)
Total bills considered or adopted	.0003*	.0005*
	(.0001)	(.0002)
Constant	−2.287#	−.941*
	(1.267)	(.424)
R^2	.15	.17
Wald chi-square	70.85	67.68
Probabilty chi-square	.000	.000
No. of cases	509	509

Note: Dependent variables are the result of pro-LGBT bills introduced minus anti-LGBT bills, and pro-LGBT minus anti-LGBT bills passed. Coefficients are regression coefficients with panel corrected standard errors. Standard errors are in parentheses. Significance levels for two-tailed tests: ** < .01; * < .05; # < .10.

total legislative volume are associated with increases in the amount of pro-LGBT legislation introduced or adopted, relative to anti-LGBT legislation.

Increases in Protestant fundamentalists, meanwhile, are associated with declines in the amount of pro-LGBT legislation introduced or adopted, relative to anti-LGBT legislation. Most important, the number of LGBT legislators is positively associated with the amount of pro-LGBT legislation introduced or adopted, relative to anti-LGBT legislation, indicating that the net effect of descriptive representation is positive for the LGBT community.

However, have these results changed since 2002, especially because there has been a significant increase in state legislative efforts to ban same-sex marriage? The results for the models from 1992 to 2007, displayed in table 6.5, reveal that there may have even been an increase in the importance of descriptive representation, LGBT households, and public opinion.[13] Meanwhile, the influence of legislature ideology and Protestant fundamentalists on the amount of pro-LGBT legislation introduced or adopted, relative to anti-LGBT legislation, appears to have declined.

Table 6.5   Determinants of the Difference between Pro-LGBT Legislation and Anti-LGBT Legislation Considered and Adopted: Overall Pro-LGBT Policy Benefit, 1992–2007

Independent Variable	Pro-Anti Introduction Model	Pro-Anti Adoption Model
LGBT legislators	.637**	.231**
	(.191)	(.056)
Legislature ideology	− .008	.005**
	(.008)	(.002)
Protestant fundamentalists	− .040**	− .014**
	(.010)	(.004)
LGBT households	3.764*	1.132*
	(1.609)	(.444)
Public support for LGBT rights	− 1.073	1.185#
	(2.285)	(.605)
Party competition	.021	.012*
	(.016)	(.005)
Total bills considered or adopted	.0008*	.0006*
	(.0003)	(.0002)
Constant	− 2.718*	− 1.117*
	(1.182)	(.404)
R^2	.23	.19
Wald chi-square	90.10	80.96
Probability chi-square	.000	.000
Number of cases	741	743

Note: Dependent variables are the result of pro-LGBT bills introduced minus anti-LGBT bills, and pro-LGBT minus anti-LGBT bills passed. Coefficients are regression coefficients with panel corrected standard errors. Standard errors are in parentheses. Significance levels for two-tailed tests: ** < .01; * < .05; # < .10.

Therefore, it appears fairly safe to conclude that the overall effect of descriptive political representation for the LGBT community is in fact positive—as the number of openly LGBT legislators increases, so too does the net pro-LGBT agenda. Although descriptive representation may generate an anti-LGBT policy backlash, the sum impact of increased descriptive representation is the increased substantive representation of the LGBT community. In addition, the pattern of results presented here and the case study evidence from chapter 4 indicate that the importance of LGBT descriptive representation in the policy process may become more important as more LGBT legislators are elected around the country.

Conclusions

This chapter has reexamined the impact of descriptive political representation in state legislatures. I suggest that although LGBT citizens are more likely to see their issues on the political agenda and achieve legislative success if they elect LGBT officials, a backlash hypothesis posits that increased descriptive representation might also result in an increase in the anti-LGBT agenda of state legislatures. To test this hypothesis I replicated analyses of pro-LGBT and anti-LGBT bill introduction and bill adoption using 1992 to 2002 data from the American states, and I expanded this analysis to include the years 1992 to 2007. Because the backlash hypothesis suggested that descriptive representation could have negative consequences for the LGBT community, I also explored the overall benefit of descriptive representation on the legislative agenda for the LGBT community.

My empirical results suggest that there is a potential backlash against descriptive representation for the LGBT community; as the number of LGBT legislators increased, so too did the number of anti-LGBT bills introduced and passed—a negative outcome for the LGBT community. Thus, consistent with a limited body of empirical research (i.e., Bratton 2002, 2006; Bratton and Haynie 1999; Preuhs 2005; Thomas 1994), the backlash hypothesis of descriptive representation was supported.

These results replicate the findings in Haider-Markel (2007) but also extended them with data through 2007. The results of the extended analysis reveal a similar pattern, but the phenomenon of backlash was less apparent, suggesting that the backlash against LGBT descriptive representation may be decreasing over time.

The backlash hypothesis was also supported with an additional analysis examining the influence of the pro-LGBT legislative agenda on the anti-LGBT legislative agenda. Both the replication and extension revealed that increases in the pro-LGBT legislative agenda are associated with increases in the anti-LGBT legislative agenda. However, this pattern can be reversed. The analysis suggests that if both LGBT representation and the pro-LGBT legislative agenda increase, an associated decrease can be seen in the anti-LGBT legislative agenda.

Furthermore, the pattern of backlash does appear to be influenced by the state legislative context, but not in a manner hypothesized. One interpretation of the backlash hypothesis would suggest that an underrepresented group that gains representation would be more likely to face a backlash in more conservative legislative contexts. However, the analysis suggests that the reverse may be true—a backlash against descriptive representation is more visible in (relatively) more liberal legislatures. In short, LGBT descriptive representative has the greatest impact of reducing anti-LGBT legislation in conservative legislatures. In more liberal legislatures, increased descriptive representation is associated with more anti-LGBT legislation. Although I suspect that we are observing the effects of ideological polarization within legislatures, and the case studies in chapter 4 appear to support this pattern, this issue must be left for future research.

Finally, I conducted additional analysis of the net effect of LGBT descriptive representation by modeling the difference between pro-LGBT legislation and anti-LGBT legislation. The results of this multivariate analysis suggest that descriptive representation for the LGBT community has a greater positive than negative effect on legislation and policy. This pattern holds even when the years 2003 to 2007 are added to the analysis. Indeed, the updated analysis suggests that the influence of anti-LGBT forces may have declined, and the importance of LGBT descriptive representation may have increased relative to these other factors. Thus, we can be fairly confident that descriptive representation will lead to net positive policy outcomes for the represented community.

Notes

1. Voss and Miller (2001) argue for and test a backlash hypothesis in the context of a state referendum vote on desegregation but they find no evidence of a white backlash against black civil rights.

2. Although Francisco (1995, 1996) and others suggest that backlash occurs when a critical mass is reached, I assume that because LGBT officeholders are so few in number, the election of even one could lead to a backlash. However, as more LGBT persons are elected, arguments concerning critical mass may become more relevant (Blalock 1967; Studlar and McAllister 2002; Thomas 1994; Yoder 1991).

3. These data are from the National Gay and Lesbian Task Force, state LGBT interest groups, and searches of state legislative websites and the LexisNexis state government universe by the author.

4. For a detailed description of the types of bills included for a variety of years, see the National Gay and Lesbian Task Force Reports, www.thetaskforce.org/reslibrary/list.cfm?pubTypeID = 2.

5. These data are from the National LGBT Task Force, the LGBT Victory Fund, and newspaper searches of LexisNexis using the keywords "gay," "lesbian," and "candidate." In a preliminary analysis I also included a measure of the number of LGBT candidates that had run for state legislative office. At no point did this measure approach statistical significance, so it was removed from the final models.

6. These data are from the U.S. Bureau of the Census (2003). In the 2000 census respondents were asked if they lived with an unmarried partner. Only those respondents who indicated that they lived with a same-sex partner are counted here. Although it is clear that this only counts those gays and lesbians living with a partner and willing to signify it, the measure is a reasonable surrogate of the size of the LGBT community (see Haider-Markel 1997; Wald, Button, and Rienzo 1996).

7. Following Haider-Markel and Meier (1996), the denominations classified as Protestant fundamentalist were Churches of God, Latter-Day Saints, Churches of Christ, Church of the Nazarene, Mennonites, Conservative Baptist Association, Missouri Synod Lutherans, Pentecostal Holiness, the Salvation Army, Seventh-Day Adventists, Southern Baptists, and Wisconsin Synod Lutherans. These data are from the Glenmary Research Center (2004) and exclude independent churches. The Catholic population was included in early models but dropped because of a lack of theoretical or empirical support.

8. Additional annual data are from the Berry et al. (1998) data update on the website of the Interuniversity Consortium for Political and Social Research, www.icpsr.umich.edu.

9. Democrats tend to be more supportive of gay civil rights than Republicans (Yang 1999). Thus, a related measure would be partisan control of the state legislature. However, my preliminary analysis found that the inclusion of a percent Democrat variable was not statistically significant, nor did it improve the models. Furthermore, given the high number of conservative Democrats in southern legislatures, a partisan control variable should be expected to perform poorly.

10. Because Louisiana is missing from the Holbrook and Van Dunk (1993) measure, I used other measures of partisanship and competition to estimate Louisiana's score as 17.07.

11. These data are from the Council of State Governments (various years).

12. The models estimated here were also estimated with a heteroskedastic corrected liner regression model, a fixed effects model, and a random effects regression model (Diggle et al. 2002). The results from these estimation techniques produce similar results to those presented here, indicating that the models are quite robust.

13. These arguments are based on a comparison of the size and significance of the coefficients across the models.

CHAPTER SEVEN

Conclusion: Out for Good

I represent 125,000 people, except, at some level, I also represent all the gay people, so it becomes a harder line to balance those different interests, because those interest groups didn't elect me.

—Openly gay New York assemblyman
Daniel O'Donnell on representation

In the past, I tried to avoid being the message and the messenger. This year I just felt that in order for it to pass I had to take on both roles. But I'm not going to lie to you. I've gotten my feelings hurt a couple of times. There were people who would not sign onto the bill and who would not be up-front with me or vote for it, and then say they want to be my friend and hug me and love me. But I know they're not supporting this bill because it has "sexual orientation" in it. That was not the most pleasant experience.

—Openly lesbian North Carolina state senator Julia Boseman
on her role in passing a pro-LGBT school antibullying bill

A S THE AMERICAN LGBT movement has expanded and matured, its policy successes have grown as well. However, as other political movements and groups have recognized, having friends at the table may not be quite the same thing as having one of your own at the table. But even with this intuitive logic, theorists of democracy have consistently suggested that there are often barriers to electing members of politically marginalized groups, and even if members of the group achieve descriptive representation, it is no guarantee of substantive representation in the policy process.

However, we know very little about potential barriers to the election of LGBT candidates. It is clear that some voters would likely oppose an LGBT candidate because of negative attitudes about homosexuality, but does this translate into enough electoral opposition to prevent LGBT candidates from being elected? Up until this point the evidence has been largely anecdotal and somewhat mixed. At the same time we know that female and minority candidates have faced voter opposition and other hurdles in their attempts to achieve elective office.

In addition there is little empirical research that evaluates whether the increased descriptive representation of LGBT Americans has in fact translated into increased substantive representation or, at a minimum, into the infusion of LGBT preferences into the policy process. Studies at the local level suggest that higher levels of LGBT descriptive representation increase the likelihood that local governments will adopt LGBT-friendly policies (Haider-Markel, Joslyn, and Kniss 2000), and case studies of national-level LGBT officials reveal that LGBT officials are able to influence the policy process (Rayside 1998). However, only limited anecdotal evidence from research on state government policymaking suggests that LGBT officials increase the political representation of LGBT interests in the state policymaking process (but see Haider-Markel 2000, 2007).

In writing this book I set out to explore these empirical questions by focusing on state legislative races and the policy process in state legislatures. I have employed both qualitative and quantitative analyses across selected state elections from 1992 to 2006, and the legislative consideration and adoption of a variety of LGBT-related policy proposals from 1990 to 2007. In this chapter I broadly interpret the findings of the previous chapters, outline important caveats, and sketch an agenda for future research.

Descriptive Representation

Analyses of state and national public opinion polls suggest that about 25 percent of the electorate is unlikely to vote for a gay or lesbian candidate for nearly any office. These individuals are more likely to be conservative, Republican, male, religious, and have less education and live in rural areas. This is a potential barrier to LGBT candidates who seek public office, but potential candidates can also take steps to assess the characteristics of the jurisdictions in which they might run for office; simply put, candidates can attempt to avoid running in districts that are disproportionately composed of individuals who tend not to support LGBT rights or LGBT candidates in surveys. Candidates can in fact strategically choose where, when, and how they run for office.

My qualitative and quantitative analysis of elections and LGBT candidates in chapters 2 and 3 suggests a counterintuitive conclusion—that sexual orientation is not a major barrier to LGBT politicians seeking public office. This is not to say that voters do not care about sexual orientation or that an LGBT candidate could run for any office in any state and be successful. Instead there is clearly a self-selection process that occurs. As chapter 2 makes clear, potential and actual LGBT candidates are cognizant of the fact that their sexual identity might play a role in determining their electoral viability. As such, and consistent with the behavior of all politicians, LGBT candidates are strategic about where, how, and when they choose to run for office. This means that LGBT candidates are, for the most part, only running for state legislative seats in districts where their sexual identity is unlikely to be a major hindrance to electoral victory. In addition, LGBT candidates appear to further mediate the potential negative consequences of their minority sexual orientation status through experience; the vast majority of LGBT candidates appear to be "quality candidates" insofar as they often have previously held a local political office or have worked for elected officials. This experience also makes it more likely that candidates can attract the support of important interest groups, as well as financial support.

LGBT candidates also do a great deal to mediate the impact of their sexual orientation by generally running as Democrats in largely Democratic districts. The evidence suggests that those voters who are most likely to oppose an LGBT candidate are also more likely to oppose a Democratic candidate, regardless of sexual orientation. This pattern is similar to what has been observed for many female candidates and candidates from ethnic and racial minority groups—likely opposition is usually not directly observed because those voters are voting based on party affiliation.

But to suggest that sexual orientation does not matter in electoral contests would be highly misleading. Clearly there are LGBT individuals who choose not to run because of real or perceived barriers and some candidates who choose to run face opponents and interest groups that at least attempt to mobilize opposition to the candidate based on his or her sexual orientation. It is also clear that there are many state legislative districts where it is unlikely that an LGBT candidate would run for a seat, and if he or she did, the candidate would very likely be unsuccessful. Therefore, there are real limits to descriptive representation for the LGBT community in many states and large parts of the country.

Conversely, to suggest that LGBT candidates face major barriers to election would also be off the mark. It seems reasonable to conclude that although sexual orientation can be a barrier to elective office, there are a variety of strategic methods to reduce the negative implications of being an LGBT candidate. And LGBT candidates for state legislative office appear to be generally astute at mediating the effects, much of the time.

One case illustrates this point. Utah, which has three openly gay or lesbian state legislators, is one of the most conservative Republican states in the union and seemingly one of the least likely places for LGBT candidates to run for office. All three of Utah's LGBT legislators ran as Democrats in relatively diverse urban districts that include portions of Salt Lake City. It seems likely that these legislators would not have been successful in other parts of the state or even in nearby states. But in and around Salt Lake City, they clearly saw fewer barriers to election and capitalized on the opportunity.

Thus, even in seemingly inhospitable states, the LGBT community may have a better opportunity for full proportional descriptive representation in state legislatures than do other groups, such as women or racial and ethnic minorities. Because the LGBT community is fairly well organized in many states, and there have been a fair number of LGBT candidates in local offices (providing a farm team for potential state office candidates), the community might be more likely to see descriptive representation of 3 percent in some state legislatures, which is probably equivalent to its representation in the general population in most states. For example, the six LGBT legislators in Washington constituted 4 percent of the state's legislative seats in 2009. Meanwhile, there is no state legislature in the country where women make up even 40 percent of legislators, even though they constitute more than 50 percent of the population in most states.

Moreover, although the historical experience of female and minority candidates suggests that LGBT candidates should also be less likely to win elections relative to their heterosexual peers, my analysis suggests that LGBT candidates are not less likely to be elected. In fact, LGBT Democratic candidates may even have a slight edge over their opponents in a general election contest. For LGBT Republicans there does not appear to be an electoral advantage or disadvantage. Likewise, LGBT candidates do not receive a lower percentage of the vote than do their heterosexual peers, and LGBT Democrats tend to receive about 7 percentage points more of the two-party vote than their heterosexual counterparts, controlling for all other factors. Interestingly, gay male candidates do not receive more support than lesbian candidates, which suggests that there is little combined bias toward sexual orientation and gender.

This does not mean that voters necessarily prefer LGBT candidates over heterosexual candidates, but it may indicate that when they do run for state legislative office, LGBT candidates are in a stronger position than their heterosexual counterparts because of where they choose to run, when they run, and how they run, such as holding a lower-level office or enlisting more support before a campaign.

But there are limits to what we know thus far. For example, we do not have systematic information on primary elections and the extent to which candidate sexual orientation may play a role in those races. The analysis in chapter 2 suggests that sexual orientation plays no greater role in primary elections than in general elections, but the evidence is not conclusive. In addition, we cannot draw conclusions about LGBT candidates for state legislative seats before 1992. Although there were few LGBT candidates before the 1990s, given generally more negative sentiment toward homosexuality during that time, it seems reasonable to conclude that a potential candidate's sexual orientation was more likely to deter him or her, and even if it did not, it likely decreased the electoral chances of those candidates.

If recent trends continue, we are likely to see more and more LGBT candidates run for state legislative seats, as well as other offices, where their ability to mediate the potentially negative effects of sexual orientation might be lower. As this occurs it could be that sexual orientation will come to play a larger role in future campaigns. We may be on the verge of seeing this pattern in some southern states, such as in Georgia and North Carolina, where there is a growing farm team of local LGBT officials who may have aspirations for state offices. Likewise, there is some growth in the number of Republican LGBT candidates, and given the likely opponents to an LGBT candidate, these candidates may find that their sexual orientation plays a more significant role in their elections.

Substantive Representation

Recall that much of the research on the impact of female and minority descriptive representation found at least some evidence that descriptive representation by these groups can be translated into substantive representation. Based on this previous research I expected that LGBT descriptive representation could also be translated into substantive representation in the state policymaking process. In chapters 4 and 5 I used qualitative and quantitative analyses of LGBT descriptive representation to explore this question. The findings in both chapters strongly suggest that increased descriptive representation translates into increased substantive representation in the policy process.

The case studies of California, Massachusetts, Minnesota, Oregon, Virginia, and Washington show a similar pattern—as LGBT legislators take office, the number of pro-LGBT bills introduced and passed increases. In addition, in some states, such as Massachusetts, Minnesota, and Washington, it seems unlikely that major advances in LGBT civil rights would have occurred when they occurred if it had not been for the actions of LGBT legislators. Some of the increase in pro-LGBT legislation is the direct result of LGBT legislators sponsoring or cosponsoring legislation, but the increase can also be attributed to LGBT legislators' efforts in supporting measures that are sometimes introduced by others as part of a broader coalition-building strategy.

The cases illustrate that although description representation can translate into substantive representation, the pattern differs across states. Likewise, the strategies of LGBT legislators differ even within the same state. Although this finding is not surprising by itself, it highlights the fact that like other politicians, LGBT politicians are strategic in terms of how and when they engage in substantive representation of the LGBT community. And it also demonstrates that even for LGBT legislators who have actively pursued LGBT issues in the legislature over multiple legislative sessions, these bills are still often a relatively small percentage of the total number of bills a legislator might sponsor or cosponsor and invest considerable time in pursuing.

In some states legislators clearly feel constrained in actively pursuing pro-LGBT legislation through sponsorship or cosponsorship. In fact, some legislators appeared to have realized that it can be advantageous to allow others to be the central proponents of pro-LGBT bills. If the LGBT legislator is the one to sponsor a given bill, it may shape who chooses to support or oppose the measure. In addition, allowing more seasoned legislators to introduce a given bill might attract more cosponsors, help passage in committee, and provide benefits in that legislator's own district.

Indeed, one clear pattern across all the cases is that LGBT legislators believe that part of their representation role is to educate other legislators on LGBT issues. Part of this occurs simply through their presence in the institution, but also through the pursuit of incremental policy change. The cases highlight many examples of LGBT legislators who introduce bills that are assured of defeat with the goal of educating other legislators on issues so that a future version of the bill might pass down the road. Some refer to this process as "softening up." We can also see that although individual legislators can be quite effective in pursing the interests of the LGBT community, there is certainly additional leverage within legislative institutions when there are multiple LGBT legislators present, especially when they are in each chamber.

In chapter 5 my statistical analysis of bills introduced and adopted across the fifty states from 1992 to 2007 confirms the pattern observed in the case studies. I find that even when controlling for other factors such as state and legislature characteristics, higher LGBT representation in state legislatures leads to greater substantive representation in terms of LGBT-related bills that are introduced and adopted. I also find that a greater number of LGBT legislators is associated with a higher probability of adopting antidiscrimination laws based on sexual orientation, a primary goal of the LGBT movement. This is consistent with previous studies of female and minority legislators, and perhaps more convincing because the legislation examined here can be more clearly linked to the goals of the LGBT movement than many of the legislative policy proposals examined in the literature on female and minority legislators.

The findings with regard to the role of state characteristics, public opinion, and the ideological leanings of legislatures also allow for some general conclusions. The importance of public preferences in the election of LGBT officials and the adoption of pro-LGBT policies was confirmed in this analysis and suggests that the process of LGBT-related policy change is unlikely unless public opinion in a state is tolerant. Other forces, such as potential interest group resources and legislature ideology, have an important role to play, but pro-LGBT policy change appears to hinge indirectly or directly on public support (see Lax and Phillips 2009).

With this in mind, LGBT activists who seek policy change must consider a broader strategy of grassroots mobilization that involves a "changing hearts and minds" strategy versus a dominance of backroom politicking in state legislatures. Interestingly, backroom procedural maneuvering may matter more for blocking anti-LGBT legislation, but it is not a long-term strategy for winning.

The analyses in chapters 4 and 5 also make clear that there is not one model of LGBT representation that LGBT legislators follow, and that all LGBT legislators spend the majority of their time on non-LGBT issues. Their allocation of time and effort appears to vary based on the needs of their district constituents, the political composition of the chamber and full legislature in which they operate, and even the level of support shown by the state's governor. In some cases LGBT representation is limited to simply reducing the impact of the anti-LGBT legislation that is likely to pass.

Interestingly, many LGBT legislators seem to operate as educators. They feel a need to educate other legislators and the public on LGBT issues through their presence in the legislature, but also through an incremental pursuit of policy goals. This strategy includes introducing bills that are certain to fail in the short term so that, for the long term, legislators can begin to be exposed to the problems faced by LGBT constituents as well as the potential remedies for these problems.

Substantive Representation and Backlash

Perhaps one of the most understudied aspects of descriptive representation is whether increases in descriptive representation can engender a political or policy backlash. In chapter 4 the historical cases and reaction to some LGBT legislators appear to support the idea that LGBT representation can lead to a policy backlash both within the legislature and in other venues, such as the citizen initiative and referenda processes. Chapter 6 systematically explores this question and whether an anti-LGBT backlash might occur because of increased success with an LGBT policy agenda in the legislature. The results support the proposition that increased LGBT descriptive representation can lead to more anti-LGBT legislation being introduced and passed. The backlash hypothesis was also supported with an additional analysis that examines the influence of the pro-LGBT legislative agenda on the anti-LGBT legislative agenda. Both the replication and extension reveals that increases in the pro-LGBT legislative agenda are associated with increases in the anti-LGBT legislative agenda. However, this pattern can be reversed. This analysis suggests that if both LGBT representation and the pro-LGBT legislative agenda increase, an associated decrease can be seen in the anti-LGBT legislative agenda.

Furthermore, the pattern of backlash appears to be influenced by the state legislative context but not in a manner hypothesized. One interpretation of the backlash hypothesis suggests that an underrepresented group that gains representation is more likely to face a backlash in more conservative legislative contexts. However, the analysis suggests that the reverse may be true—a backlash against descriptive representation is more visible in (relatively) more liberal legislatures. In short, LGBT descriptive representation has the greatest impact of reducing anti-LGBT legislation in conservative legislatures. In more liberal legislatures, increased descriptive representation is associated with more anti-LGBT legislation. Put differently, when LGBT legislators are elected to conservative legislatures, their influence may come in terms of decreasing anti-LGBT legislation, at least relative to what it would be predicted to be given the ideology of the legislature. In more liberal legislatures, LGBT legislators appear to increase the amount of anti-LGBT legislation relative to what would be predicted. Although I suspect that we are observing the effects of ideological polarization within legislatures, and the case studies in chapter 4 appear to support this pattern, this issue must be left for future research.

It is also clear from the historical case studies that political backlashes to LGBT representation are not limited to actions in the legislature, and in fact the actions in the legislature may be relatively trivial when compared with measures passed with direct democracy techniques (see Haider-Markel, Querze, and Lindaman 2007). My analysis also highlights the fact that a political backlash is not limited to those things that occur within one state's boundaries. Clearly much of the anti-LGBT legislation introduced in state legislatures through the 2000s was a direct result of both court decisions on same-sex marriage in other states and the U.S. Supreme Court's decision in *Lawrence v Texas*, but some might also be attributed to the legislative successes of the LGBT movement in other states. Thus, a full understanding of backlash in the context of descriptive representation must take a broader array of forces into account.

Representation as Reality

Some readers might be troubled by the evidence that suggests that descriptive representation might incur negative political consequences. Certainly one should interpret the evidence with caution, but the additional analysis in chapter 6 suggests that the political benefits of increased descriptive representation outweigh the costs. For this analysis I modeled the difference between pro-LGBT legislation and anti-LGBT legislation introduced and passed. The results of this multivariate analysis suggest that descriptive representation for the LGBT community has a greater positive than negative effect on legislation and policy. This holds throughout the period 1992–2007, but my analysis indicates that the influence of anti-LGBT forces may have declined over time, and the importance of LGBT descriptive representation may have increased. Thus, we can be fairly confident that descriptive representation will lead to positive policy outcomes for the represented community, and the potential for this is likely to grow in the short term.

Directions for Future Research

I have pointed out the many limitations of the research presented in this book, but it is worthwhile to highlight a few more general directions for future research. First, we still know very little about LGBT representation at the local level. Although my results suggest that LGBT candidates will likely choose to run for office in areas that will be less hostile toward LGBT people, we do not know if the same is true of potential candidates for local offices. These candidates are more likely to differ in terms of "quality," and one might expect that we would see a great many candidates who run for office but have little chance for success. Unfortunately local races receive less media attention and are also generally more difficult to study.

Second, future research should attempt to better explain how and when potential LGBT candidates run for office. My analysis does not systematically explore primary elections and is entirely reliant on the pool of individuals who ran for office. As Fox and Lawless (2004, 2005) make clear, many potential female candidates for office self-select out of the process because they misperceive the hurdles to success. The same might be true for LGBT candidates but future researchers should explore this question by identifying pools of potential candidates for public office.

Third, this issue gives rise to yet another: What is the dynamic between openly LGBT candidates and legislators and those LGBT candidates and legislators who choose not to go public with their sexual orientation? In many states the closeted LGBT candidates and legislators are known to many individuals, and their support on LGBT issues in legislatures might often be crucial, yet we know almost nothing about their roles, except through rumor and the few cases where such legislators have later publicized their sexual orientation. Although difficult, it may be possible to identify these individuals for a qualitative anonymous study of candidates' and/ or legislators' behavior.

Fourth, my analysis of political backlash against increased descriptive representation is clearly narrow. But given that there is evidence that other groups have faced similar circumstances (Bratton 2002; Sanbonmatsu 2008), researchers should develop research designs that can incorporate the dynamic nature of this process and account for the forces both external and internal to a state. This is especially relevant in LGBT politics but it would also likely be important for understanding a backlash against increased descriptive representation of women, African Americans, and Latinos.

Finally, through the book I do not distinguish between candidates and legislators who belong to more than one group. For example, little note is made of a black, gay male or a Latina lesbian. I found little evidence of differences in electoral support for gay versus lesbian candidates but I could not systematically explore the influence of an LGBT candidate's race. Currently, LGBT candidates and legislators who belong to more than one group are limited to a handful, but these numbers will surely increase considerably in the next decade. How these candidates and legislators come to understand and act upon their multiple identities could provide important new insights for representation theory.

Implications for Groups and Movements

My suggestions for future research also point to some of the broader relevance some might draw from the findings presented in this book. In particular, what implications do these findings have for the LGBT movement as well as other movements and groups?

All movements certainly attempt to influence the policy process, and there is a reasonable debate over whether descriptive representation is the best means for pursuing policy change. On the basis of what I have learned from this project, I would suggest that the question here is actually broader than substantive policy representation. The real question for the objective observer is: Given a variety of movement goals, should considerable effort and resources be expended to elect representatives of the movement? I believe the answer is yes, for several reasons.

First, the evidence suggests that policy representation can be increased, even if in fits and starts. Pursuing policy change solely through the sympathetic efforts of friends of a movement is tenuous, and when political pressure mounts, these friends may abandon movement goals. Examples abound, but some of the most dramatic are, of course, President Bill Clinton's backtracking on gays serving openly in the military and his secretive signing of the Defense of Marriage Act in 1996. More recently, in 2009 liberal New Jersey legislators backed off passing a law to allow same-sex marriage following the defeat of the state's Democratic governor who had championed the bill.

Second, as evidenced by my qualitative analysis of candidates and legislators, the LGBT people who run for office as well as those who win have profound effects on LGBT people in general and, perhaps to a lesser extent, on heterosexuals. Harvey Milk's campaigns, success, and murder are the most dramatic examples, but others abound. (The reaction of the LGBT community to the historic election of lesbian Annise Parker as the mayor of Houston in December 2009 also provides a vivid example.) As a stigmatized minority, LGBT people—and especially LGBT youth—need role models who make it clear that the political process can be successfully engaged. Many voters are willing to support LGBT candidates, and the LGBT community sometimes succeeds in the policy process. Because the possibility of same-sex marriage has been used to inflame the far right of American politics since 2003, this message seems especially important; it is often elected officials who serve as the most visible role models on political issues, and if LGBT officials are not present in these debates, the outcome is more likely to be damaging to the LGBT community.

Finally, movements need leaders and organization. The LGBT movement's leaders might become political candidates, and LGBT political candidates might inspire the next generation of movement leaders. But perhaps more important, movements tend to be sustained when they achieve measurable success. Although there are significant LGBT groups working at the national level to influence national and state policies, my research suggests that movement gains in leadership, organization, and policy success might be more achievable at the local and state levels. Grassroots organizing and a strategy of changing public attitudes might be the best means for achieving long-term policy goals and may also build a lasting foundation for tolerance and understanding in the broader civic culture. Recall that LGBT activist groups in states such as California, Oregon, and Washington were able to build lasting organizations during anti-LGBT ballot initiative campaigns or following significant defeats in the legislature. These grassroots mobilizing efforts may have the greatest long-term impact on the lives of LGBT people. And indeed, the pattern of results for successful pro-LGBT legislation and policy suggests that changing public attitudes, both indirectly and directly, is the most important factor for achieving long-term policy goals.

Appendix A for Chapter 2:
Survey of 2003–2004
State Legislative Candidates

1. Please assess the level of support for candidates from your political party in your district (for example, what percentage of voters typically votes for your party).

2. How did you decide to run for a state legislative seat? Did you decide on your own? Did a group or political party approach you about running? More generally, what were the circumstances surrounding your decision to run for office?

3. How supportive was the gay and lesbian community of your candidacy? Did you speak at any gay or lesbian events or before any gay or lesbian organizations? Did you face any opposition from the political left in the gay community?

4. Have any religious-based or conservative groups actively campaigned against you? If so, are these organizations based in your district? Are any of these groups state-level or national groups?

5. Assess the treatment you have received in the media. Do you think the media's coverage of your campaign has been fair and accurate? Do you believe the race received much attention compared to other election campaigns? Do you believe media coverage of your sexual orientation was (1) excessive, and (2) influential in the campaign?

6. Did you have problems raising money for your campaign? If yes, to what do you attribute these problems? What was the major source of funding for your campaign? Did you receive any funding from Political Action Committees? If so, which ones? What was the average dollar amount of contributions to your campaign?

7. Were you publicly endorsed by any local, state, or national organizations? If so, which ones?

8. Was your party supportive of your candidacy? Were leaders in the legislature supportive of your candidacy? Did you receive any campaign funds from legislative leadership PACs? Did you receive any public funding for you campaign?

9. Have you held public office previously? If so what positions and for how long?

10. What are or were the four central issues in your campaign?

11. Are gay civil rights issues important to your campaign? Please describe.

12. During the primary election, please assess the campaign, spending levels, and tactics of your opponent(s).

13. During the general election, please assess the campaign, spending levels, and tactics of your opponent(s).

14. If you could name one issue or event that had the most influence on the outcome of the election, what would it be?

15. What role (if any) do you think a candidate's sexual orientation is playing or played in the campaign?

16. As an openly LGBT candidate running for state office, what lessons have you learned that would be valuable to other LGBT people considering campaigns for state office?

17. How do you think the campaign may have been different if you ran in another district or another state?

18. How have you been influenced (if at all) by other LGBT candidates running for public office?

Appendix B for Chapters 5 and 6:
Political Representation
Descriptive Statistics

Variable	Mean	Standard Deviation	Minimum	Maximum	No.
Pro-LGBT bills introduced	3.905	7.636	0	77	750
Pro-LGBT bills adopted	.512	1.354	0	14	750
Anti-LGBT bills introduced	2.533	3.947	0	51	750
Anti-LGBT bills passed	.300	.677	0	4	750
LGBT legislators	.728	1.246	0	9	800
Legislature ideology	45.722	26.106	0	97.92	800
Protestant fundamentalists	13.392	12.985	.8	72	800
LGBT households	.5095	.1446	.0047	.8021	800
Public support for LGBT rights	.58	10.071	− 24.00	19.00	800
Party competition	38.589	11.596	9.26	56.58	800
Total bills considered	2,162	2,546	202	1,700	741
Total bills adopted	418	311	7	2,325	743

BIBLIOGRAPHY

Alexander, Deborah, and Kristi Andersen. 1993. Gender as a Factor in the Attributions of Leadership Traits. *Political Research Quarterly* 46 (3): 527–45.

Altman, Dennis. 1974. *Homosexual Oppression and Liberation*. London: Allen Lane.

Ambrosius, Margery M., and Susan Welch. 1984. Women and Politics at the Grassroots. *Social Science Journal* 21 (1): 29–42.

Ammons, David. 1997. Locke Vetoes Gay Marriage Ban. Associated Press, February 22.

———. 2003. Gay Civil Rights Bill Passes House; Faces Tough Fight in Senate. *Seattle Times*, March 18.

Anderson, Ellen Ann. 2005. *Out of the Closets & into the Courts: Legal Opportunity Structure and Gay Rights Litigation*. Ann Arbor: University of Michigan Press.

Arceneaux, Kevin. 2001. The "Gender Gap" in State Legislative Representation: New Data to Tackle an Old Question. *Political Research Quarterly* 54 (1): 143–60.

Associated Press. 1998. Bill Would Aid Homosexuals. *St. Louis Post-Dispatch*, March 20.

———. 2000. Problem Worse Than Statistics Say. November 5.

Atkeson, Lonna Rae. 2003. Not All Cues Are Created Equal: The Conditional Impact of Female Candidates on Political Engagement. *Journal of Politics* 65 (4): 1040–61.

Bajko, Matthew S. 2006. LGBT Caucus Could Fold by 2008. *Bay Area Reporter*, June 22.

Baker, S., and P. Kleppner. 1986. Race War Chicago Style: The Election of a Black Mayor, 1983. In *Research in Urban Policy*, ed. T. N. Clark, vol. 2, 215–38. Greenwich, CT: JAI Press.

Baldwin, Tammy. 2000. Speech: Keep Flame Alive for Rights. *Capital Times*, May 15.

Banaszac, Lee Ann. 1996. When Waves Collide: Cycles of Protest and the Swiss and American Women's Movements. *Political Research Quarterly* 49 (4): 837–61.

Bandler, James. 2000. Anger over Civil-Union Law Shapes Vt. Governor Race. *Wall Street Journal*, September 27.

Banducci, Susan A., Todd Donovan, and Jeffrey A. Karp. 2004. Minority Representation, Empowerment, and Participation. *Journal of Politics* 66 (2): 534–56.

Barker, Lucius J., Mack H. Jones, and Katherine Tate. 1999. *African Americans and the American Political System*. Upper Saddle River, NJ: Prentice Hall.

Barlow, Gary. 1999. New White House GLBT Liaison Chats with *Windy City Times*. *Windy City Times*, December 23.

Barna, Mark. 2008. Ritter Signs Bill Giving Equal Access to Accommodations. *Gazette* May 29.

Barreto, Matt A. 2005. Latino Immigrants at the Polls: Foreign Born Voter Turnout in the 2002 Election. *Political Research Quarterly* 58 (1): 79–86.

———. 2007. Sí Se Puede! Latino Candidates and the Mobilization of Latino Voters. *American Political Science Review* 101 (3): 425–41.

Barrett, Edith J. 1995. The Policy Priorities of African American Women in State Legislatures. *Legislative Studies Quarterly* 20 (2): 223–47.

———. 1997. Gender and Race in the State House: The Legislative Experience. *Social Science Journal* 34 (2): 131–44.

Barreto, Matt A., Gary M. Segura, and Nathan D. Woods. 2004. The Mobilizing Effect of Majority-Minority Districts on Latino Turnout. *American Political Science Review* 98 (1): 65–75.

Baxter, Sandra, and Marjorie Lansing. 1980. *Women and Politics: The Invisible Majority*. Ann Arbor: University of Michigan Press.

Bay Windows. 2008. Editorial: Sonia Chang-Diaz for Senate, Re-elect State Rep. Carl Sciortino. September 11.

Becker, J. F., and E. E. Heaton Jr. 1967. The Election of Senator Edward W. Brooke. *Public Opinion Quarterly* 31 (2): 346–58.

Beckwith, Karen, and Kimberly Cowell-Meyers. 2007. Sheer Numbers: Critical Representation Thresholds and Women's Political Representation. *Perspectives on Politics* 5 (3): 553–65.

Beggs, Charles E. 1995. Court Upholds Ban on Local Anti-Gay Ordinances. Associated Press, April 13.

Belluck, Pam. 2006. Gain for Same-Sex Marriage in Massachusetts. *New York Times*, November 10.

Berkman Michael B., and Robert E. O'Connor. 1993. Do Women Legislators Matter?: Female Legislators and State Abortion Policy. *American Politics Quarterly* 21 (1): 102–24.

Berrill, Kevin T. 1992. *Countering Anti-Gay Violence through Legislation*. Washington, DC: National Gay and Lesbian Task Force Policy Institute.

Berry, William D., Evan J. Ringquist, Richard C. Fording, and Russell L. Hanson. 1998. Measuring Citizen and Government Ideology in the American States, 1960–93. *American Journal of Political Science* 42 (1): 327–48.

Blalock, H. 1967. *Toward a Theory of Minority-Group Relations*. New York: Wiley.

Bobo, Lawrence, and Franklin Gilliam Jr. 1990. Race, Sociopolitical Participation and Black Empowerment. *American Political Science Review* 84 (2): 377–94.

Boles, Janet K., and Katherine Scheurer. 2007. Beyond Women, Children, and Families: Gender, Representation, and Public Funding for the Arts. *Social Science Quarterly* 88 (1): 39–50.

Bowman, Karlyn, and Adam Foster. 2006. *Attitudes about Homosexuality & Gay Marriage, May 31, 2006*. Washington, DC: American Enterprise Institute.

Box-Steffensmeier, Janet M., David C. Kimball, Scott R. Meinke, and Katherine Tate. 2003. The Effects of Political Representation on the Electoral Advantages of House Incumbents. *Political Research Quarterly* 56 (3): 259–70.

Boyce, Ed. 1998. R.I. Gov Almond Wins Re-election; Democrat York's Defeat Blamed on Ignoring "Core Constituencies." *Newsweek*, November 11.

Bratton, Kathleen A. 2001. Legislative Collaboration and Descriptive Representation. In *Representation of Minority Groups in the U.S.*, ed. Charles E. Menifield, 289–311. Lanham, MD: Austin & Winfield.

———. 2002. The Effect of Legislative Diversity on Agenda Setting: Evidence from Six State Legislatures. *American Politics Review* 30 (2): 115–42.

———. 2005. Critical Mass Theory Revisited: The Behavior and Success of Token Women in State Legislatures. *Politics & Gender* 1 (1): 97–125.

———. 2006. The Behavior and Success of Latino Legislators: Evidence from the States. *Social Science Quarterly* 87 (1): 1136–57.

Bratton, Kathleen A., and Kerry L. Haynie. 1999. Agenda-Setting and Legislative Success in State Legislatures: The Effects of Gender and Race. *Journal of Politics* 61 (3): 658–79.

Bratton, Kathleen A., and Leonard P. Ray. 2002. Descriptive Representation, Policy Outcomes, and Municipal Day-Care Coverage in Norway. *American Journal of Political Science* 46 (2): 428–37.

Brelis, Matthew. 1998. Politics: From Closet to Campaign Trail—Being Gay Once Defined a Candidate; Now the Issues Do. *Boston Globe*, August 30.

Brewer, Paul R. 2002. Framing, Value Words, and Citizens' Explanations of Their Issue Opinions. *Political Communication* 19 (3): 303–16.

———. 2003a. The Shifting Foundations of Public Opinion about Gay Rights. *Journal of Politics* 65 (4): 1208–20.

———. 2003b. Values, Political Knowledge, and Public Opinion about Gay Rights. *Public Opinion Quarterly* 67 (2): 173–201.

Brians, Craig Leonard. 2005. Women for Women? Gender and Party Bias in Voting for Female Candidates. *American Politics Research* 33 (3): 357–75.

Brooks, Clem, and David Brady. 1999. Income, Economic Voting, and Long-Term Political Change in the U.S., 1952–1996. *Social Forces* 77 (4): 1339–74.

Browning, Rufus P., Dale R. Marshall, and David H. Tabb. 1984. *Protest Is Not Enough: The Struggle or Blacks and Hispanics for Equality in Urban Politics*. Berkeley: University of California Press.

Bull, Chris, and John Gallagher. 1996. *Perfect Enemies: The Religious Right, the Gay Movement, and the Politics of the 1990s*. New York: Crown.

Bullock, Charles S., III. 1987. Redistricting and Changes in the Partisan and Racial Composition of Southern Legislatures. *State and Local Government Review* 19:62–67.

———. 2000. Partisan Changes in the Southern Congressional Delegation and the Consequences. In *Continuity and Change in House Elections*, ed. David W. Brady, John F. Cogan, and Morris Fiorina, 39–64. Stanford, CA: Stanford University Press.

Bullock, Charles S., III, and Richard E. Dunn. 1999. The Demise of Racial Districting and the Future of Black Representation. *Emory Law Journal* 48:1209–53.

Bullock, Charles S., III, and R. K. Gaddie. 1993. Changing from Multimember to Single-Member Districts: Partisan, Racial, and Gender Consequences. *State and Local Government Review* 25:155–63.

Burrell, Barbara. 1994. Campaign Finance: Women's Experience in the Modem Era. In *Women and Elective Office*, ed. Susan Thomas and Clyde Wilcox. New York: Oxford University Press.

———. 1997. The Political Leadership of Women and Public Policymaking. *Policy Studies Journal* 25 (4): 565–68.

———. 1998. *A Woman's Place Is in the House: Campaigning for Congress in the Feminist Era*. Ann Arbor: University of Michigan Press.

Button, James, and David Hedge. 1996. Legislative Life in the 1990s: A Comparison of Black and White State Legislators. *Legislative Studies Quarterly* 21:199–218.

Button, James W., Barbara A. Rienzo, and Kenneth D. Wald. 1997. *Private Lives, Public Conflicts: Battles over Gay Rights in American Communities*. Washington, DC: CQ Press.

Caldeira, G. A., and S. C. Patterson. 1982. Bringing Home the votes: Electoral Outcomes in State Legislative Races. *Political Behavior* 4:33–67.

Calhoun, Craig. 1991. The Problem of Identity in Collective Action. In *Macro–Micro Linkages in Sociology*, ed. Joan Huber. Newbury Park, CA: Sage.

Cammisa, Anne Marie, and Beth Reingold. 2004. Women in State Legislative Research: Beyond Sameness and Difference. *State Politics and Policy Quarterly* 4 (2): 181–210.

Campbell, David, and Joe R. Feagin. 1977. Black Politics in the South: A Descriptive Analysis. *Journal of Politics* 37:129–59.

Carey, John M., Richard G. Niemi, and Lynda W. Powell. 2000. Incumbency and the Probability of Reelection in State Legislative Elections. *Journal of Politics* 62 (4): 671–700.

Carlson, Brian. 1998. Republican Gubernatorial Forum Focuses on Spending. *Daily Nebras-kan*, April 17.

Carrier, Paul. 1995. Withdrawn Gay-Rights Bill Faced Slim Odds of Passing. *Portland Press Herald*, December 29.

Carroll, Susan J. 1994. *Women as Candidates in American Politics*, 2nd ed. Bloomington: Indiana University Press.

———, ed. 2001. *The Impact of Women in Public Office*. Bloomington: Indiana University Press.

Carroll, Susan, and Wendy Strimling. 1983. *Women's Routes to Elective Office: A Comparison with Men's*. New Brunswick, NJ: Center for the American Woman and Politics.

Carsey, Tom M. 1995. The Contextual Effects of Race on White Voter Behavior: The 1989 New York City Mayoral Election. *Journal of Politics* 57 (1): 221–28.

Carson, Jamie L., Erik J. Engstrom, and Jasosn M. Roberts. 2007. Candidate Quality, the Personal Vote, and the Incumbency Advantage in Congress. *American Political Science Review* 101 (2): 289–301.

Cassels, Peter. 1999. Gay Elected Officials Gather in Providence; Annual INLGO Confab Draws 75 Leaders. *Bay Windows*, November 26.

Chibbaro, Lou, Jr. 1997. Gay Republican Lawmaker Forces Vote On Bill; Oregon Representative Bucks Party Line on Employment Bill. *Washington Blade*, May 9.

Chong, Dennis. 1991. *Collective Action and the Civil Rights Movement*. Chicago: University of Chicago Press.

Citrin, Jack, Donald Philip Green, and David O. Sears. 1990. White Reactions to Black Candidates: When Does Race Matter? *Public Opinion Quarterly* 54 (1): 74–96.

Clark, Janet. 1994. Getting There: Women in Political Office. In *Different Roles, Different Voices*, ed. Marianne Githens, Pippa Norris, and Joni Lovenduski. New York: HarperCollins.

Clark, Janet, and Cal Clark. 1984. Women in New Mexico Politics. *Social Science Journal* 21 (1): 57–66.

Clark, Janet, Robert Darcy, Susan Welch, and Margery Ambrosius. 1984. Women as Candidates in Six States. In *Political Women: Current Roles in State and Local Government*, ed. Janet Flammang. Beverly Hills, CA: Sage.

Cockerham, Sean. 2007. Washington Gives Domestic Partnership Rights to Gay Couples. *News Tribune*, April 21.

Colbert, Chuck. 1997. Clinton Inaugural Ushers in Gay and Lesbian Optimism. *New America News Service*, January 22.

Colby, David C., and David G. Baker. 1988. State Policy Responses to the AIDS Epidemic. *Publius* 18:113–30.

Cole, Leonard. 1976. *Blacks in Power: A Comparative Study of Black and White Elected Officials*. Princeton, NJ: Princeton University Press.

Council of State Governments. Various Years. *The Book of the States*. Lexington, KY: Council of State Governments.

Crea, Joe. 2005. Va. Poised to Become "Most Anti-Gay State": Lone Gay Lawmaker Battles Flurry of Bills. *Washington Blade*, February 11.

Crowley, Jocelyn Elise. 2004. When Tokens Matter. *Legislative Studies Quarterly* 29 (1): 109–36.

Dahlerup, Drude. 1988. From a Small to a Large Minority. *Scandinavian Political Studies* 11 (4): 275–98.

Darcy, Robert, Margaret Brewer, and Judy Clay. 1984. Women and Men Candidates in Oklahoma Elections. *Social Science Journal* 21 (1): 67–78.

Darcy, Robert, Charles D. Hadley, and Jason F. Kirksey. 1993. Election Systems and the Representation of Black Women in American State Legislatures. *Women and Politics* 13 (2): 73–89.

Darcy, Robert, Susan Welch, and Janet Clark. 1985. Women Candidates in Single- and Multi-Member Districts: American State Legislative Races. *Social Science Quarterly* 66 (4): 945–53.

———. 1994. *Women, Elections and Representation*, 2nd ed., revised. Lincoln: University of Nebraska Press.

Davila, Florangela. 2001. Civil-Union Law for Gays Is Goal of Proposed Bills. *Seattle Times*, February 11.

Dawson, Michael C. 1994. *Behind the Mule: Race and Class in African-American Politics*. Princeton, NJ: Princeton University Press.

DeBold, Kathleen. ed. 1994. *Out for Office: Campaigning in the Gay Nineties*. Washington, DC: Gay and Lesbian Victory Fund.

Deber, Raisa. 1982. "The Fault Dear Brutus": Women as Candidates in Pennsylvania. *Journal of Politics* 44 (2): 463–79.

D'Emilio, John. 1983. *Sexual Politics Sexual Communities*. Chicago: University of Chicago Press.

Desroches, Steve. 2007. Peake on the Hill. *Cape Codder*, January 25.

Diggle, Peter J., Patrick J. Heagerty, Kung-Lee Liang, and Scott L. Zeger. 2002. *Analysis of Longitudinal Data*, 2nd ed. New York: Oxford University Press.

Dodson, Debra L., and Susan J. Carroll. 1991. *Reshaping the Agenda: Women in State Legislatures*. New Brunswick, NJ: Center for the American Woman and Politics.

Dolan, Kathleen. 1997. Gender Differences in Support for Women Candidates: Is There a Glass Ceiling in American Politics? *Women and Politics* 17 (2): 27–41.

———. 1998. Voting for Women in the "Year of the Woman." *American Journal of Political Science* 42 (1): 272–93.

———. 2004. *Voting for Women: How the Public Evaluates Women Candidates*. Boulder, CO: Westview Press.

———. 2005. Do Women Candidates Play to Gender Stereotypes? Do Men Candidates Play to Women? Candidate Sex and Issue Priorities on Campaign Websites. *Political Research Quarterly* 58 (1): 31–44.

———. 2006. Symbolic Mobilization? The Impact of Candidate Sex in American Elections. *American Politics Research* 34 (6): 687–704.

Dolan, Kathleen, and Lynne Ford. 1997. Change and Continuity among Women State Legislators: Evidence from Three Decades. *Political Research Quarterly* 50 (1): 137–51.

Dower, Erin. 2005. Poster Boy for Gay Weds Ready to Tackle other Issues. *Somerville Journal*, September 22.

Dunbar, Elizabeth. 2008. Ex-Minn. Legislator Allan Spear, Gay Pioneer, Dies. Associated Press, October 12.

Edwards, George C., III, Andrew Barrett, and Jeffrey Peake. 1997. The Legislative Impact of Divided Government. *American Journal of Political Science* 41 (2): 545–63.

Egan, Patrick J., and Kenneth Sherrill. 2005. Neither an In-Law Nor an Outlaw Be: Trends in Americans' Attitudes toward Gay People. *Public Opinion Pros* (February). www.publicopinionpros.com/.

Eisinger, Peter K. 1982. Black Employment in Municipal Jobs: The Impact of Black Political Power. *American Political Science Review* 76 (2): 380–92.

Ekstrand, Laurie E., and William Eckert. 1981. The Impact of Candidate's Sex on Voter Choice. *Western Political Quarterly* 34 (1): 78–87.

Eleveld, Kerry. 2006. Huge Victories for Our Community. *New York Blade*, November 13.

———. 2007. Strategies for Marriage Equality: State's Gay Lawmakers Take Different Approaches. *New York Blade* , February 2.

Epstein, Michael J., Richard Niemi, and Lynda W. Powell. 2005. Do Women and Men State Legislators Differ? In *Women and Elective Office*, ed. Sue Thomas and Clyde Wilcox, 94–109. New York: Oxford University Press.

Esteve, Harry. 1997. House Republicans Bolted Monday from the State Capital. *Register-Guard*, April 15.

———. 1998. Money Can't Always Buy You Election. *Register-Guard*, July 2.

Eulau, Heinz, and Paul D. Karps. 1977. The Puzzle of Representation: Specifying Components of Responsiveness. *Legislative Studies Quarterly* 2 (1): 233–54.

Fairbanks, Madelyn. 2009. Work on Gay Rights Just Getting Started; Partnership Bill's Sponsors Say Marriage Equality Is Next. *Seattle Post-Intelligencer*, January 29.

Faludi, Susan. 1991. *Backlash: The Undeclared War against American Women*. New York: Crown.

Flammang, Janet. 1997. *Women's Political Voice: How Women Are Transforming the Practice and Study of Politics*. Philadelphia: Temple University Press.

Florida, Richard. 2002. *The Rise of the Creative Class: And How It's Transforming Work, Leisure, Community and Everyday Life*. New York: Perseus.

Foster, Heath. 1998. Lawmakers Unite, Override Veto on Gay-Marriage Ban. *Seattle Post Intelligencer*, February 7.

Fox, Richard L. 1997. *Gender Dynamics in Congressional Elections*. Thousand Oaks, CA: Sage.

———. 2000. Gender and Congressional Elections. In *Gender and American Politics*, ed. S. Tolleson-Rinehart and J. Josephson. Armonk, NY: M. E. Sharpe.

Fox, Richard L., and Jennifer L. Lawless. 2004. Entering the Arena? Gender and the Decision to Run for Office. *American Journal of Political Science* 48 (2): 264–80.

———. 2005. To Run or Not to Run for Office: Explaining Nascent Political Ambition. *American Journal of Political Science* 49 (3): 642–59.

Fox, Richard L., and Zoe M. Oxley. 2003. Gender Stereotyping in State Executive Elections: Candidate Selection and Success. *Journal of Politics* 65 (3): 833–50.

Fraga, Luis Ricardo. 1988. Domination through Democratic Means: Nonpartisan Slating Groups in City Electoral Politics. *Urban Affairs Quarterly* 23 (2): 528–55.

Fraga, Luis Ricardo, Kenneth J. Meier, and Robert E. England. 1986. Hispanic Americans and Educational Policy: Limits to Equal Access. *Journal of Politics* 48 (4): 850–76.

Francisco, Ronald A. 1995. The Relationship between Coercion and Protest: An Empirical Evaluation in Three Coercive States. *Journal of Conflict Resolution* 39 (2): 263–82.

———. 1996. Coercion and Protest: An Empirical Test in Two Democratic States. *American Journal of Political Science* 40 (4): 1179–1204.

Frank, Barney. 1994. Reaching a Broader Audience. In *Out for Office: Campaigning in the Gay '90s*, ed. Kathleen DeBold. Washington, DC: Gay And Lesbian Victory Fund.

Freiberg, Peter. 1998. Utah Legislature to Get Its First Openly Gay Member; Massachusetts Man Loses Statewide Bid. *Washington Blade*, November 6.

———. 2000a. Name-Dropping in San Francisco; ACT UP Chapter Changes Moniker to Distinguish from Other Group. *Washington Blade*, March 31.

———. 2000b. A Vote of Confidence: Openly Gay Candidates Nearly Double Compared to Number on 1998 Ballots. *Washington Blade*, October 27.

Freyer, Felice J. 1999. Officials Say Being Openly Gay Isn't a Detriment. *Providence Journal-Bulletin*, November 21.

Friederich, Steven. 2003. Push On in State Senate for Anti-Discrimination Bill. *Seattle Post-Intelligencer*, April 12.

Galloway, Angela. 2002. Gay Members of House Claim a Low-Key Victory. *Seattle Post Intelligencer*, February 26.

Gardner, Michael. 2004. Kehoe Sees Equal-Rights Issue; Same-Sex Marriage Debate May Shadow Her Campaign. *San Diego Union-Tribune*, May 17.

Gay, Claudine. 1999. Choosing Sides: Black Electoral Success and Racially Polarized Voting. Paper presented at Annual Meeting of American Political Science Association, Atlanta.

———. 2001. The Effect of Black Congressional Representation on Political Participation. *American Political Science Review* 95 (3): 589–602.

———. 2002. Spirals of Trust? The Effect of Descriptive Representation on the Relationship between Citizens and Their Government. *American Journal of Political Science* 46 (4): 717–32.

Gay and Lesbian Victory Fund. 1998. *Political Extremists Target Openly Gay Legislator: Press Release from the Gay and Lesbian Victory Fund, 4/9/98*. Washington, DC: Gay and Lesbian Victory Fund.

Gelineau, Kristen. 2005. Openly Gay Lawmakers Often Fight Alone. Associated Press, March 7.

Georgia Log Cabin Republicans. 2000. January 19th: News Update. Atlanta.

Gerber, Elisabeth R., Rebecca B. Morton, and Thomas A. Rietz. 1998. Minority Representation in Multimember Districts. *American Political Science Review* 92 (1): 127–44.

Gierzynski, A., and D. Breaux. 1991. Money and Votes in State Legislative Elections. *Legislative Studies Quarterly* 16:203–17.

———. 1993. Money and the Party Vote in State House Elections. *Legislative Studies Quarterly* 18:515–33.

Gilliam, Frank. 1996. Exploring Minority Empowerment: Symbolic Politics, Governing Coalitions, and Traces of Political Style in Los Angeles. *American Journal of Political Science* 40 (1): 56–81.

Githens, Marianne, and Jewell Prestage, eds. 1977. *A Portrait of Marginality: The Political Behavior of American Women*. New York: David McKay.

Glenmary Research Center. 2004. *Churches and Church Membership in the United States, 1960–2000 (Data CD)*. Atlanta: Glenmary Research Center.

Golebiowska, E. A. 2001. Group Stereotypes and Political Evaluation. *American Politics Research* 29:535–65.

———. 2002. Political Implications of Group Stereotypes: Campaign Experiences of Openly Gay Political Candidates. *Journal of Applied Social Psychology* 32:590–607.

Golebiowska, E. A., and C. J. Thomsen. 1999. Group Stereotypes of Individuals: The Case of Gay and Lesbian Political Candidates. In *Gays and Lesbians in the Democratic Process: Public Policy, Public Opinion and Political Representation*, ed. E. D. B. Riggle and B. Tadlock. New York: Columbia University Press.

Grofman, B., and Handley, L. 1991. The Impact of the Voting Rights Act on Black Political Representation in Southern State Legislatures. *Legislative Studies Quarterly* 16:111–28.

Grofman, B., M. Migalski, and N. Noviello. 1986. Effects of Multimember Districts on Black Representation in State Legislatures. *Review of Black Political Economy* 14:65–78.

Grose, Christian R. 2005. Disentangling Constituency and Legislator Effects in Legislative Representation: Black Legislators or Black Districts? *Social Science Quarterly* 86 (2): 427–43.

Grow, Doug. 2000. Allan Spear, Gay Senator Who Educated Minnesota, Retiring. *Minneapolis Star Tribune*, May 17.

Guerrero, M. A. James. 1997. Affirmative Action: Race, Class, Gender, and *Now*. *American Behavioral Scientist* 41 (2): 246–56.

Gunnison, Robert B. 1996. Setback for Foes of Gay Unions Senate Panel Dilutes Bill against Same-Sex Marriages. *San Francisco Chronicle*, July 10.

Haas-Wilson, Deborah. 1993. The Economic Impact of State Restrictions on Abortion: Parental Consent and Notification Laws and Medicaid Funding Restrictions. *Journal of Policy Analysis & Management* 12 (3):498–512.

Haeberle, Steven H. 1996. Gay Men and Lesbians at City Hall. *Social Science Quarterly* 77:190–97.

Haider-Markel, Donald P. 1997. Interest Group Survival: Shared Interests Versus Competition for Resources. *Journal of Politics* 59 (3): 903–12.

———. 1999a. AIDS and Gay Civil Rights: Politics and Policy at the Ballot Box. *American Review of Politics* 20:349–75.

———. 1999b. Redistributing Values in Congress: Interest Group Influence under Sub-Optimal Conditions. *Political Research Quarterly* 52 (1): 113–44.

———. 2000. Lesbian and Gay Politics in the States: Interest Groups, Electoral Politics, and Public Policy. In *The Politics of Gay Rights*, ed. Craig Rimmerman, Kenneth Wald, and Clyde Wilcox. Chicago: University of Chicago Press.

———. 2001a. Policy Diffusion as a Geographical Expansion of the Scope of Political Conflict: Same-Sex Marriage Bans in the 1990s. *State Politics and Policy Quarterly* 1(1): 5–26.

———. 2001b. Shopping for Favorable Venues in the States: Institutional Influences on Legislative Outcomes of Same-Sex Marriage Bills. *American Review of Politics* 22:27–54.

———. 2007. Political Representation and Policy Backlash: The Positive and Negative Influence of Descriptive Representation in State Legislatures. *Legislative Studies Quarterly* 32 (1): 107–34.

Haider-Markel, Donald P., and Mark Joslyn. 2005. Attributions and the Regulation of Marriage: Considering the Parallels between Race and Homosexuality. *PS: Political Science and Politics* 38 (2): 233–40.

———. 2008. Understanding Beliefs about the Origins of Homosexuality and Subsequent Support for Gay Rights: An Empirical Test of Attribution Theory. *Public Opinion Quarterly* 72 (2): 291–310.

Haider-Markel, Donald P., Mark R. Joslyn, and Chad J. Kniss. 2000. Minority Group Interests and Political Representation: Gay Elected Officials in the Policy Process. *Journal of Politics* 62 (2): 568–77.

Haider-Markel, Donald P., and Matthew S. Kaufman. 2006. Public Opinion and Policymaking in the Culture Wars: Is There a Connection between Opinion and State Policy on Gay and Lesbian Issues? In *Public Opinion in State Politics*, ed. Jeffrey Cohen. Stanford, CA: Stanford University Press.

Haider-Markel, Donald P., and Kenneth J. Meier. 1996. The Politics of Gay Rights: Expanding the Scope of the Conflict. *Journal of Politics* 58 (2): 352–69.

———. 2003. Legislative Victory, Electoral Uncertainty: Explaining Outcomes in the Battles over Lesbian and Gay Civil Rights. *Review of Policy Research* 20 (4): 671–90.

Haider-Markel, Donald P., Alana Querze, and Kara Lindaman. 2007. Lose, Win, or Draw? A Reexamination of Direct Democracy and Minority Rights. *Political Research Quarterly* 60 (2): 304–14.

Hajnal, Zoltan L. 2007. *Changing White Attitudes toward Black Political Leadership*. New York: Cambridge University Press.

Hamm, Keith E., and Gary F. Moncrief. 2008. Legislative Politics in the States. In *Politics in the American States*, 9th edition, ed. Virginia Gray and Russell L. Hanson, 154–91. Washington, DC: CQ Press.

Hargrove, Thomas, and Guido H. Stemple III. 2003. Anti-Gay Attitudes Found in Survey on Elections, Marriages." *Seattle Post Intelligencer*, Dec. 12.

Harris, Jamie H., and John F. Zipp. 1999. Black Candidates, Roll-Off, and the Black Vote. *Urban Affairs Review* 34 (4): 489–98.

Haynie, Kerry L. 2000. *African American Legislators in the American States*. New York: Columbia University Press.

Hawkesworth, Mary. 2003. Congressional Enactments of Raced-Gender: Toward a Theory of Raced-Gendered Institutions. *American Political Science Review* 97 (4): 529–50.

Heath, Roseanna Michelle, Leslie A. Schwindt-Bayer, and Michelle M. Taylor-Robinson. 2005. Women on the Sidelines: Women's Representation on Committees in Latin American Legislatures. *American Journal of Political Science* 49 (2): 420–36.

Hedge, David, James Button, and Mary Spear. 1996. Accounting for the Quality of Black Legislative Life: The View from the States. *American Journal of Political Science* 40 (1): 82–98.

Henshaw, Jake. 2008. For Laird, a Time to Reflect. *Californian.com*, November 29.

Herek, Gregory M. 2002. Gender Gaps in Public Opinion about Lesbians and Gay Men. *Public Opinion Quarterly* 66 (1): 40–66.

Herrick, Rebekah, and Sue Thomas. 1999. The Effects of Sexual Orientation on Citizen Perceptions of Candidate Viability. In *Gays and Lesbians in the Democratic Process*, ed. Ellen D. B. Riggle and Barry Tadlock. New York: Columbia University Press.

Herrnson, Paul S., J. Celeste Lay, and Atiya Kai Stokes. 2003. Women Running "as Women": Candidate Gender, Campaign Issues, and Voter-Targeting Strategies. *Journal of Politics* 65 (1): 244–55.

Herron, Michael C., and Jasjeet S. Sekhon. 2005. Black Candidates and Black Voters: Assessing the Impact of Candidate Race on Uncounted Vote Rates. *Journal of Politics* 67 (1): 154–77.

Highton, Benjamin. 2004. White Voters and African American Candidates for Congress. *Political Behavior* 26 (1): 1–25.

Hogan, Robert E. 2001. The Influence of State and District Conditions on the Representation of Women in U.S. State Legislatures. *American Politics Research* 29 (1): 4–24.

———. 2003. The Effects of Primary Divisiveness on General Election Outcomes in State Legislative Elections. *American Politics Research* 31:27–47.

———. 2007. The Effects of Candidate Gender on Campaign Spending in State Legislative Elections. *Social Science Quarterly* 88 (5): 1092–1105.

———. 2008. Policy Responsiveness and Incumbent Reelection in State Legislatures. *American Journal of Political Science* 52 (4): 858–73.

Holbrook, T. M., and C. M. Tidmarch. 1993. The Effects of Leadership Positions on Votes for Incumbents in State Legislative Elections. *Political Research Quarterly* 46:897–909.

Holbrook, Thomas M., and Emily Van Dunk. 1993. Electoral Competition in the American States. *American Political Science Review* 87 (4): 955–62.

Howlett, Deborah. 2006. Mercer Assemblyman Acknowledges He's Gay; Gusciora Cites State's "Tolerant" Attitude. *Star-Ledger*, December 5.

Huddy, Leonie, and Nayda Terkildsen. 1993a. The Consequences of Gender Stereotypes for Women Candidates at Different Levels and Types of Office. *Political Research Quarterly* 46 (3): 503–25.

———. 1993b. Gender Stereotypes and the Perception of Male and Female Candidates. *American Journal of Political Science* 37 (1): 119–47.

Ivers, Kevin. 1998. *Carpenter Defeated in Oregon: Narrow Loss a Warning Sign to Gay Community, Log Cabin Says, 5/28/98*. Washington, DC: Log Cabin Republicans.

Jacobs, Ethan. 2008a. Peake Performance. *Bay Windows*, October 30.

———. 2008b. Power Surge. *Bay Windows*, August 6.

———. 2009. Advocates Focus Narrowly in New Legislative Session. *Bay Windows*, January 8.

Jenkins, Shannon. 2007. A Woman's Work Is Never Done? Fund-Raising Perception and Effort among Female State Legislative Candidates. *Political Research Quarterly* 60 (2): 230–39.

Jewell, M. E. 1994. State Legislative Elections: What We Know and Don't Know. *American Politics Quarterly* 22:483–509.

Jewell, M. E., and S. M. Morehouse. 2001. *Political Parties and Elections in American States*, 4th ed. Washington, DC: CQ Press.

Johnson, Chris. 2008. Virginia Gays on Offense as Lawmakers Return: Medical Decision-Making Rights Bill Introduced. *Washington Blade*, January 11.

———. 2009. Marriage on the March; Vermont, N.J. Seen as Most Likely to Legalize Same-Sex Unions This Year. *Washington Blade*, January 30.

Jones, Jeffrey M. 2007. Some Americans Reluctant to Vote for Mormon, 72-Year-Old Presidential Candidates. Gallup Poll News Service, February 20.

Jones-Correa Michael. 2001. Institutional and Contextual Factors in Immigrant Citizenship and Voting. *Citizenship Studies* 5 (1): 41–56.

Kahn, Kim Fridkin. 1996. *The Political Consequences of Being a Woman: How Stereotypes Influence the Conduct and Consequences of Political Campaigns*. New York: Columbia University Press.

Kane, Melinda D. 2003. Social Movement Policy Success: Decriminalizing State Sodomy Laws, 1969–1998. *Mobilization* 8 (3): 313–34.

Kanter, Rosabeth M. 1977. Some Effects of Proportion on Group Life: Skewed Sex Ratios and Response to Token Women. *American Journal of Sociology* 82 (5): 965–90.

———. 1994. *Men and Women of the Corporation*. New York: Basic Books.

Kathlene, Lyn. 1994. Power and Influence in State Legislative Policymaking: The Interaction of Gender and Position in Committee Hearing Debates. *American Political Science Review* 88 (3): 560–76.

Keech, William R. 1968. *The Impact of Negro Voting*. Chicago: Rand McNally.

Keen, Lisa. 1996. Marriage Vote to Fall on Hawaii Trial's Eve; California's Anti-Gay Measure Stalls. *Washington Blade*, August 30.

Key, V. O. 1964. *Politics, Parties and Pressure Groups*, 5th ed. New York: Thomas Y. Crowell.

Kinder, D., and D. O. Sears. 1981. Prejudice and Politics: Symbolic Racism versus Racial Threats to the Good Life. *Journal of Personality and Social Psychology* 40:414–31.

King, James D. 2002. Single-Member Districts and the Representation of Women in American State Legislatures: The Effects of Electoral System Change. *State Politics and Policy Quarterly* 2 (2): 161–75.

Kingdon, John. 1989. *Congressmen's Voting Decisions*, 3rd ed. New York: Harper & Row.

King-Meadows, Tyson D., and Thomas F. Schaller. 2001. Black State Legislators: A Case Study of North Carolina and Maryland. In *Representation of Minority Groups in the U.S.*, ed. Charles E. Menifield, 163–88. Lanham, MD: Austin & Winfield.

Kiritsy, Laura. 2002. Barrios Seeks a Seat in the Senate. *Bay Windows*, March 28.

———. 2004. Rep. Rivera Speaks Out. February 19.

———. 2007. Pressing the Flesh. *Bay Windows*, July 5.

———. 2008. Dressing for Success, from Somerville to P'town. *Bay Windows*, July 30.

Kittilson, Miki Caul. 2008. Representing Women: The Adoption of Family Leave in Comparative Perspective. *Journal of Politics* 70 (2): 323–34.

Klarman, Michael J. 1994. How Brown Changed Race Relations: The Backlash Thesis. *Journal of American History* 81:81–119.

Knuckey, Jonathan, and Byron D'Andra Orey. 2000. Symbolic Racism in the 1995 Louisiana Gubernatorial Election. *Social Science Quarterly* 81 (4): 1027–35.

Krebs, T. B. 1998. The Determinants of Candidates' Vote Share and the Advantages of Incumbency in City Council Elections. *American Journal of Political Science* 42:921–35.

Krueger, Brian S., and Paul D. Mueller. 2001. Moderating Backlash: Racial Mobilization, Partisan Coalitions, and Public Policy in the American States. *State Politics and Policy Quarterly* 1 (2): 165–79.

La Corte, Rachel. 2007. State's Gay Lawmakers Won't Stop Until Same-Sex Marriage Is Reality. *Daily World*, January 12.

———. 2008. State's Gay Caucus Is 2nd-Largest in U.S. *Seattle Times*, January 24.

Law, Steve. 2007. Oregon Senate OKs Bill Granting Domestic Partnerships for Same-Sex Couples. *Statesman Journal*, May 2.

Lawless, Jennifer L. 2004. Women, War, and Winning Elections: Gender Stereotyping in the Post-September 11th Era. *Political Research Quarterly* 57 (3): 479–90.

Lawless, Jennifer L., and Richard L. Fox. 2005. *It Takes a Candidate: Why Women Don't Run for Office*. Cambridge: Cambridge University Press.

Lax, Jeffrey R., and Justin H. Phillips. 2009. Gay Rights in the States: Public Opinion and Policy Responsiveness. *American Political Science Review* 103 (3): 367–86.

Layman, Geoffrey C., and Edward G. Carmines. 1997. Cultural Conflict in American Politics: Religious Traditionalism, Postmaterialism, and U.S. Political Behavior. *Journal of Politics* 59 (3): 751–77.

Layman, Geoffrey C., and Thomas M. Carsey. 2002. Party Polarization and "Conflict Extension" in the American Electorate. *American Journal of Political Science* 46 (4): 786–802.

Leal, David, Valerie Martinez-Ebers, and Kenneth Meier. 2004. The Politics of Latino Education: The Biases of At-Large Elections. *Journal of Politics* 66 (4): 1224–44.

Lee, Ryan. 2008. Quiet Campaign Helps Two Pro-Gay Bills Pass Ala. House. *Southern Voice*, May 16.

Levine, Charles H. 1974. *Racial Conflict and the American Mayor*. Lexington, MA: Lexington Books.

Lewis, Gregory B., and Jonathan L. Edelson. 2000. DOMA and ENDA: Congress Votes on Gay Rights. In *The Politics of Gay Rights*, ed. Kenneth D. Wald, Craig A. Rimmerman, and Clyde Wilcox. Chicago: University of Chicago Press.

Liias, Marko. 2008. *Press Release: Governor Signs Domestic Partnership Expansion into Law*. March 12. Olympia: Office of Representative Liias, Washington State.

Lilley, William, III, Laurence J. Defranco, Mark F. Bernstein, and Karl L. Ramsby. 2008. *The Almanac of State Legislative Elections*. Washington, DC: CQ Press.

Lilley, William, III, Laurence J. Defranco, William M. Diefenderfer, and William Lilley. 1998. *The Almanac of State Legislatures*. Washington, DC: CQ Press.

Lindsey, J. K. 1999. *Models for Repeated Measurements*, 2nd ed. New York: Oxford University Press.

Liu, Baodong, and James M. Vanderleeuw. 2001. Racial Transition and White-Voter Support for Black Candidates in Urban Elections. *Journal of Urban Affairs* 23 (3–4): 309–22.

Lofton, Katie, and Donald P. Haider-Markel. 2007. The Politics of Same-Sex Marriage vs. the Politics of Gay Civil Rights: A Comparison of Public Opinion and State Voting Patterns. In *The Politics of Same-Sex Marriage*, ed. Craig Rimmerman and Clyde Wilcox. Chicago: University of Chicago Press.

Lublin, David, and Sarah E. Brewer. 2003. The Continuing Dominance of Traditional Gender Roles in Southern Elections. *Social Science Quarterly* 84 (2): 379–96.

Lublin, David, and Voss, D. S. 2000. Racial Redistricting and Realignment in Southern State Legislatures. *American Journal of Political Science* 44:792–810.

MacDonald, John, and Robert J. Stokes. 2006. Race, Social Capital, and Trust in the Police. *Urban Affairs Review* 41 (3): 358–76.

MacKay, Scott. 1998. Move to Repeal Sex Law Sparks Contentious Debate. *Providence Journal-Bulletin*, March 12.

Maier, Scott. 1995. Gay Groups Split on Own Initiative; Job Bias Is the Target, but Tactic Is Questioned. *Seattle Post Intelligencer*, March 10.

Mansbridge, Jane, and Shauna L. Shames. 2008. Toward a Theory of Backlash: Dynamic Resistance and the Central Role of Power. *Politics & Gender* 4 (4): 623–34.

Mapes, Lynda V. 1998. Spotlight Is Often on Gay Lawmaker: Ed Murray, Partner Unwitting Symbols. *Seattle Times*, February 15.

Marschall, Melissa J., and Anirudh V. S. Ruhil. 2007. Substantive Symbols: The Attitudinal Dimension of Black Political Incorporation in Local Government. *American Journal of Political Science* 51 (1): 17–33.

Marschall, Melissa, and Paru R. Shah. 2007. The Attitudinal Effects of Minority Incorporation: Examining the Racial Dimensions of Trust in Urban America. *Urban Affairs Review* 42 (5): 629–58.

Matier, Phillip, and Andrew Ross. 2004. Undaunted Leno Revs Up Marriage Issue. *San Francisco Chronicle*, November 7.

Matland, Richard E., and Deborah Dwight Brown. 1992. District Magnitude's Effect on Female Representation in U.S. State Legislatures. *Legislative Studies Quarterly* 17 (3): 469–92.

Matson, Marsha, and Terri Susan Fine. 2006. Gender, Ethnicity, and Ballot Information: Ballot Cues in Low-Information Elections. *State Politics and Policy Quarterly* 6 (1): 49–72.

McDermott, Monika L. 1997. Voting Cues in Low-Information Elections: Candidate Gender as a Social Information Variable in Contemporary United States Elections. *American Journal of Political Science* 41 (1): 270–83.

———. 1998. Race and Gender Cues in Low-Information Elections. *Political Research Quarterly* 51 (4): 895–918.

McGann, Chris. 2006. Gay Rights Bill Passes in Legislature; Amid Celebration, Governor Promises to Sign Law. *Seattle Post-Intelligencer*, January 27.

———. 2007a. Gay Rights Advocates Expect a Productive Session. *Seattle Post-Intelligencer*, December 9.

———. 2007b. Rep. Pedersen "Hits the Ground Running" in First Year as Lawmaker. *Seattle Post-Intelligencer*, April 29.

Meier, Kenneth J., Warren S. Eller, Robert D. Wrinkle, and Jerry L. Polinard. 2001. Zen and the Art of Policy Analysis: A Response to Nielsen and Wolf. *Journal of Politics* 63 (2): 616–29.

Meier, Kenneth J., Eric Gonzalez Juenke, Robert D. Wrinkle, and J. L. Polinard. 2005. Structural Choices and Representational Biases: The Post-Election Color of Representation. *American Journal of Political Science* 49 (4): 758–68.

Menifield, Charles E. 2001. Hispanics Representation in State and Local Governments. In *Representation of Minority Groups in the U.S.*, ed. Charles E. Menifield, 223–45. Lanham, MD: Austin & Winfield.

Menifield, Charles E., and Regina C. Gray. 2001. A Wave of Change: Women in State and Local Governments. In *Representation of Minority Groups in the U.S.*, ed. Charles E. Menifield, 187–222. Lanham, MD: Austin & Winfield.

Menifield, Charles E., and Charles E. Jones. 2001. African American Representation in Congress: Then and Now." In *Representation of Minority Groups in the U.S.*, ed. Charles E. Menifield, 13–36. Lanham, MD: Austin & Winfield.

Mladenka, Kenneth R. 1989. Blacks and Hispanics in Urban Politics. *American Political Science Review* 83 (1): 165–91.

Moncrief, Gary F., and Joel A. Thompson. 1992. Electoral Structure and State Legislative Representation: A Research Note. *Journal of Politics* 54 (1): 246–56.

Mooney, Christopher Z., and Mei-Hsien Lee. 1995. Legislating Morality in the American States: The Case of Pre-*Roe* Abortion Regulation Reform. *American Journal of Political Science* 39:599–627.

Morse, Rob. 1999. Same Old City, but Different, 21 Years after Horror. *San Francisco Examiner*, November 26.

Moskowitz, David, and Patrick Stroh. 1994. Psychological Sources of Electoral Racism. *Political Psychology* 15 (2): 307–29.

Mucciaroni, Gary. 2008. *Same Sex, Different Politics*. Chicago: University of Chicago Press.

Newport, Frank, and Joseph Carroll. 2007. *Analysis: Impact of Personal Characteristics on Candidate Support, March 13, 2007*. Lincoln, NE: Gallup News Service.

Nichols, Larry. 2007. A Talk with Elaine Noble. *Windy City Times*, October 10.

Niven, David. 1998. Party Elites and Women Candidates: The Shape of Bias. *Women and Politics* 19 (2): 57–80.

Norrander, Barbara, and Clyde Wilcox. 1999. Public Opinion and Policymaking in the States: The Case of Post-Roe Abortion Policy. *Policy Studies Journal* 27 (4): 707–22.

Orey, Byron D'Andra, L. Marvin Overby, and Christopher W. Larimer. 2007. African-American Committee Chairs in U.S. State Legislatures. *Social Science Quarterly* 88 (3): 619–39.

Overby, L. Marvin, Robert D. Brown, John M. Bruce, Charles E. Smith, Jr., and John W. Winkle, III. 2005. Race, Political Empowerment, and Minority Perceptions of Judicial Fairness. *Social Science Quarterly* 86 (2): 444–62.

Oxley, Zoe M., and Richard L. Fox. 2004. Women in Executive Office: Variation across the American States. *Political Research Quarterly* 57 (1): 113–20.

Palmer, Barbara, and Dennis M. Simon. 2005. When Women Run against Women: The Hidden Influence of Female Incumbents in Elections to the U.S. House of Representatives, 1956–2002. *Politics & Gender* 1 (1): 39–63.

Pantoja, Adrian D., and Gary M. Segura. 2003. Does Ethnicity Matter? Descriptive Representation in Legislatures and Political Alienation among Latinos. *Social Science Quarterly* 84 (2): 441–60.

Paolino, Phillip. 1995. Group-Salient Issues and Group Representation: Support for Women Candidates in the 1992 Senate Elections. *American Journal of Political Science* 39 (2): 294–313.

Penhale, Ed, and Anne R. Williams. 1993. Backers Work to Reroute Gay-Rights Bill. *Seattle Post Intelligencer*, April 7.

Perry, Elizabeth. 2007. Calif. Passes Another Gay Marriage Bill. *Washington Blade*, September 14.

Petrow, Steven. 2009. Julia Boseman Won't Back Down. *IndyWeek.com*, September 23. www.indyweek.com/indyweek/julia-boseman-wont-back-down/Content?oi d = 1218138.

Pew Research Center for People and the Press. 2007. Republicans Lag in Engagement and Enthusiasm for Candidates, February 23. Washington, DC.

Philpot, Tasha S., and Hanes Walton Jr. 2007. One of Our Own: Black Female Candidates and the Voters Who Support Them. *American Journal of Political Science* 51 (1): 49–62.

Pitkin, Hanna F. 1967. *The Concept of Representation*. Berkeley: University of California Press.

Plutzer, Eric, and John F. Zipp. 1996. Identity Politics, Partisanship, and Voting for Women Candidates. *Public Opinion Quarterly* 60 (1): 30–57.

Polman, Dick. 1998. Openly Gay Candidates the Hot Topic in U.S. Politics; Seeing a More Tolerant America, They Want Straight Voters to Know They Share Concerns. *Philadelphia Inquirer*, May 3.

———. 2000. New Clout for Gays in Fall Election. *Philadelphia Inquirer*, January 17.

Postman, David. 2001. New Tack Taken in Gay-Rights Struggle. *Seattle Times*, February 9.

Preuhs, Robert. 2002. Black and Latino Representation, Institutional Position and Influence. Paper presented at annual State Politics and Policy Conference, Milwaukee.

———. 2005. Descriptive Representation, Legislative Leadership, and Direct Democracy: Latino Influence on English Only Laws in the States, 1984–2002. *State Politics and Policy Quarterly* 5 (3): 203–24.

———. 2007. Descriptive Representation as a Mechanism to Mitigate Policy Backlash: Latino Incorporation and Welfare Policy in the American States. *Political Research Quarterly* 60 (2): 277–92.

Price, Deb. 2007. Breakthrough Gay Advances in Past Three Weeks. *Detroit News*, April 30.

Rapp, Andrew. 2003. Cheryl Jacques to Lead HRC. *Bay Windows*, October 30.

Rayside, David Morton. 1998. *On the Fringe: Gays and Lesbians in Politics*. Ithaca, NY: Cornell University Press.

Reeves, Keith. 1997. Voting Hopes or Fears? *White Voters, Black Candidates & Racial Politics in America*. New York: Oxford University Press.

Reingold, Beth. 2000. *Representing Women: Sex, Gender, and Legislative Behavior in Arizona and California*. Chapel Hill, NC: North Carolina University Press.

Rimmerman, Craig A. 2008. *The Lesbian and Gay Movements: Assimilation or Liberation?* Boulder, CO: Westview Press.

Rizzo, Katherine. 1999. Democrats Seek Gays; Party Sets Quota of Five Gay People for Ohio Delegation at 2000 Convention. *Akron Beacon Journal*, December 9.

Rojas, Aurelio. 2009. California Democrats Driving Gay-Rights Measures. *Sacramento Bee*, January 19.

Rosenthal, Alan. 1998. *The Decline of Representative Democracy: Process, Participation, and Power in State Legislatures*. Washington, DC: CQ Press.

Rudman, Laurie A., and Peter Glick. 1999. Feminized Management and Backlash toward Agentic Women: The Hidden Costs to Women of a Kinder, Gentler Image of Middle Managers. *Journal of Personality and Social Psychology* 77 (4): 1004–11.

Rule, Wilma. 1990. Why More Women Are State Legislators: A Research Note. *Western Political Quarterly* 43 (3): 437–48.

———. 1992. Multimember Legislative Districts: Minority and Anglo Women's and Men's Recruitment Opportunity. In *United States Electoral Systems: Their Impact on Women and Minorities*, ed. Wilma Rule and Joseph F. Zimmerman. New York: Greenwood Press.

Rybka, Ted. 2006. It's Aboud Time: Tucson Lesbian Paula Aboud Appointed to Fill Senate Seat. *Echo Magazine*, January 30.

Saad, Lydia. 2005. Gay Rights Attitudes a Mixed Bag: Broad Support for Equal Job Rights, but Not for Gay Marriage. Gallup News Service, May 20.

Saint-Germain, Michelle A. 1989. Does Their Difference Make a Difference? The Impact of Women on Public Policy in the Arizona Legislature. *Social Science Quarterly* 70 (4): 956–68.

Saltzstein, Grace Hall. 1989. Black Mayors and Police Policies. *Journal of Politics* 51 (3): 525–44.

Sanbonmatsu, Kira. 2002a. Gender Stereotypes and Vote Choice. *American Journal of Political Science* 46 (1): 20–34.

———. 2002b. Political Parties and the Recruitment of Women to State Legislatures. *Journal of Politics* 64 (3): 791–809.

———. 2006. *Where Women Run: Gender and Party in the American States*. Ann Arbor: University of Michigan Press.

———. 2008. Gender Backlash in American Politics? *Politics & Gender* 4 (4): 634–42.

Sanchez, Samantha. 2005. *Money and Diversity in State Legislatures, 2003*. Helena, MT: Institute on Money in State Politics.

Santos, Adolfo, and Carlos Huerta. 2001. An Analysis of Descriptive and Substantive Latino Representation in Congress. In *Representation of Minority Groups in the U.S.*, ed. Charles E. Menifield, 57–75. Lanham, MD: Austin & Winfield.

Savage, Dan. 1998. Don't Blame Murray for Marriage Ban. *Seattle Times*, April 7.

Schaffner, Brian, and Nenad Senic. 2006. Rights or Benefits? Explaining the Sexual Identity Gap in American Political Behavior. *Political Research Quarterly* 59 (1): 123–32.

Scheck, Tom. 2004. Debate over Gay Marriage Ban Begins at Capitol. *Minnesota Public Radio*, March 9.

Schiller, Wendy J. 1995. Senators as Political Entrepreneurs: Using Bill Sponsorship to Shape Legislative Agendas. *American Journal of Political Science* 39:186–203.

Schwindt-Bayer, Leslie A. 2005. The Incumbency Disadvantage and Women's Election to Legislative Office. *Electoral Studies* 24 (2): 227–44.

———. 2006. Still Supermadres? Gender and the Policy Priorities of Latin American Legislators. *American Journal of Political Science* 50 (3): 570–85.

Schwindt-Bayer, Leslie A., and William Mishler. 2005. An Integrated Model of Women's Representation. *Journal of Politics* 67 (2): 407–28.

Searcey, Dionne. 1999. Bill Pushes School Policy against Gay Harassment. *Seattle Times*, March 11.

Sears, D. O., J. Citrin, and R. Kosterman. 1987. Jesse Jackson and the Southern White Electorate in 1984. In *Blacks in Southern Politics*, ed. L. W. Moreland, R. P. Steed, and T. A. Baker, 209–25. New York: Praeger.

Seltzer, Richard A., Jody Newman, and Melissa Voorhees Leighton. 1997. *Sex as a Political Variable: Women as Candidates and Voters in US. Elections*. London: Lynne Rienner.

Shaffer, Robert. 1994. As We Look Back, Prop. One Has Strengthened Idaho's Gay and Lesbian Community. *Diversity*, November.

Shannon, Brad. 2009. Same-Sex Rights Might Expand. *Olympian*, January 4.

Shapiro, Robert, and Harpreet Mahajan. 1986. Gender Differences in Policy Preferences: A Summary of Trends from the 1960s to the 1980s. *Public Opinion Quarterly* 50 (1):42–61.

Sharp, Elaine B. 1997. A Comparative Anatomy of Urban Social Conflict. *Political Research Quarterly* 50 (2): 261–80.

Shibley, Gail. 1994. Coming Out on Every Doorstep. In *Out For Office: Campaigning in the Gay '90s*, ed. Kathleen DeBold. Washington, DC: Gay and Lesbian Victory Fund.

Shilts, Randy. 1982. *The Mayor of Castro Street: The Life and Times of Harvey Milk*. New York: St. Martin's Press.

Sigelman, Carol K., Lee Sigelman, Barbara J. Walkosz, and Michael Nitz. 1995. Black Candidates, White Voters: Understanding Racial Bias in Political Perceptions. *American Journal of Political Science* 39 (1): 243–65.

Sigelman, Lee, and Carol K. Sigelman. 1982. Sexism, Racism, and Ageism in Voting Behavior: An Experimental Analysis. *Social Psychology Quarterly* 45:263–69.

Sigelman, Lee, and Susan Welch. 1984. Race, Gender, and Opinion toward Black and Female Presidential Candidates. *Public Opinion Quarterly* 48 (2): 467–75.

Skelton, George. 1997. A Remarkable Floor Debate on Gay Rights. *Los Angeles Times*, June 5.

Smith, Raymond A., and Donald P. Haider-Markel. 2002. *Gay and Lesbian Americans and Political Participation*. Denver: ABC-CLIO Publishers.

Staff, *Seattle Post Intelligencer*. 2002. Locke Signs School Bully Bill. *Seattle Post Intelligencer*, March 28, 2002.

Stein, Robert M., Stacy G. Ulbig, and Stephanie Shirley Post. 2005. Voting for Minority Candidates in Multiracial/Multiethnic Communities. *Urban Affairs Review* 41 (2): 157–81.

Stone, Andrea. 2006. Gay Candidates Look to Further Rights at State Level. *USA Today* May 9.

Stoutenborough, James W., Donald P. Haider-Markel, and Mahalley D. Allen. 2006. Reassessing the Impact of Supreme Court Decisions on Public Opinion: Gay Civil Rights Cases. *Political Research Quarterly* 59 (3): 419–33.

Straube, Trenton. 2007. Assembly Member Daniel O'Donnell Talks about Sponsoring the Marriage Bill. *New York Blade*, May 25.

Studlar, Donley, and Ian McAllister. 2002. Does a Critical Mass Exist? A Comparative Analysis of Women's Legislative Representation since 1950. *European Journal of Political Research* 41 (2): 233–53.

Swain, Carol. 1993. *Black Faces, Black Interests: The Representation of African Americans in Congress*. Cambridge, MA: Harvard University Press.

Swers, Michele L. 1998. Are Women More Likely to Vote for Women's Issue Bills Than Their Male Colleagues? *Legislative Studies Quarterly* 23 (3): 435–48.

———. 2001. Research on Women in Legislatures: What Have We Learned, Where Are We Going? *Women & Politics* 23 (1–2): 167–85.

———. 2002. *The Difference Women Make: The Policy Impacts of Women in Congress*. Chicago: University of Chicago Press.

Tadlock, Barry L., and Ann Gordon. 2003. Political Evaluations of Lesbian and Gay Candidates: The Impact of Stereotypic Biases in Press Coverage. Paper presented at annual meeting of American Political Science Association, Philadelphia, August.

Takeda, Okiyoshi. 2001. The Representation of Asian Americans in the U.S. Political System. In *Representation of Minority Groups in the U.S.*, ed. Charles E. Menifield, 77–109. Lanham, MD: Austin & Winfield.

Tate, Katherine. 2001. The Political Representation of Blacks in Congress: Does Race Matter? *Legislative Studies Quarterly* 26 (4): 623–38.

———. 2003. *Black Faces in the Mirror: African Americans and Their Representatives in the U.S. Congress*. Princeton, NJ: Princeton University Press.

Terkildsen, Nayda. 1993. When White Voters Evaluate Black Candidates: The Processing Implications of Candidate Skin Color, Prejudice, and Self- Monitoring. *American Journal of Political Science* 37 (4): 1032–53.

Terkildsen, Nayda, and David F. Damore. 1999. The Dynamics of Racialized Media Coverage in Congressional Elections. *Journal of Politics* 61 (3): 680–99.

Thomas, Sue. 1989. Voting Patterns in the California Assembly: The Role of Gender. *Women & Politics* 9 (4): 43–56.

———. 1991. The Impact of Women on State Legislative Policies. *Journal of Politics* 53 (4): 958–76.

———. 1994. *How Women Legislate*. New York: Oxford University Press.

———. 1997. Why Gender Matters: The Perceptions of Women Officeholders. *Women & Politics* 17 (1): 27–51.

———. 2008. "Backlash" and Its Utility to Political Scientists. *Politics & Gender* 4 (4): 615–23.

Thomas, Sue, and Susan Welch. 1991. The Impact of Gender on Activities and Priorities of State Legislators. *Western Political Quarterly* 44 (2): 445–56.

Thomas, Sue, and Clyde Wilcox, eds. 2005. *Women and Elective Office: Past, Present, and Future*. New York: Oxford University Press.

Thompson, J. A., and G. F. Moncrief, eds. 1998. *Campaign Finance in State Legislative Elections*. Washington, DC: Congressional Quarterly.

Times Staff. 1996. Assembly OKs Bill That Opposes Gay Marriages. *Los Angeles Times*, August 21.

Tolbert, Caroline J., and Gertrude A. Steuernagel. 2001. Women Lawmakers, State Mandates, and Women's Health. *Women & Politics* 22 (1): 1–39.

Tucker, H. J., and R. E. Weber. 1987. State Legislative Election Outcomes: Contextual Effects and Legislative Performance Effects. *Legislative Studies Quarterly* 12:537–53.

Ulbig, Stacy G. 2007. Gendering Municipal Government: Female Descriptive Representation and Feelings of Political Trust. *Social Science Quarterly* 88 (5): 1106–23.

U.S. Bureau of the Census. 2003. *2000 Census of Population. Social and Economic Characteristics*. Washington, DC: U.S. Government Printing Office.

Vaid, Urvashi. 1995. *Virtual Equality: The Mainstreaming of Gay and Lesbian Liberation*. New York: Anchor Books.

Vandenbosch, Sue. 1996. A Negative Relationship between Religion and the Percentage of Women State Legislators in the United States. *Journal of Legislative Studies* 2 (3): 322–38.

Vanderleeuw, James M., and Baodong Liu. 2002. Political Empowerment, Mobilization, and Black Voter Roll-Off. *Urban Affairs Review* 37 (3): 380–96.

Van Der Veen, Kari. 2006. A Personal Battle. *Downtown Journal*, April 17.

Vengroff, Richard, Zsolt Nyiri, and Melissa Fugiero. 2003. Electoral System and Gender Representation in Sub-National Legislatures: Is There a National—Sub-National Gender Gap? *Political Research Quarterly* 56 (2): 163–73.

Victory Fund. 2005. Illinois Passes Non-Discrimination Act. *Outlines*, January 14.

Voss, D. Stephen, and David Lublin. 2001. Black Incumbents, White Districts: An Appraisal of the 1996 Congressional Elections. *American Politics Research* 29:141–82.

Voss, D. Stephen, and Penny Miller. 2001. Following a False Trail: The Hunt for White Backlash in Kentucky's 1996 Desegregation Vote. *State Politics and Policy Quarterly* 1 (1): 62–80.

Wahlke, John C. 1971. Policy Demands and System Support: The Role of the Represented. *British Journal of Political Science* 1 (3): 271–90.

Wald, Kenneth D., James W. Button, and Barbara A. Rienzo. 1996. The Politics of Gay Rights in American Communities: Explaining Antidiscrimination Ordinances and Policies. *American Journal of Political Science* 40 (4): 1152–78.

Warren, Jenifer. 2001. Capitol Gains for Gay Pols; Legislature's Four Lesbians Help Push California to the Forefront in the Fight for Equal Rights. *Los Angeles Times*, December 10.

Washington, Ebonya. 2006. How Black Candidates Affect Voter Turnout. *Quarterly Journal of Economics* 121 (3): 973–98.

Wasson, David. 2000. Move to Moderation Has Backers' Backs Up. *Tampa Tribune*, September 2.

Weintraub, Daniel M. 1997. California to Battle over Discrimination against Gays in Schools. *Orange County Register*, February 5.

Welch, Susan. 1990. The Impact of At-Large Elections on the Representation of Blacks and Hispanics. *Journal of Politics* 52 (4): 1050–76.

Welch, Susan, Margery M. Ambrosius, Janet Clark, and Robert Darcy. 1985. The Effect of Candidate Gender on Electoral Outcomes in State Legislative Races. *Western Political Quarterly* 38 (3): 464–75.

Welch, Susan, and Lee Sigelman. 1982. Changes in Public Attitudes toward Women in Politics. *Social Science Quarterly* 63 (2): 312–22.

Welch, Susan, and Donley T. Studlar. 1990. Multi-Member Districts and the Representation of Women: Evidence from Britain and the United States. *Journal of Politics* 52 (2): 391–412.

———. 1996. The Opportunity Structure for Women's Candidacies and Electability in Britain and the United States. *Political Research Quarterly* 49 (4): 861–74.

Weldon, S. Laurel. 2002. Beyond Bodies: Institutional Sources of Representation for Women in Democratic Policymaking. *Journal of Politics* 64 (4): 1153–74.

Wiest, Jason. 2007. Gay Lawmaker's Agenda Includes Environment, Health Care. *Morning News*, May 15.

Wilcox, Clyde, and Robin Wolpert. 2000. Gay Rights in the Public Sphere: Public Opinion on Gay and Lesbian Equality. In *The Politics of Gay Rights*, ed. Craig A. Rimmerman, Kenneth D. Wald, and Clyde Wilcox. Chicago: University of Chicago Press.

Williams, Linda. 1989. White/Black Perceptions of the Electability of Black Political Candidates. *National Political Science Review* 2:45–64.

Witt, Linda, Karen Paget, and Glenna Matthews. 1995. *Running as a Woman: Gender and Power in American Politics*. New York: Free Press.

Witt, Stephanie L., and Suzanne McCorkle, eds. 1997. *Anti-Gay Rights: Assessing Voter Initiatives*. Westport, CT: Praeger.

Wolbrecht, Christina, and David E. Campbell. 2007. Leading by Example: Female Members of Parliament as Political Role Models. *American Journal of Political Science* 51 (4): 921–39.

Wyman, Hastings. 2002. Gay Liberation Comes to Dixie—Slowly. *American Review of Politics* 23:167–92.

Yang, Alan S. 1999. *From Wrongs to Rights: Public Opinion on Gay and Lesbian Americans Moves toward Equality, 1973–1999*. Washington, DC: National Gay and Lesbian Task Force.

Yang, John E. 1997. Gays in a Conservative Closet; Some GOP Congressional Aides Experience Dissonance between Personal, Political. *Washington Post*, November 7.

Yoder, Janice D. 1991. Rethinking Tokenism: Looking beyond Numbers. *Gender and Society* 5:178–92.

Zipp, John F., and Eric Plutzer. 1985. Gender Differences in Voting for Female Candidates: Evidence from the 1982 Election. *Public Opinion Quarterly* 49 (2): 179–97.

INDEX

abortion, 3, 45, 48

Aboud, Sen. Paula (AZ), 84

ACT UP, 20. *See also* activism

active representation, 9, 15. *See also* representation

activism: and LGBT politics ix, 18, 20, 58, 114

adoption legislation, 107

affect, towards gays and lesbians and homosexuality 27, 32, 34, 35, 69, 71, 74

African American: attitudes of, 13, 31n6; candidates 4, 5, 6, 7, 14, 31, 38, 64n1, 65n3; constituencies, 10; groups, 17; legislators, xii, 10, 11, 16, 132; officials, xii, 2, 13, 85, 131; and political incorporation, xii, 11, 13; population, 7, 10, 73, 74, 75, 76, 77, 80, 90, 109; representation, 2, 7–8, 9, 10, 11, 16, 85, 119, 131, 142; voters, 2, 7, 22, 131

age, as a predictor variable, 35, 41, 43, 45, 49, 52,

AIDS, 19, 20, 21, 56, 90, 95, 97, 98, 99, 103, 104, 110

Alabama, 1, 88

amendment process: and LGBT-related legislation, 90, 91, 94, 95, 96, 97, 98, 99, 100, 101, 102, 103, 104, 107, 108, 111, 114, 120, 121, 127, 129, 133, 135

Amendment 2, 22

American Family Association, 23

Americans with Disabilities Act, 21

Ammiano, Rep. Tom (CA), 93

Anderson, Sen. Calvin (Cal) (WA), 20, 22, 110, 111, 115

antidiscrimination: policy, xii, 24, 27, 34, 86, 88, 91, 95, 98, 104, 106, 110–12, 116, 120, 121, 125–28, 130, 135, 141, 153; and public opinion 27, 34, 125

anti-LGBT groups, 23, 25, 107

anti-LGBT legislation: xii, 88, 90, 93, 94, 95, 100, 101, 104, 107, 108; and LGBT descriptive representation, xii, 94, 95, 99, 100, 127, 129, 130, 132, 133, 134, 135, 136, 137, 138, 139, 140, 141, 142, 143, 145, 153, 154, 155

Arizona, 11, 30, 70, 84, 87

Arkansas, 84, 88, 129, 142

Asian American, 10, 38

assimilationist philosophy, 18

at-large elections, 8, 10

attorney general: 50; and lesbian candidate 48, 49

backlash: theory, xi, xii, 15, 31, 94, 130, 133, 146n2; and LGBT politics, 19, 30, 31, 56, 94, 99, 130–45, 146n2, 153–56; and blacks, xii, 131, 132, 133, 146, 156; and Latinos 16, 133, 156; and public opinion 29, 30; and women, xii, 16, 131, 132, 133, 156

Baehr v. *Lewin*, 23

Baldwin, Rep. Tammy (D-WI), 25

ballot initiative, 19, 21, 56, 90, 106, 107, 111, 157. *See also* direct democracy

Barrios, Rep. Jarrett (MA), 96, 97, 98, 116

bill introduction, analysis of, 119, 123, 124, 125, 127, 130, 138, 145

bisexual, ix, 1, 56, 105, 106, 116

Biskupski, Rep. Jackie (UT), 88, 133

black candidate. *See* African American

black legislators. *See* African American

black voters. *See* African American

born-again, Christians, 41, 43, 52. *See also* Protestant fundamentalist

Boseman, Sen. Julia (NC), 148

Bowers v. *Hardwick*, 20